Wonders of a Golden Age

Painting at the Court
of the Great Mughals

Indian art of the
16th and 17th centuries
from collections
in Switzerland

by B.N. Goswamy
and Eberhard Fischer

1987
Museum Rietberg
Zurich

Table of contents

Concept (exhibition and catalogue):
Prof. B.N. Goswamy (Panjab University, Chandigarh)
and Dr. Eberhard Fischer (Museum Rietberg Zürich)
Assistance: Andrea Isler
Proofs: Jacqueline Isler
Administration: Lilly Burgherr
Publicity: Dr. Brigit Bernegger
Lay-out (catalogue and exhibition):
Dr. Eberhard Fischer, Isabelle Wettstein and Brigitte
Kammerer
Exhibition mounted by: Ernst Bär, David Staub
Photographs:
Wettstein + Kauf (Museum Rietberg Zürich)
Stephen Wakeham, London, and others
Cover design: Fred Bauer, Küsnacht
Photolithographs: Cliché und Litho AG, Zürich
Printing and production of the catalogue:
J.E. Wolfensberger AG, Zürich

Catalogue of an exhibition held at the Museum Rietberg Zürich, May 30th to September 27th, 1987 in
conjunction with "India in Switzerland '87".

Distributed by:
Museum Rietberg Zürich
Gablerstrasse 15
CH-8002 Zürich
Switzerland

Printed in Switzerland
© Text: Publikationsstiftung für das Museum Rietberg
Zürich
Illustrations: Owners of the works

ISBN 3-907070-14-3

Honorary Committee

Mr. Pierre Aubert,
   President of the Swiss Confederation

His Excellency Mr. Ramaswami Venkataraman,
   Vice-President of the Republic of India

Mrs. Elisabeth Kopp,
   Federal Councillor

His Most Serene Highness The Hereditary Prince Hans-Adam of Liechtenstein

His Excellency Mr. Ashoke Sen Chib,
   Ambassador of the Republic of India

Mr. Alfred Gilgen,
   President of the Government Council of the Canton of Zurich

His Excellency Jean Cuendet,
   Ambassador of Switzerland to India

Mr. Thomas Wagner,
   Mayor of the City of Zurich

His Highness The Prince Sadruddin Aga Khan

Mr. Hashem Khosrovani,
   President of Chempetrol Group, Geneva

Mrs. Georgette Boner

Mr. Prakash Hinduja,
   Chairman of AMAS S.A., Geneva

Mr. Spiro Latsis,
   President of SETE S.A., Geneva

Mr. Balthasar Reinhart

Mrs. Lucy Rudolph

Mr. Pierre Uldry,
   President of the Rietberg Society

A word from the Hinduja Foundation

Fifty years ago, Parmanand Deepchand Hinduja made a commitment to fund cultural, educational, medical and other humanitarian projects in, and linked with his motherland, India. The Hinduja Foundation was established in 1968 as an umbrella organisation to support and coordinate the activities of the various charitable trusts set up by the Hinduja family in India. Similar Foundations were also established in Europe and in the United States at that time.

It has been our endeavour to build bridges of different kinds – bridges between the past and the present, between India and the West, between the generations that are and the generations that are to come. It is our belief that one such bridge is that of culture, for it remains firm and stands the test of time. But its structure needs to be carefully studied and any serious attempt to do this is worthy of generous support.

The Hinduja Foundation is aware, and deeply appreciative, of the tireless efforts of the City of Zurich and the Honorary Committee to bring about cultural understanding. Among the latest undertakings of the city of Zurich is the presentation of Indian art in the Mughal period at the Rietberg Museum, and the Foundation is proud to associate itself with this exhibition of "Wonders of a Golden Age". It hopes that this remarkable effort to present a facet of the rich tapestry of India will not only be welcomed by connoisseurs of art the world over, but also contribute to a real understanding of what India of the past was and stood for.

Words of thanks

by the Mayor of Zurich, Dr. Thomas Wagner

"India in Switzerland 1987" – "India permanently at the Rietberg Museum Zurich": Zurich is the only city in Switzerland which has been presenting classical Indian art for more than 30 years at the Rietberg Museum. It is now especially welcome that through a whole range of events such as special exhibitions, theatre and music performances a wide section of the public will have the opportunity this year of coming face to face with the varied and fascinating heritage of India, an encounter that can only help us in enriching ourselves further.

The great Mughal exhibition at the Rietberg Museum is the first of its kind in Switzerland. However, let us not forget the fact that already two centuries ago a Swiss called Antoine Polier collected noteworthy albums with calligraphy and miniatures by indigenous artists (a picture of Polier from ca. 1780 is shown in this exhibition), nor the fact that yet another century earlier Rembrandt owned Mughal paintings and drew upon them for his own work, or that the empress Maria Theresia had one entire hall in Schloss Schönbrunn decorated exclusively with Indian pictures. Mughal paintings had been collected in Europe from very early on in fact, so that many Indian works now in Europe have been there for a very long time. Thus this exhibition of Mughal painting could be seen as a rediscovery; but for most it offers a new possibility of an encounter with high-quality Indian paintings.

Firstly I would like to thank both authors of the catalogue and exhibition, Prof. B.N. Goswamy (Panjab University, Chandigarh) and Dr. Eberhard Fischer (Director of the Rietberg Museum Zurich). An exhibition of such refinement and a catalogue so ably conceived and written can come only from an exceptionally wide knowledge of Indian culture and languages, sensitivity to works of art and extensive museum experience. The authors have presented new insights into Mughal painting, especially into the painters' artistic concerns in this eventful period. Together they have opened up pictures of an alien time and culture.

Without the generous cooperation and help of the collectors, this remarkable exhibition would not have been conceivable. My warm thanks go especially to Prince Sadruddin Aga Khan, whose collection of Islamic works of art, based on his fine awareness of quality, is of world renown. A number of his remarkable Mughal paintings in this show are exhibited for the first time in Europe. Further loans come from various private collections in Switzerland as well as from the Bernisches Historisches Museum and the Rietberg Museum in Zurich.

My special thanks go to the distinguished ladies and gentlemen, who kindly agreed to join the Honorary Committee of the Mughal exhibition, especially the Vice-President of India, H.E. Shri R. Venkataraman, the president of the Swiss Confederation, Mr. Pierre Aubert, Mrs. Elisabeth Kopp, member of the Swiss Council, Prince Sadruddin Aga Khan and Mr. Hashem Khosrovani whose unbounded interest and support have contributed greatly to the making of this exhibition.

The City of Zurich and the Rietberg Museum wish to express their sincere gratitude to the Hinduja Foundation for their very generous sponsorship of this English edition of the catalogue. My warmest thanks therefore go to Mr. Prakash Hinduja in Geneva. I also thank Mrs. Lucy Rudolph, Mr. and Mrs. Pierre Uldry as well as Mr. and Mrs. Balthasar Reinhart who have enabled the Rietberg Museum to acquire Mughal paintings of highest quality, and Mrs. Georgette Boner, president of the Alice Boner Foundation, for the bequest of a distinguished collection of Indian miniatures to the Rietberg Museum. I am also grateful that H.H. Hans-Adam von und zu Liechtenstein agreed to join the Committee, especially considering his role as the President of the Swiss-Liechtenstein Foundation for Archeological Research Abroad.

Special mention needs to be made of the deep interest taken in this exhibition project by the Indian Ambassadors to Switzerland, H.E. Mr. Thomas Abraham and H.E. Mr. Ashoke S. Chib as well as of the Swiss Ambassadors to India, Mr. Peter Erni and Mr. Jean Cuendet who supported this Mughal show from the very beginning.

My thanks also go to Mr. Lalit Mansingh of the Indian Council for Cultural Relations in New Delhi and Mr. Luc Boissonnas of Pro Helvetia, Zurich, who made the events accompanying this Mughal exhibition possible.

I should not forget the staff at the Rietberg Museum through whose dedication and commitment this elaborate project, "Wonders of a Golden Age", was realised. Dr. Brigit Bernegger, Mrs. Lilly Burgherr, Ms. Andrea Isler, the photographers Isabelle Wettstein and Brigitte Kammerer, Mr. Ernst Bär and others have for months been occupied with preparations for the exhibition, the catalogue and for many performances. Special research assistance was supplied by Mrs. Ursula Ferrar and Mrs. Liliane Tivolet in Geneva; also most kindly by Mrs. Nanni Boller, Barbara Fischer, Rashna Imhasly, Sheila Ledergerber, Danielle Porret and Prem Wach

as well as Mrs. Maria Zehnder and Mr. Nicolas Baerlocher of my own offices.

With the help of innumerable friends of India in Switzerland the beauty of one of India's most important periods is going to light up Zurich for an entire summer through this exhibition, "Wonders of a Golden Age – Painting at the Court of the Great Mughals". I am certain that a new fire will burn in many a viewer's heart through it!

Zurich, May 1987   Dr. Thomas Wagner
                                   Mayor of Zurich

Authors' note

The work presented here needs a word of explanation. This is an exhibition catalogue, not a history of Mughal painting, and all that we set out to do is to place the works included here in a context. Splendid as the material we were working with is, it is drawn only from collections in Switzerland, public and private, a fact which has strongly influenced the design of the exhibition and our emphasis on certain themes and styles. We have made no attempts here at examining any segment of time in great, dense detail or reconstructing the style of individual painters. There are no fresh attributions here, nor do we present a different view of the chronology of Mughal painting. We have chosen, on the other hand, to draw attention through this distinguished group of paintings to what we believe were some of the dominant concerns of the Mughal painters.

For the average European viewer, conversant only with the art that belongs to his own immediate world, Mughal painting is still a closed book, tantalizing but somewhat opaque, touched by a distant, alien kind of beauty. In awareness of this, therefore, we have aimed at providing, to the extent possible, a key to the understanding of the world to which this beauty belonged; to make it accessible. In the introductory essay, we have also aimed at presenting some new insights into the world of the Mughal painter, and raised some questions that we hope will lead to discussion. The catalogue entries document individual works for the most part, but also draw attention, wherever relevant, to the principal art-historical issues that they raise.

Many art historians have turned their attention, ably and with imagination, to Mughal painting in the past, and we have gratefully drawn upon their work. We would like especially to mention our indebtedness to the more recent work of several colleagues: Milo C. Beach, Stuart Cary Welch, Anthony Welch, Pramod Chandra, Glenn Lowry and Michael Brand in America; Ananda Krishna, Karl Khandalavala and Asok Das in India; Robert Skelton, Toby Falk and Jeremiah Losty in England. To the excellent catalogue of Prince Sadruddin Aga Khan's collection by Anthony Welch and Stuart C. Welch we have gone back very often, as we have to Toby Falk's valuable information on many other paintings, and to the relevant entries in the catalogues published by Christie's, Colnaghi, Sotheby's and Spink's.

The making of this catalogue has been possible only with the help of our colleagues, especially Andrea Isler who worked with ability and patience on the text, and Isabelle Wettstein and Brigitte Kammerer who designed the production. Our thanks are also due to Michael Glünz in Berne who gave generous help in the translation of many passages from Persian.

Finally: diacritical marks have been dispensed with in the text in the interest of easier reading. Indian and Persian words have been italicized and frequently provided with English equivalents. Indian versions of spellings (thus, *Shahnama* instead of *Shahnameh*) have been followed. We do hope that all this has been at least consistently done, so that no confusion is caused to the reader. Wherever possible, the paintings have been reproduced in their original size, and colours closely checked.

Zurich, April 1987   B.N. Goswamy
                               Eberhard Fischer

The Great Mughals and their Painters

The world to which the court painters of the Great Mughals belonged – men who occasionally carried splendid titles like 'Wonder of the Age', 'Rarity of the Realm' – had a name with a magical ring to it: an empire whose glitter had already become a by-word by the end of the 16th century. Accounts of the untold riches of the Mughals ('Moguls') and their great sense of style had reached far beyond the frontiers of India, and when travelers from the West wrote about what they saw in this land with dazzled, unbelieving eyes, those endless processions and displays of royal panoply, the sheen and lustre of innumerable pearls and diamonds and emeralds that were a daily sight at the court – this was already the stuff that fables are made of. Even sober accounts such as those of Sir Thomas Roe, the English ambassador to the court of the Emperor Jahangir, placed the territory of the Great Mughal in 1616 as "far greater than the Persians', and almost equal, if not as great as, the Turks'... His means of money, by revenue, custom of presents, and inheriting all men's goods, above both." At the imperial court, the receiving of presents like the one from the Deccani king of Bijapur (that Roe reports) – "of six and thirtie Elephants, of two whereof the chaines and all tackles were of beaten Gold, to the weight of foure hundred pounds, two of siluer, of the same fashion, the rest of copper; fiftie Horses richly furnished, and ten *Leckes* of *Rupias* in Iewels, great Pearles, and Balasse Rubies. Euerie *Lecke* is a hundred thousand *Rupias*, euery *Rupia* two shillings and six pence sterling; so tenne *Leckes* is a Million of *Rupias*" – seems to have been no unusual occurrence at all.

But this had not always been so. When Babur, tracing his descent from the great Timur on the one side and Chingiz Khan on the other, won the decisive battle at Panipat in 1526, defeating the then weak Sultan of Delhi, he was a man of but few means. It was his intrepidity as a campaigner, his restless, untiring spirit of adventure that had gained him a foothold in India on which the great Mughal empire was to be built later. His four years in India (1526–1530) saw much activity: battles and conquests, construction and organisation, but it was a limited kingdom that he left to his son Humayun. The span of Humayun's rule was longer than that of his father, but truly only in name, for determined resistance from several quarters, including a very gifted Afghan in India, Sher Shah, never allowed him to consolidate the kingdom that he had inherited. He was, in fact, forced to flee India in 1540, and he spent long years in virtual exile, some of them at the court of Shah Tahmasp of Persia, and some at Kabul where he prepared to march back to India to reclaim it. This reconquest he was able to effect in 1555;

but again, like his father, he did not live long enough to enjoy it, dying in 1556 of a fall from the stairs of his library, leaving the kingdom to his eldest son Akbar, then not yet fourteen years of age.

But with Akbar a decidedly different era began, and it is with justice that he is regarded as the true founder of the Mughal empire in India. Raised as he was in the school of adversity, from his very young years onwards he seems to have decided not to allow what had happened to his cultivated but indecisive father to happen again. With prodigious energy he set about winning back areas that had been lost, adding voraciously to his possessions and pushing the confines of his empire remarkably far while knitting it closely together like no one before had done in India for close to a thousand years. Akbar did not simply enlarge the empire; he imparted greatness to it. In the course of the fifty years for which he ruled (1556–1605), he sought to give India a different turn, a new profile. Babur, the grandfather whose memory he loved so dearly, had possessed great personal courage and ambition; Humayun shared a measure of persistence; but Akbar possessed a vision. Sharply aware of the fact that he ruled over a remarkable diversity of people and hostile factions at the court, he seems to have concluded that no kingdom, however extensive, could survive for long if it was built on slender foundations, on ground that had marked subterranean faults. Despite the establishment of Muslim rule as early as in the 11th century, the vast majority of the population of India continued to consist of Hindus, who had lived as subjected people under the authority of the conquering Muslims for nearly five hundred years wherever that authority obtained. This could only have bred resentment, deep dissatisfaction and, wherever possible, armed insurgency. At the level of the common people, however, Akbar did not fail to notice that the followers of the two major religions in India, the Hindus and the Muslims, had learned to live together, even showing signs of making accommodations to each other, the mystic or *Sufi* thread, in particular, building a bridge between them. There were reachings-out and, unless things were unnecessarily pushed towards a point of exciting passions, a certain civil, peaceful co-existence obtained at the ground-level. Essentially then, if confrontation could be avoided, if the harsh attitude of official authority were to be softened and modified, much could be achieved in the direction of turning India from two hostile camps into a different kind of land.

The pattern of rule established by the Muslim sultans in the first five hundred years of Islamic rule in northern India clearly needed to be discarded, and while power did not have to be given up or even substantively shared, the footing of power could be dramatically secured by patiently pulling out the numerous thorns. With this conviction, Akbar brought about major changes in state policy. A clear measure of tolerance was introduced at all levels: the much hated *jiziya* or poll-tax on Hindus was abolished; the emperor himself took Rajput princesses in marriage; Hindus of distinction and talent were raised to the highest rank in the state. The Mughal structure of power was being re-designed to rest on more than one pillar. One only has to read the accounts of Akbar's reign – especially those left by his friend and companion, Abul Fazl – of his life and his regulations, to get a sense of how much was undertaken and at how many levels. The remarkable conquests of Akbar's armies apart, conquests that brought a far greater part of India under one rule than had ever been the case since the third century B.C., a brilliantly conceived administrative structure was designed. Great undertakings like roads and irrigation projects and monuments were started, serving as symbols of authority and benevolence at the same time. The task was protean, but the energies of the emperor and his able lieutenants were clearly up to it. By the last quarter of the 16th century, the profile of a new India was emerging. In the nature of things there was turmoil and recalcitrance, challenge and resistance; but by now the empire had vast resources, and the emperor was capable of looking far into the future. Akbar was by no means unaware that stout resistance would come from within the ranks of Islam itself, from the orthodox *mullas* (Muslim learned) and nobles who had grown used to the exercising of total authority; but much of this resistance he was able to contain or circumvent. One does get the feeling that the murmurs of dissent never quite died out, but neither did they ever succeed in keeping a clear, new voice from being heard.

Personally, Akbar was deeply inwardly inclined, possessing a clear philosophical bent of mind. This, combined with his inexhaustible curiosity about phenomena and things that belonged to the domain of the spirit, led him to look in a systematic fashion for the hard core of truth in all religions, inquiries that ran into serious opposition from the orthodox Muslims at his court, but that clearly broadened his vision and gave him inner strength and resilience. The concerns of the mind, however, did not inhibit Akbar from turning his prodigious energies into taking a deep interest in the material aspects of the world around him. If Abul Fazl is to be believed, virtually nothing, no aspect

Formerly I persecuted men into conformity with my faith and deemed it Islam. As I grew in knowledge, I was overwhelmed with shame. Not being a Muslim myself, it was unmeet to force others to become such. What constancy is to be expected from prose-lytes on compulsion?
(Akbar quoted by Abul Fazl, Ain-i Akbari, transl. H.S. Jarret, vol. III, 1949:429)

His Majesty forms matrimonial alliances with princes of Hindustan, and of other countries; and secures by these ties of harmony the peace of the world. As the sovereign, by the light of his wisdom, has raised fit persons from the dust of obscurity, and appointed them to various offices, so does he also elevate faithful persons to the several ranks in the service of the seraglio.
(Abul Fazl, Ain-i Akbari, transl. H. Blochmann, vol. I, 1873:5)

The killing of animals on the first day of the week was strictly prohibited, because this day is sacred to the Sun... and on several other days, to please the Hindus.
(Badauni, Muntakhabu-t-Tawarikh, transl. W. Haig, vol. II, 1973:331)

His Majesty has appointed fourteen zealous, experienced, and impartial clerks, two of whom do daily duty in rotation... Their duty is to write down the orders and the doings of His Majesty and whatever the heads of the departments report; what His Majesty eats and drinks; when he sleeps, and when he rises; the etiquette in the State hall; the time His Majesty spends in the Harem; when he goes to the general and private assemblies; the nature of hunting-parties; the slaying of animals; when he marches, and when he halts... his remarks; what books he has read out to him; what alms he bestows; what presents he makes; the daily and monthly exercises which he imposes on himself; appointments to mansabs; contingents of troops; salaries; jagirs... the increase or decrease of taxes; contracts; sales, money transfers; peshkash (trib-ute receipts); dispatch; the issue of orders; the papers which are signed by His Majesty; the arrival of reports; the minutes thereon; the arrivals of courtiers; their departures; the fixing of periods; the inspection of the guards; battles, victories; and peace... the harvests of the year; the reports on events.
(Abul Fazl, Ain-i Akbari, vol. I:268f)

of life, escaped his attention, he becoming personally involved in the processes of production and organisation at all levels. The improvement of colours was as important to him as the regulations for recruitment in the army; the training of hunting falcons as vital as perfecting the system of record-keeping for the empire. The remarkable organisation of the innumerable *karkhanas* or work-shops that employed thousands of craftsmen drawn from all over the country and beyond is recorded in some detail by Abul Fazl. Every possible trade or craft was taken into account, its methods reorganised, its scope expanded and brought within the mainstream of national life. Markedly inclined towards learning but ironically unable to read or write himself, the emperor attached great importance to his library, and promoted a remarkable amount of literary activity that spanned the writing of histories and chronicles and poetry, but also translations from other languages into Persian that was now the language of the court.

With Persia, that refined and civilised Islamic power west of India, there was evident contact. One reads of a great deal of coming and going between Persia and India, especially at the level of common men. As the power and the fame of the Mughal empire grew, several men of talent were drawn to India from other parts, including Persia. But Akbar himself entertained no intentions of turning India culturally into an extension of Persia. He had clearly different thoughts, and for him the idea of a marked Indian identity held powerful appeal. Rejecting nothing, he took ideas from a whole range of sources; but he was intent upon merging them together with a view to developing a different kind of alloy. One reads, in the Hindu context, of the importance attached to images made from using as many as eight different metals, the *ash-tadhatu*, for they are especially auspicious. Akbar's vision seems to have been formed by this idea of an *ashtadhatu*-India.

Akbar's remarkable attention to matters of detail seems to have stemmed from his belief that what is often seemingly insignificant has bearing on much larger things, sometimes on whole modes of thought. Abul Fazl also carefully records many of the new 'inventions' of the emperor that reveal as much the innovative as the playful side of his nature: we hear of him inventing phosphorescent balls with which *chaugan* or polo can be played at night, of devising different and new methods of catching and training leopards, of revising regulations for the feeding of elephants in the imperial stables, of discussing new dyes for woollen shawls, of devising different costumes and giving entirely new names to known articles of apparel. While some of this simply reflects a mind that absorbs remarkably well and is interested in an incredible range of things and activities, behind some of it lurks a faith in the power of 'small' things. An interesting example is the emperor's renaming of several dresses. The names that he substitutes for old ones combine Persian and Hindi terms in a careful, conscious manner. Thus, when he renames a jacket called *nimtana* as *tanzeb* or a shawl as *param naram,* it is not an idle play with words but a reflection of a different kind of thought. When he devises a turban for himself, the turban that we see ordinarily in Akbari paintings and that established a fashion for nearly everyone at his court, he consciously rejects alike the 'foreign looking' *Chaghatai-*turban that his father Humayun had invented and the fuller turban with a *kulah* (skull cap) that his grandfather Babur preferred. Akbar's turban sits flat on the head, and consists essentially of a long, narrow strip artfully wrapped and bound. This turban distinguished itself quite remarkably from the earlier Turkish-looking headgears, and was obviously much more suited to the Indian climate. Even more remarkable than this is the simple manner in which the emperor himself dressed, occasionally even sporting, Hindu fashion, a *dhoti* tied around the waist, leaving the upper part of the body bare. For a Muslim ruler to wear this garment, even if in the privacy of his own apartments within the palace, could only have been regarded as an act of courage or defiance.

It would seem as if this very kind of thought, the same attention to detail, went into Akbar's whole view of what is of primary concern to us here: painting. In that important field, conscious decisions were taken and a direction determined. But to this matter we return a little later. Meanwhile it is of interest to remember that things that appear initially to be peripheral to an empire and its identity, were here obviously the subject of close and careful thought by the emperor himself.

The last years of the great empire that Akbar had built were clouded by an estrangement between him and his eldest son Salim, the future Jahangir. There was defiance on the prince's part, even the setting up of a 'court' of his own at Allahabad, in 1599; but eventually there was a reconciliation, and the empire, with its vast resources, its superb administrative machinery, passed on intact to Jahangir in 1605. Possessed of remarkable taste but unfortunately neither of the same energy nor the same vision as his father, Jahangir continued to remain in firm control of his domains. But what he was able to add to was the richness and the splendour of the

And in these days, when reproach began to spread upon the doctrines of Islam, and all questions relating thereto, and ever so many wretches of Hindus and Hinduizing Musalmans brought unmitigated reviling against the Prophet… this matter became the cause of general disgrace, and the seeds of depravity and disturbance began to lift their heads in the empire.
(Badauni, Muntakhabu-t-Tawarikh, vol. II:277)

Although I am the master of so vast a kingdom, and all the appliances of government are to my hand, yet since true greatness consists in doing the will of God, my mind is not at ease in this diversity of sects and creeds, and my heart is oppressed by this outward pomp of circumstance; with what satisfaction can I undertake the conquest of empire? How I wish for the coming of some pious man, who will resolve the distractions of my heart.
(Akbar quoted by Abul Fazl, Ain-i Akbari, vol. III:433)

At this time when the capital (Fathepur Sikri) was illuminated by his glorious advent, H.M. ordered that a house of worship (libadatkhana) should be built in order to the adornment of the spiritual kingdom… A general proclamation was issued that, on that night of illumination, all orders and sects of mankind – those who searched after spiritual and physical truth, and those of the common public who sought for an awakening, and the inquirers of every sect – should assemble in the precincts of the holy edifice, and bring forward their spiritual experiences, and their degrees of knowledge of the truth in various and contradictory forms in the bridal chamber of manifestation.
(Abul Fazl, Akbarnama, transl. H. Beveridge, vol. III, 1921:157)

It would take me too long to describe the chiras, fawtas, *and* dupattas, *or the costly dresses worn at feasts or presented to the grandees of the present time. Every season, there are made one thousand complete suits for the imperial wardrobe, and one hundred and twenty, made up in twelve bundles, are always kept in readiness.*
(Abul Fazl, Ain-i Akbari, vol. I:96)

image of the empire: its style, not its substance. His years as emperor were marked by his share of troubles, including those from his sons – something that was emerging as an unhappy dynastic pattern (for Humayun had had his trouble with his brothers, Akbar with his son, and Shahjahan in the next generation was to reap the same harvest) – but his own personal lifestyle and the magnificence of his court left a clear impress.

In terms of outward grandeur, however, the empire seemed to reach some kind of peak under Shahjahan, Jahangir's son who succeeded him in 1627. The momentum that the Mughal empire had gained in the 16th century continued to keep it in majestic motion, but the vision that lay behind it was by this time beginning to dim slowly. A slow but perceptible shift in attitudes and policies became apparent: a new tilt towards Islamic orthodoxy was seen, and that wonderful human warmth, that great sense of compassion that had marked Akbar, was in the process of being replaced by a certain aloofness, as if it were necessary to cultivate an attitude of cool distance for maintaining a great imperial image. But there is little doubt that Shahjahan understood, more perhaps than any other Mughal emperor, the true meaning of magnificence. A whole apparatus of grandeur marked his period, and so much in it is of a piece: the construction of great architectural monuments like the Taj Mahal and the whole city of Shahjahanabad (Delhi), the fabled peacock-throne, those superb albums of paintings that were assembled for him. Remarkable wealth seems to have belonged to the imperial court of which the jewels, the precious stones of which the emperor was so inordinately fond, served as perfect symbols. Shahjahan's last years were deeply troubled, and there are signs of his withdrawing into himself, as if to seek a certain solace within, but little of this inward-turning led to a process of deep thought which could have affected the fortunes of the empire. He lived to see a sanguine war of succession break out between his four sons that resulted in the murder of his favourite, Dara Shukoh, the eldest and the most scholarly, and his own imprisonment at the hands of Aurangzeb, who declared himself emperor in 1658.

The new emperor's rule was nearly as long as that of his great-grandfather Akbar, but nothing could be more different than the tenor of the two reigns. In its physical extent, the empire was now perhaps at its widest, but its strength was slowly being sapped, as much from the narrow policies established by the emperor as from a combination of outside factors. The emperor's personal piety as a devout Muslim was one thing, but his evident lack of sympathy for the vast numbers of his Hindu subjects did not help to keep the empire together unlike before. But this is not to say that the Great Mughal's was no longer a name that was feared and respected. Aurangzeb's personal style was quite different from that of his predecessors, he being a man of austere habits, but the domains he ruled were still enormously wealthy, and the resources of the empire still vast and remarkable.

It was in the 18th century, however, after the death of Aurangzeb in 1707, that the true decline of the Mughal empire began. The cracks that had been visible earlier now turned into cleavages. No longer did a 'Great Mughal' sit on the throne of Delhi: it became a story of small men, manipulated by endemic intrigue and determined invaders that drew to its inexorable end: first, with the virtual take-over by the new power in India, the English East India Company, and then the formal extinction of the empire with its last ruler, Bahadur Shah Zafar, who was dethroned on the charge of being involved in the 'Mutiny' of 1857, and exiled to Burma where he was to die, a destitute, lonely figure. But from the point of view of painting, except for a sporadic flare, there is little of true interest in the fortunes of the Mughals after 1700. The last 150 years did little more than simply preserve a memory of a line of rulers whose empire had been among the most remarkable in the long history of India, and under whom great art was produced.

II

Beginnings are seldom without interest and, in the case of Mughal painting, they certainly help one understand the art better, especially, if one were to consider the different options open and available to those who laid its foundations. The story of Mughal painting does not begin with Babur, for remarkably cultivated as he was – a poet himself, a writer of remarkable prose as evidenced by his famous *Tuzuk* written originally in Turki – there is certainly nothing to link him with painting in India. The few remarks that his celebrated work contain on painting, especially in connection with the great Persian master Bihzad, show marked sensitivity, but his tumultuous career certainly did not afford him the right opportunities. Humayun, his son, however, was not only aware of painting and its beauties, but became personally involved in the art. There is an incidental but very early reference to his having had a painter in his retinue, even when he was fleeing India and in less than fortunate cir-

It should be stated that the Great Mogul has seven magnificent thrones, one wholly covered with diamonds, the others with rubies, emeralds, or pearls. The principal throne, which is placed in the hall of the first court, is nearly of the form and size of our camp beds; that is to say, it is about 6 feet long and 4 wide. Upon the four feet, which are very massive, and from 20 to 25 inches high, are fixed the four bars which support the base of the throne, and upon these bars are ranged twelve columns, which sustain the canopy on three sides, there not being any on that which faces the court. Both the feet and the bars, which are more than 18 inches long, are covered with gold inlaid and enriched with numerous diamonds, rubies, and emeralds. In the middle of each bar there is a large balass ruby, cut en cabuchon, with four emeralds round it, which form a square cross. Next in succession, from one side to the other along the length of the bars there are similar crosses, arranged so that in one the ruby is in the middle of four emeralds, and in another the emerald is in the middle and four balass rubies surround it. The emeralds are table-cut, and the intervals between the rubies and emeralds are covered with diamonds, the largest of which do not exceed 10 to 12 carats in weight, all being showy stones, but very flat. There are also in some parts pearls set in gold, and upon one of the longer sides of the throne there are four steps to ascend it…
The underside of the canopy is covered with diamonds and pearls, with a fringe of pearls all round, and above the canopy, which is a quadrangular-shaped dome, there is to be seen a peacock with elevated tail made of blue sapphires and other coloured stones, the body being of gold inlaid with precious stones, having a large ruby in front of the breast, from whence hangs a pear-shaped pearl of 50 carats or thereabouts, and of a somewhat yellow water. On both sides of the peacock there is a large bouquet of the same height as the bird, and consisting of many kinds of flowers made of gold inlaid with precious stones. On the side of the throne which is opposite the court there is to be seen a jewel consisting of a diamond of from 80 to 90 carats weight, with rubies and emeralds round it, and when the King is seated he has this jewel in full view.
(J. B. Tavernier, Travels in India 1676, *transl. V. Ball, vol. II, 1889:381–384)*

The king undressed, and ordered his clothes to be washed, and in the meanwhile he wore his dressing gown; while thus sitting, a beautiful bird flew into the tent, the doors of which were immediately closed, and the bird caught; His Majesty then took a pair of scissors and cut some of the feathers off of the animal; he then sent for a painter, and had a picture taken of the bird, and afterwards ordered it to be released.
(Jauhar Aftabchi, Tazkirat al-Vaqiat, *transl. Ch. Stewart, cit. in Brand, Lowry, 1985:43)*

cumstance. There are indications that he even practised the art himself. Certainly when, as a virtual refugee from India, he was resident at the court of Shah Tahmasp of Persia with its remarkable galaxy of painters, he established early contacts with painters some of whom were later to return to India with him.

One can visualise Humayun submerging himself in the refinements of Persian culture. In the midst of all his misfortunes and personal uncertainties, we find him deeply concerned about his collection of rare and precious books, a camel-load of which he lost in the course of a campaign: fortunately to recover it later. As soon as he had some breathing space and had established the semblance of a court at Kabul, while he prepared to march back into India, he sent for the great Persian masters of painting with whom he had formed an understanding while in Persia earlier. The arrival of the painters and other gifted men at Kabul was evidently quite an event, for it is spoken of in detail and with some enthusiasm. Humayun took obvious pride in the work of his artists and craftsmen, and an oft-cited letter that he wrote from Kabul to the ruler of Kashghar, sending along with it some specimens of the remarkable work produced by his men, says a great deal about his private passion for painting. The period is so thinly documented that our information on painting under Humayun is sketchy, although one suspects that, considering his circumstances, he undertook a great deal and laid a splendid foundation. The Persian masters clearly moved on to India with Humayun in 1555, but the emperor's early death left much that was incomplete.

It is of interest to remark that there is nothing in the attitude either of Babur or of Humayun that concedes, even remotely, the orthodox Islamic objection to figural or representational art. Considering the pride with which some early Timurid princes had maintained ateliers of painters, and considering the remarkable state of painting at the Shi'ite court of Persia, this does not sound surprising; but in the context of early Islamic rule in India, this openness of attitude represents a marked departure. While there is increasing evidence that painting in a derived Persian style, designated now as 'Sultanate' or 'Indo-Persian', was practised at least from the 15th century on, if not earlier, at some of the minor centres of power like Mandu or Jaunpur or Bengal in northern India, there is nothing that clearly links the Muslim sultans of Delhi with painting. Barely a work or manuscript produced for one of the Delhi sultans has surfaced so far and, if one were to go by the evidence from the reign of a sultan like Feroze Shah Tughlaq, who ordered all traces of representation to be removed not only from his palace walls but even from the utensils in use in the royal kitchen, and who had a Hindu who was carrying around 'painted devices' publicly burnt, the official view towards painting was a narrow and orthodox one. The rulers who sat on the throne of Delhi perhaps saw themselves as the upholders of Islamic authority in a land that they had conquered and subdued, and nothing less than the strictest following of the Islamic injunctions could have been seen as proper by them. When Babur supplanted the rule of the Lodis and founded the Mughal dynasty in India, he remained, however, unburdened by this attitude. The same holds true for Humayun, considering all the evidence that we have of his enthusiasm for painting.

One needs to recall to one's mind the fact that when young Akbar succeeded to the Mughal throne, in the matter of painting many clear options were available to him. That he would be indifferent to painting, and take no interest in it can easily be ruled out; for not only was he aware of his father's enthusiasm for the art: he himself had taken lessons in drawing as a child, judging from a well-known painting showing him presenting a work to his father. The kind of pious staying away from figural art that the Tughlaq Sultans of Delhi had cultivated also held obviously no meaning for him; in fact, if one sees the development of his whole attitude towards orthodoxy in later years, this would have been unthinkable. However, even if one takes his interest in painting from the very beginning as granted, one can be sure that many different roads were still open to him. The easiest, perhaps the one most easily warranted by circumstances, would have been to ask the Persian masters whom he inherited from his father to continue painting as they had always done: in the true Persian manner, harking back to the glories of the work of masters like Bihzad or Sultan Muhammad or Aqa Mirak. Akbar could, at the same time, have availed himself of the services of such painters as were working in the 'Indo-Persian' style, at regional centres like Malwa or Jaunpur. It is more than likely that their work was known to him and that some of them converged upon the court of the young monarch in the hope of finding patronage. Yet another possibility for Akbar would have been, given his remarkably liberal attitudes, to patronise work in the native Indian tradition, like Jaina or early Rajasthani: styles which had roots in the soil and were possessed of remarkable vitality, each in its own way.

Forty days had passed since His Majesty's return from the Balkh campaign when Mir Sayyid Ali, Mulla Abd al-Samad, and Mulla Fakhr, in the company of Khwaja Jalal al-Din Mahmud, arrived in Kabul and humbly presented themselves before His Majesty, who honoured them with many favours. At that time among the most notable painters there was one Mulla Dost, who could not give up wine at the time His Majesty did, and who had, without His Majesty's permission, joined the service of Mirza Kamran. He was declared by the connoisseurs to have drawn trees and mountains better than Mani. And God knows best...
(The Memoirs of Bayazid, transl. C.M. Naim, cit. in P. Chandra, 1976:172)

From among those matchless artists who had presented themselves before me in Iraq and Khurasan and were generously rewarded, a group came and joined my service in Shawwal A.H. 959 / September–October 1552. One of them is the painter Mir Sayyid Ali, the nadir al-asr, *who is matchless in painting (taswir). He has painted on a grain of rice a polo scene – two horsemen stand within the field, a third comes galloping from one corner, while a fourth horseman stands at one end receiving a mallet from a footman; at each end of the field are two goal posts; and at each corner of the rice is written the following couplet:*
'A whole granary lies within a grain/ and an entire world inside a bubble.' And at the bottom he has written, 'the humble servant Sayyid Ali, in the month of Rajab A.H. 959 / June–July 1552.
Another of these rare craftsmen is Maulana Fakhr the book-binder, who has made twenty-five holes in a poppy seed... and there is the unique craftsman Ustad Wais, the gold-wire drawer (zar-kash), who has made twenty-five gold and silver wires so thin that Mulla Fakhr could draw them through the holes in the poppy seed. These few things made by these talented people are being sent.
(The Memoirs of Bayazid, transl. C.M. Naim, cit. in P. Chandra, 1976:172 f)

Bigoted followers of the letter of the law are hostile to the art of painting; but their eyes now see the truth. One day at a private party of friends, His Majesty, who had conferred on several the pleasure of drawing near him, remarked: "There are many that hate painting; but such men I dislike. It appears to me as if a painter had quite peculiar means of recognizing God; for a painter in sketching anything that has life, and in devising its limbs, one after the other, must come to feel that he cannot bestow individuality upon his work, and is thus forced to think of God, the giver of life, and will thus increase in knowledge."
(Abul Fazl, Ain-i Akbari, vol. I:115)

If the emperor did not take any of these straight options, then, it is because he evidently had ideas of his own, ideas that were much more in consonance with the much larger ideas of an empire with a different identity. Our information on the early years of Akbar's reign is not as full as from the middle years onwards, but it is more than likely that very early on, the notion of extensive *karkhanas* or workshops was conceived and put into practice. This concerned not only painting but a whole remarkable range of products and activities. In painting, clearly the Persian *ustads* or masters were not only retained in service but paid due homage by being asked to head the workshops which began to be filled with artists drawn from far corners of India. The names of a great many of the artists employed in the imperial ateliers have survived, a large number of them Hindus, the second parts of their names indicating their extraction or regional affiliation. From these lists one notices that artists and craftsmen came from Kashmir and Lahore, from Gujarat and Gwalior; to these one must add the Persian masters who had come from far-off Tabriz and Shiraz. One can be sure that if more names in all their fullness had survived, more regions or stylistic affiliations would have been seen as represented in the imperial ateliers. But even this limited list is impressive enough.

The process by which these artists were recruited to the atelier is not documented, but one can make guesses. Some of the artists were, to be sure, formally invited, as had been Mir Sayyid Ali, Khwaja Abd-al Samad, Dust Muhammad, Maulana Yusuf, Maulana Darvish Muhammad by Humayun while he was still in Kabul. Other artists on their own must have been drawn to the court, much in the manner that any major court with strong cultural interests had always acted as a magnet for poets and writers, painters and calligraphers and craftsmen of various descriptions. One can even visualise painters pressing their claims upon imperial attention by presenting works for approval, in support of their hopes. We have Abul Fazl's evidence about Akbar himself, alert as ever, being on the look-out for talent: the great Daswant, a palanquin bearer by caste and family profession, was thus 'spotted'. And then, obviously, the ranks of painters were always swelling through the inclusion of gifted family members or relations whose talents were recommended by those already in employ.

There can be little doubt that the painters drawn from such widely dispersed areas, and belonging to mature, well-established traditions, brought initially their own styles or manner with them. But in the imperial atelier, the idea that each of the painters should continue working in his own 'inherited' manner was not seriously entertained. That might have been of interest, but not necessarily of significance. It could have meant a certain continuance, an extension in time of a style already extant; but it was new beginnings that were being aimed for. It would seem as if no one, not even the great Persian masters who had brought with them such prestige, was encouraged to go on doing exactly what he had grown up doing. Something different had to be attempted, a merging of opposites, a vital coming together of different elements, in the belief that a new identity was not only possible but necessary. Understandably, this process could only have been an uneasy one to begin with, a little confused, perhaps a little contrived; but there was evidently enough energy and resolve behind the attempt at establishing a new identity for it to succeed.

Interestingly, almost at the very beginning of painting activity under Akbar, in 1562 or thereabouts, a remarkable enterprise was undertaken, the painting of the *Hamzanama*, pseudo-historical tales of the adventures of an uncle of the Prophet Muhammad: this was conceived as consisting of 1,400 unusually large paintings in fourteen volumes of one hundred paintings each. Not only was the scale of the entire enterprise without precedent: the size of each painting was truly large, 94 x 75 cm, and the material on which it was to be done was cotton. It is as if in the taking of these decisions, everything had been carefully calculated – the volume, the size, the material – so as to make continuing to do things that artists had done for so long virtually impossible. One senses that within the extended format, new ground was being prepared for ideas, for experiments to be tried out, and, hopefully, for new understandings to be arrived at.

It is somewhere in the course of this, and certainly from this point onwards, that a new entity emerges which can broadly be referred to as Mughal painting, distinguishable with swift ease from the painting of Persia on the one hand and Rajput work on the other. Fortunately, no dead uniformity was to belong to the new style, for many men of remarkable gifts were to work in it and develop their own personal idioms within the general framework of the style; new impulses were to keep coming in, some from Europe, others in a renewed form from Persia or the Deccan; these things were absorbed and subsumed with majestic ease. A language had been fashioned. Within it, individual styles, dialects, personal and idiosyncratic turns of phrase, were all to exist,

Among the wonderful events and unusual traits of H.M. Shahinshah which came forth from the ambush of secrecy and displayed their splendours in the theatre of manifestation, there was this that when H.M. Jahanbani Jannat Ashiyani had come to Delhi after the victory over Sikandar, he (Akbar) there practised drawing in accordance with a sublime suggestion (of Humayun?). The skilful artists such as Mir Saiyid Ali and Khwaja Abdul-Samad Shiringalam, who were among the matchless ones of this art, were in his service and were instructing him. One day this cyclopaedia of Divine things was in the library of H.M. Jahanbani and in order to sharpen his mind was employing himself in drawing…
(Abul Fazl, Akbarnama, vol. II:67)

Among the forerunners on the high road of art I may mention:
1. Mir Sayyid Ali of Tabriz. From the time of his introduction at Court, the ray of royal favour has shone upon him.
2. Khwaja Abd-al Samad, styled Shiringalam or 'sweet pen'. He comes from Shiraz. From the instruction they received, the Khwaja's pupils became masters.
3. Daswanth … In a short time he surpassed all painters, and became the first master of the age.
4. Basawan. In back grounding, drawing of features, distribution of colours, portrait painting, and several other branches, he is most excellent, so much so that many critics prefer him to Daswanth.
The following painters have likewise attained fame: Kesu, Lal, Mukund, Mushkin, Farrukh the Qalmaq (Calmuck), Madhu, Jagan, Mohesh, Khemkaran, Tara, Sawla, Haribas, Ram. It would take me too long to describe the excellencies of each. My intention is "to pluck a flower from every meadow, an ear from every sheaf."
(Abul Fazl, Ain-i Akbari, vol. I:114)

Daswanth. He is the son of a palkee-bearer. He devoted his whole life to the art, and used, from love of his profession, to draw and paint figures even on walls. One day the eye of His Majesty fell on him; his talent was discovered, and he himself handed over to the Khwaja. In a short time he surpassed all painters, and became the first master of the age. Unfortunately the light of his talents was dimmed by the shadow of madness; he committed suicide. He has left many masterpieces.
(Abul Fazl, Ain-i Akbari, vol. I:114)

but a structure of grammar had been laid down.

III

It is tempting, though not without hazard, to try and reconstruct the manner, the steps, through which artists drawn from various traditions and used to working in different styles – Persians as well as Hindus, those who came from Shiraz or from Gujarat – were encouraged to see and render things differently. As an absorbing example, one can take the representation, or understanding, of time as reflected in painting. In the Persian tradition it was the norm, within the frame of a single painting, to refer to a given moment of time. Different episodes, whether taken from epic works or poetical compositions or historical narratives, and covering sometimes a number of actions, were encompassed within a single painting, but only such actions as were happening or could have happened at a given moment. In the Hindu tradition, however, no specific importance was attached to a moment, for things were naturally understood to be happening within the flux, the uninterrupted flow of time. For more than 1500 years the Hindu artist like his Buddhist and Jaina counterpart, had rendered within the same frame, in sculpture and painting alike, different or succeeding moments of time; because to him they naturally belonged to a sequence in a given narrative. Thus, the same figure, within a single frame – a roundel in stone, a segment of a painting on a wall, a page of an illustrated manuscript – could be shown twice or even more often: moving from one point to another, or engaged in a succession of activities. What was represented through this was not simultaneity, not different things happening at the same moment, but a progression, a movement in time. In a substantial way this reflected the Hindu understanding of time which had always been conceived of not as linear, with a given beginning and a given end, but as cyclical: possessed of a *chhanda*, a rhythm, of its own. Clearly, not every single artist worked these ideas out before sitting down to paint or carve: they came in because they were an integral part of the thinking of a whole people and were therefore naturally reflected in their art. To the Islamic mind which takes a 'rational', at least a different, view of time, more in line with the Judaeo-Christian modes of thought, such a rendering would be illogical, confused; at any rate unacceptable.

It is entirely likely that questions like this came up at the workshops, and one can visualise a Hindu painter from Gujarat or

Gwalior initially working out a design, a composition, in which, following his usual manner, he would show the same figure two or three times within the same frame: a lion leaping from one end of a painting and being cut down by a sword at another; a man setting out from his house, and seen first leaving from the outer door and then again at a distance walking along the bank of a river or resting under a tree. But clearly, since everything had to be controlled in a workshop situation, one can then visualise the Persian master, with his own given and strict view of these matters, looking at this composition with unconcealed disapproval, pointing out to the painter its lack of logic, and asking him to work the composition out again, differently. The Hindu painter might have been startled by this, even dissatisfied, but was unlikely to have had any option. Something approaching this must have happened at the very outset, for the sequential rendering of the same figure (or figures) within a single frame finds no place in Mughal painting: it is with great difficulty that one can think of examples of Mughal work in which this continuous, narrative method of Hindu India figures. In this matter, Mughal and Hindu painting clearly part company.

To be sure, within the Mughal tradition one sees paintings that refer to more than a real, fixed moment and seemingly take a different view of time: for example one knows of works in which several generations of the same family are represented seated together. The princes of the house of Timur, drawn from as many as six generations, might thus be brought together within the same painting: an 'illogical' rendering of time, a clear anachronism. But these works are of another order than the ones from the Hindu tradition in which the flow of time is conceived differently. These are in the nature of visual renderings of genealogical 'trees of descent', and not actual assemblages. The occasional groups of *shaikhs* or holy men, drawn from different regions and belonging to different periods of time but seated in the same gathering as if conversing, are also not very different from genealogical or dynastic representations, for in them a spiritual connection, a collective 'auspiciousness', is sought to be evoked. These are works done self-consciously, not in defiance of logical, linear time, but as statements of connection: they serve a different end.

Not in the same measure as regards time but in the treatment of space too, some new ideas seem to have been worked out in Mughal painting, distancing it both from Persian and Hindu approaches. The manner in which depth had been virtually eliminated

It is now seven years that the Mir has been busy in the royal bureau of books (kitab khana-i ali), *as commanded by His Majesty* (hazrat-i ala), *in the decoration and painting of the large compositions* (taswir-i majalis) *of the story of Amir Hamza* (qissa-i amir hamza), *and strives to finish that wondrous book which is one of the astonishing novelties that His Majesty has conceived of. Verily it is a book the like of which no connoisseur has seen since the azure sheets of the heavens were decorated with brilliant stars, nor has the hand of destiny inscribed such a book on the tablet of the imagination since the discs of the celestial sphere gained beauty and glamour with the appearance of the moon and the sun. His Majesty has conceived of this wondrous book on the following lines. The amazing descriptions and the strange events of that story will be completed in twelve volumes, each volume consisting of one hundred leaves* (waraq); *each leaf being one 'yard'* (zar) *by one 'yard', containing two large compositions* (majlis-i taswir). *Opposite each illustration, the events and incidents relative to it, put into contemporary language, have been written down in a delightful style … Although, during the aforesaid period, thirty painters, equal to Mani and Bihzad, have constantly been devoted to the task, no more than four volumes have been completed. One can imagine just from that its grandeur and perfection. May God bring their work to completion under the sublime and majestic shade.*
(Mir Ala al-Daula, *Nafais al-Maasir, transl. C. M. Naim, cit. in P. Chandra, 1976:180)*

Murder scene, Akbar period, c. 1590
Staatsbibliothek Preussischer Kulturbesitz, Berlin

from pre-Mughal paintings in the Indian tradition, in Rajput or Jaina work for instance, with their strong preferences for flat, evenly coloured backgrounds and no statements about depth, was now discarded, except in formal, single portraits that required no necessary relationship to a given space. The shallowness of space that belonged to the tradition of Persian paintings was, in essence, retained; but in the new, emerging style, there was no reluctance to establish depth: the eye was invited to move not only along smooth surfaces on one or several planes, but to travel in and out apart from up and down, the major consideration being the needs of the situation in a composition. Things were no longer seen uniformly at more or less eye-level against flat backgrounds, or in vertical projection from a bird's eye view: a new favourite viewpoint emerged, something that can be roughly designated as a 'view from a balcony', like that which women, often seen peering down from their palace windows, must have had. This view enabled the painter, if a scene inside an enclosure like a palace courtyard were to be represented, first to show what was happening outside the outer wall of the palace; then to lead the eye to the 'lower part' of the courtyard inside and gradually up to the chambers where, most often, the major focus of activity rested. Essentially this 'view from the balcony' was retained over a considerable period of time and even when that major incursion, the arrival of European paintings and engravings, occurred, only limited accomodations to the new ways of seeing were made. A certain depth was experimented with; distant views of towns in a bluish aerial haze were inducted into standard compositions; but linear perspective of the kind that had been painstakingly established by this time in European art was never really adopted as such. The Mughal understanding of space is thus not 'scientific'; it is not even constant; it is, in its own way, pragmatic. Evidently, artists who came from different backgrounds and traditions must have had to make major adjustments in their own visions to conform to this new comprehension of space that was in part intellectual and in part visual.

In the matter of observation, of establishing a visible link with reality and taking cognizance of natural appearances, the ideas that were worked out in the Mughal imperial atelier entailed major departures from their own points of view and ways of seeing, alike for those trained in the Persian manner and those who came from Hindu backgrounds. The painters from both these traditions had, in their own ways, always been clear-eyed, possessed of remarkable powers of observation; but their concerns were not 'naturalistic'. The minuteness of the Persian painters' observation, so often combined with an extraordinary dexterity of hand, had always been subordinated to the demands of the overall design, the surface rhythms of a work. The painters from the native Indian traditions had also always observed well, but their interest was not so much in the appearance of things as in their true nature, their essence: the emphasis being on a kind of reality or truth, different from the one ordinarily seen by the eye. The view of reality that emerged in Mughal painting was not uninformed by either of these viewpoints, but it aimed at grounding that reality, making it earth-bound.

One sees it nowhere better than in Mughal portraits. Here was a whole genre of painting that had never entered the ken of the Hindu painter, his interests being entirely different. To the Persian painter, portraiture was by no means unknown, but his figures tended to be only elements in what was essentially conceived as a design: elegant, rhythmic, superbly drawn, but primarily surface-bound, tending constantly towards abstraction. Mughal portraits, on the other hand, at least in the 16th century, are possessed of a certain weight, an earth-bound quality, a sense of immediacy. The sharpness of observation that we see in them is remarkable but, the intention not being 'realistic' in the ordinary sense of the word, statements remain discreet and subtle; the painter does not ever wander away from the subject, but he is not intent upon laying it bare either. These portraits are possessed of remarkable incisiveness, of penetration, but this incisiveness is nearly always tempered with a certain human warmth. It is only well into the 17th century that Mughal portraiture acquires a measure of aloofness, even some coldness; in its early stages it is alive and warm to the touch.

All these aspects of Mughal paintings – renderings of time and of space, relationships to natural appearances and the like – represent decisions. The manner in which these 'decisions' were taken, the process of working them out, however, remains obscure. Judging from Abul Fazl's brief but sharp statement about the extent of interest taken in painting by the Emperor Akbar, one would not be surprised if he was personally involved in discussions with his master painters, offering suggestions if not necessarily laying down clear directions. It is also possible that compromises were worked out between the artists themselves, and one can think of animated discussions being held, sharp disagreements being aired, all under

The first thing he (Akbar) did was to go into the church, which was well appointed with its perfumes and fragrance. On entering he was surprised and astonished and made a deep obeisance to the picture of Our Lady that was there, from the painting of St. Luke, done by Brother Manuel Godinho, as well as to another beautifully executed representation of Our Lady brought by Fr. Martin da Silva from Rome, which pleased him no end. After stepping outside briefly to discuss these pictures with his attendants, he came back in with his 'chief painter' and other painters, 'and they were all wonderstruck and said that there could be no better paintings nor better artists than those who had painted the said pictures.'
(Letter from Father Henriques, April 1580, cit. in Brand, Lowry, 1985:98)

The birth of Prince Salim, Akbarnama, c. 1590
Victoria and Albert Museum, London

the aegis of the heads of the workshops, the master painters. But we do not know enough. The silences even of this ordinarily well-documented period are too dense to penetrate.

IV

Being a painter in the Mughal atelier must have been a task at once challenging and exciting. Apart from the intellectual and technical demands of working in a style that set out to be different, the painters must always have had to keep their perceptions sharp and all their senses alert. The situation was highly competitive, for the number of artists who pressed their claims upon imperial patronage could not but have been large, considering that patronage at this level brought with it not only security and rewards but decided prestige. From the surviving inscriptions or annotations on paintings and leaves of illustrated manuscripts, one knows that roles were constantly being shifted. Work on large undertakings like the illustration of an extensive manuscript was often collaborative in nature: in these situations a painter might be asked to work on the composition of one page but only fill in the colours in another, or paint in the more important faces on a third one. For a painter, then, commissions or assigned tasks carried with them necessarily a measure of uncertainty. Relationships with the masters, those superintending work at the ateliers, and with fellow artists needed to be carefully tended, and opportunities, whenever they presented themselves, had to be seized. One can sense challenge being in the air nearly all the time: the arrival at the court of a distinguished painter; the coming in of totally 'alien' work like that from Europe in which the patron was seen to take obvious interest and delight; the need to pit one's skills against those of another when different versions of a given subject were suddenly commissioned. It could not but have been necessary in these situations for a painter to keep his hand in fine trim, perhaps even to aim at showing off his virtuosity. Those prodigies of fine workmanship that had held such appeal in the Persian world might not have been expected of the Mughal painter, but there could be little doubt that, as ideals, they were alive in Mughal India. And whenever a painter were to approximate to those skills, like painting whole compositions on a grain of rice, it could only have added to his status and prestige. When Khwaja Abd-al Samad paints, at the age of 85 years, a picture of fighting camels in the manner of Bihzad, he might have been fulfilling an inner need; but he might equally be out to demonstrate that, despite his modest statement in the inscription on the painting (no. 19) saying his hand was now infirm and his eyes weak, he was in some manner still very much in control.

Even more than this, given our understanding that patronage was a crucial factor in the situation, the painter must have intuitively had to know and perceive the inner needs of the patron, his true preferences. The personalities of the men that the painter worked for, whether at the imperial level or that of the grandees who maintained ateliers of their own, were naturally different, and there was a need for a painter to be sensitive to these differences. If we see the temper of Mughal painting change from the Akbar period to that of Jahangir, and on to Shahjahan – in fact even within Jahangir's own ambit, from the time that he was prince to the time that he became emperor – the change comes about not because the cast of painters had suddenly changed: painters from one reign ordinarily went on to paint in the next, but only those that sensitively picked up the spirit of the new times could have survived long. It is easy to see that some interests and concerns remained constant. Each of the ruling monarchs was interested in the imperial image; each was interested in the past and through that a proclamation of pride in ancestry; each also in the present with all its ceaseless tumult of activity. But all of these concerns were capable of being expressed and articulated differently, and each patron undoubtedly had his own ideas and his personal preferences. It is to these that the painter must have had to be responsive. The bustling sense of energy that might have delighted Akbar in a work was perhaps too noisy, too uncontrolled for the taste of Shahjahan; the feeling of preciousness in a single stalk of a flower painted for Jahangir, on the other hand, his father might have found to be too remote and aloof.

The painter had to keep firmly within his ken (if not necessarily always in his favoured repertoire) a wide range of subjects and themes. The emphases shifted somewhat from reign to reign, but throughout the high period of Mughal art, strong interest in contemporary events did not ever wane; the chronicles of the past, illustrations of poetic works, copies or adaptations of European works, many of them of Christian content, 'natural history' paintings, were other favourites. But the painter had always to weigh the extent of shift in emphasis. This is not to suggest that the themes were always chosen by the painter himself: sometimes they were, but in the ordinary course they would either be suggested or approved of by the patron;

His name is Sharif, and he is the son of Khwaja Abd-al Samad the painter. He is a youth lately come to man's estate, and he is unrivalled in beauty of penmanship and in painting. It is well known that his father wrote in full, and in a good and legible hand, on one side of a poppy seed, the Suratu-l-Ikhlas, *and on the other side of it the argument of the chapter; and they say that his son, Sharif, bored in one poppy seed eight small holes, and passed wires through them, and that he drew, on a grain of rice, a picture of an armed horseman, preceded by an outrider, and bearing all the things proper to a horseman such as a sword, a shield, a polo-stick, et cetera.*
(Badauni, Muntakhabu-t-Tawarikh, *vol. III:229 f)*

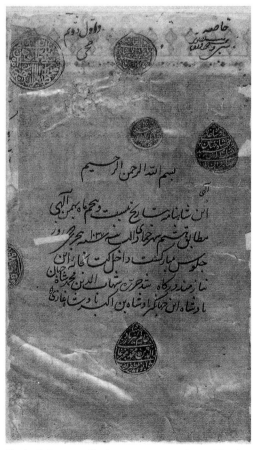

Fly-leaf from a Shahnama-*manuscript, with the seals of the Emperors Babur, Humayun, Jahangir, Shahjahan and Aurangzeb*
Royal Asiatic Society, London

or, alternatively, by the *ustad* or master painter who directed the production of an atelier. But, given all this, some changes are likely to have come about through the sheer fact of the organisation of the workshops changing from the 16th century to the 17th. Extensive collaborative enterprises, like the production of the great *Hamzanama,* or the histories for Akbar, in which a host of painters worked on the same manuscript collectively – and two or more on a single painting – yielded gradually to a different mode of production in which the individual painter came more sharply into focus. Under Jahangir, and later under Shahjahan, collaboration was obviously not unknown, but far more often works were conceived, drawn, and completed by one artist. Given this changed situation, in respect of where the initiative rested in the matter of choosing a theme, a shift would ordinarily have come about. While this must have given the artist a certain freedom, it also placed upon him a new responsibility. He could now set about achieving virtuoso effects in his work, but failure could be his as much as success.

Whatever the situation in regard to themes and the initiative of the painter, it is more than certain that he could not take his patron lightly. For in a very real way, the Mughals were highly discerning patrons, passionately involved in painting and keenly conscious of quality. Connoisseurship was a matter of pride. The Mughal emperors had great taste, each in his own fashion: taste that reflected itself not only in painting but in all of their thought processes. Whether it was in the laying of gardens or planning great architectural complexes, in founding workshops where objects of the most exquisite quality were produced or in surrounding themselves with institutions, procedures and rules of conduct and etiquette, a fine aestheticism marked the decisions of the Mughals. One may pick at random any object that has survived from the Mughal period, and one would be able to see in it an inner integrity and a mark of refined taste. It is therefore not surprising that the style that the Mughals surrounded themselves with became, for the rest of India, a standard against which to measure quality for close to three hundred years. This was not simply a matter of expensive materials and precious stones, of gold and jade, pearls and rubies, but of refined sensibilities reflected in the shapes and forms of even the most commonplace things. The sensitivity with which Babur described flowers and birds, and planned orderly water courses in gardens that he founded, from Kabul (in the North-West) to Dholpur (near Agra), the poetic flair with which Humayun planned elaborate feasts that delighted the eye as much as the palate, are of a piece with Akbar's passion in these matters, too. The elaborate procedures and finenesses of detail in all matters, down to the wearing of dresses and perfumes appropriate to certain days and occasions and zodiacal signs, make one feel as if everything were being orchestrated in the most careful and precise manner possible.

When Abul Fazl states that the work of the painters was laid 'weekly before His Majesty', he is not likely to be exaggerating. There may not be many verbal statements about Akbar's great taste in painting, but the general quality of work done for him gives an accurate idea of how demanding his standards were. The reference to painting in Jahangir's own words are quite remarkable, for he returns to the subject again and again, now praising the work of an individual painter, now stating that he gave specific orders for a dying man in his employ to be drawn from life, now taking great pride in his own connoisseurship. When connoisseurship of this order was combined with that consuming, insatiable curiosity that marked nearly all the Great Mughals, the task of the painter could by no means have been easy. He could have survived only if he brought to his work all, absolutely everything, that he was capable of. He must also have been asked to do all kinds of things, take lightning turns as it were, expected now to turn out faithful copies of European works, now to envision an episode from the 9th century when the Barmakis (Barmecides) were active, now to record the brilliant plumage of a turkeycock recently brought in from Goa, now to render a splendid portrait of the emperor fit for formal presentation.

All this speculation about the painter's circumscription by the patron's taste does not take into account the artist who did not conform, the gifted eccentric who had his own view of art and of life. But even he had a place in the scheme of things, for the parameters within which the painters were expected to stay were remarkably broad. There was always room for innovation: this alone could explain the sudden incursion, and seeming success, of a painter arriving from outside and working for the emperor while standing slightly outside of the mainstream of Mughal art.

V

Reading works of art from the past is never easy, and there is much that remains elusive. Mughal painting poses in this respect even more than the usual problems perhaps, for it

When within two miles of the Ab-i-istada, we saw a wonderful thing, – something as red as the rose of the dawn kept shewing and vanishing between the sky and the water. It kept coming and going. When we got quite close we learned that what seemed the cause were flocks of geese, not 10,000, not 20,000 in a flock, but geese innumerable which, when the mass of birds flapped their wings in flight, sometimes shewed red feathers, sometimes not.
(Babur, Baburnama, transl. A.S. Beveridge, 1922: 240)

His Majesty, from his earliest youth, has shown a great predilection for this art, and gives it every encouragement, as he looks upon it as a means both of study and amusement. Hence the art flourishes, and many painters have obtained great reputation. The works of all painters are weekly laid before His Majesty by the Daroghas and the clerks; he then confers rewards according to excellence of workmanship, or increases the monthly salaries.
(Abul Fazl, Ain-i Akbari, vol. I:113)

As regards myself (Jahangir), my liking for painting and practice in judging it have arrived at such a point that when any work is brought before me, either of deceased artists or of those of the present day, without the names being told me, I say on the spur of the moment that it is the work of such and such a man. And if there be a picture containing many portraits, and each face be the work of a different master, I can discover which face is the work of each of them. If any other person has put in the eye and eyebrow of a face, I can perceive whose work the original face is, and who has painted the eye and eyebrows.
(Jahangir, Tuzuk-i-Jahangiri, transl. A. Rogers and H. Beveridge, 1909–1914, vol. II:20f)

One of the wonderful inventions of that holy mind was a cap (taj) which was alike magnificent and agreeable to wear. The border (or margin) which went round the taj had two divisions (furja), and each of these was in the form of the figure seven (V), and thus by there being two figures 7 (VV) the number 77 was produced, which was the numerical value of the word aizz. Here it was called the taj-iaizzat or cap of honour. This was invented in Badakhshan...
(Abul Fazl, Akbarnama, vol. I:648f)

stems from and describes a culture that had gone to great lengths in building a structure of relationships and hierarchies that was at once highly complex and subtle. There was much meaning attached to seemingly small things: who stood at what distance from the emperor; whether a person was inside a railing or outside it; at what point was gaze directed; how hands were disposed and what was carried in them. These were all carefully studied matters that stated quite definite things and placed a person in a hierarchy of relationships. The more obvious among these things would be difficult to miss, but one would really have to be intimately familiar with the structure of the court and its highly formal etiquette, with not only personalities but politics at the court, to be able to catch the right nuances that belong to scenes related to the Mughal *darbars,* for instance. Since feelings and emotions are rarely registered on the face, one has to be alert to pick up attitudes and gestures, the tilt of the head, and the direction of the eyes, for they are seldom without meaning.

Like everywhere else, dresses in Mughal paintings tell a great deal. It is not merely a matter of the expensiveness of material or the source from which a dress comes: clearly these help establish status or extraction; it is also the manner of wearing a dress that needs to be noticed, for it often contains valuable clues. As an example one could take the turban, that ubiquitous headgear that one sees in Mughal painting of all periods. It is possible to quickly pick up the fact that the turban styles were established individually by each monarch, and they are quite distinct and easily identifiable. The rather heavy turban of Babur with a small projecting skull cap or *kulah* is different from the *Chaghatai-* cap and turban of Humayun, for its loops are more relaxed and curling, and the *kulah* rises proudly in the air. The Akbari turban is small, as we have seen, and sits relatively lightly on the head, and is made up of a narrow, long strip of cloth, two or three loops of which sometimes adorn the back of the head. But the Jahangiri turban is somewhat fuller and looser, covering the forehead slightly and extending to the back of the head with its end, made of the same material as the turban, serving as a kind of crossband, tied diagonally from the middle of the top of the head and rimming the turban along its lower edge towards the back. The Shahjahani turban becomes even more elaborate and loses the relaxed air that the Jahangiri turban had, with more importance given to the crossband; the Aurangzeb period turban accentuates that profile still further and moves considerably far away from the simple, lightly-tied turban of the

Akbar period. Being able to recognise these turbans is helpful, for not only do they communicate something of the personal style of the emperor who obviously set a fashion; they also help in placing a work within a time frame.

But the whole matter is more complex than this, for while the emperor's own manner of wearing a turban is immediately recognisable (since it would be normal to expect this style to be followed by the nobles and grandees at the court), one sees a certain mixture of turban styles at least in the first few years of a new reign. Nobles and ministers who had grown old in the service of the monarch in the preceding reign evidently did not change their style of wearing the turban overnight: one sees, therefore, Jahangiri turbans co-existing with Akbari turbans at least for a period of time. Sometimes even affiliations were expressed through this, for clearly there were factions at the court, and those that were loyal to a prince who had ideas of his own during his father's reign would proclaim their loyalties by wearing a turban in the style of their patron, the prince, rather than in the style followed by the emperor, his father. There are further elements in this sartorial situation that might appear to us complicated even though to contemporaries they would have been perfectly clear. Thus visitors from outside, ambassadors and envoys and others, quite naturally stuck to the style of headgear that was their own, so that at a court like that of Jahangir, one might find European hats, large Persian turbans, conical furcaps that came from Afghanistan and Central Asia, easily intermingling with the turbans sported by men who belonged to the court. These 'odd' headgears suffice in themselves to establish the foreign extraction of the people wearing them. But the situation remains always a trifle beyond our grasp. It is certain that the great splash of colour that turbans make in large, elaborately composed scenes had other dimensions.

In the matter of dress, at least of equal interest as the turban, is the *jama,* that long and elegant gown-like dress that remains constant virtually throughout this period. But the length and the style of the *jama* varied and there is much discussion about one particular type of *jama,* that with slit and pointed ends called the *'chakdar'.* The point of controversy is from where it originates and when it goes decidedly out of use, for that could be seen as a useful clue to the dating of paintings. This is an arcane area (and one that cannot be gone into without a detailed examination of conflicting evidence). But at least one culturally significant detail that is

Babur

Humayun

Akbar

Jahangir

Shahjahan

absolutely necessary to pick up is the manner of tying the *jama.* Being an open-fronted kind of garment, the front panels of which overlapped and had to be fastened under the arm, the *jama* as a rule was tied under the left arm with tie-cords by the Hindus and under the right by Muslims. At a court where personal appearance and the general style of dress did not necessarily help distinguish a Hindu from a Muslim, this distinction, drawn by the emperor Akbar, must have been a necessary one for eliminating the possibilities of social faux-pas, if for nothing else. Though externally often similar in private habits and modes of behaviour, the Hindus and the Muslims bore distinct identities, and there was eminent reason behind laying down this convention. In the context of painting, it is of interest to see how alertly the painters pay attention to this detail. Even in the telling of those long and involved tales in the *Tutinama* that belong to no specific time, the painters very quickly switched from one style of wearing the *jama* to another, the moment the principal figure in that tale, a king or a prince, is specified by the narrative as a Hindu or a Muslim. To this rule of fastening the *jama* – the actual number of strings or lappets, and the height at which these were placed, were often a matter of personal taste – there must be remarkably few exceptions in the range of Mughal painting from the Akbar period onwards.

It is useful to remember that details like the style, the length, the manner of fastening the *jama* were not things that the painter was inventing: he was simply rendering with veracity what he observed. Our need to pay close attention to these today arises from the fact that we are removed from those times and therefore sometimes liable to misread what is represented in a situation.

Yet another item of apparel that deserves careful notice in this context is the length and the design of the *patka,* that elegant sash or waistband, which almost every person of rank is seen wearing. This underwent a clear change over a period of time. The *patkas* of the Akbar period tend to be a little long, with both ends falling evenly in front, and the design on them relatively simple, mostly consisting of horizontal bars and lozenges or chevrons. At this time, the *patka* does not call too much attention to itself. In the Jahangir period, the fashion changes slightly, with the usual *patka* often being added to by a sash of fine muslin perhaps, that falls along the decorative *patka* but serves to support it. The *patka* seen mostly in the Shahjahan period paintings is far more decorative, with prominent, highly formalised and elegant floral sprigs occupying the lower ends, set against a bare ground and placed neatly between narrow, horizontal floral borders above and below. Some of the elegant 'herbal' designs on these *patkas* are remarkably reminiscent of those superb floral decorations in pietra dura on the great Shahjahan architectural monuments. There is much work with gold thread in these *patkas* which are worn relatively short, but the effect is one of sophistication and elegance, not of unbearable richness.

In the matter of richness of dress in general, it is of interest to notice the marked difference in the paintings of the Akbar period from those of the succeeding reigns: very few persons in the Akbar period are seen wearing rich dresses and generally one sees remarkably few dresses made of brocaded material with those fine stripes and floral patterns that one encounters as a matter of course in the Jahangir and the Shahjahan periods. In Akbari paintings, an occasional member of the court, a high dignitary like a minister, sometimes an ambassador, and oddly enough sometimes even a (specially favoured?) personal attendant of the emperor, wears these richly patterned dresses: but these are so few that they stand out in a large group of people who dress elegantly, but not with ostentation. This comes as somewhat of a surprise, for there can be little doubt that the age was extremely rich in splendid materials and Abul Fazl's evidence on the interest that the emperor himself took in designs, and the wide range of stuffs produced and imported for the court is singularly detailed. One can only conclude from this 'disparity' between verbal descriptions of rich materials and textiles and the visual records of the period that the emperor's personal preferences must have had something to do with defining and laying down a trend. Rarely, if ever, do we see, in a contemporary work, the emperor himself dressed as richly as his son or grandson were to do later. In this respect one clearly has to take seriously the casual statement made by a visitor to the Akbari court that the emperor "dressed plainly". In contrast, the blaze of colours and patterns that one sees in the court assemblages in palace settings under Jahangir and Shahjahan is quite striking. In the Akbar period, a richly dressed figure is an exception; in the Jahangir-Shahjahan periods, the exception is a plainly dressed one. Here once again, the painters could only have been recording what they observed – as always sensitively and with clear eyes.

(The Emperor Akbar is)... of good stature, sturdy body, arms and legs, broad-shouldered. The configuration of his face is ordinary, and does not reflect the grandeur and dignity of the person because, besides being Chinese-like as the Mughals usually are, it is lean, sparse of beard, wrinkled and not very fair. The eyes are small but extremely vivid and when he looks at you it seems as if they hurt you with their brightness, and thus nothing escapes his notice, be it a person or something trivial, and they also reveal sharpness of mind and keenness of intellect. And so he is very much feared by his subjects. To his people he displays a certain amount of cheerfulness which in no way detracts from his imperial bearing. He dresses plainly.
(Letter from Father Monserrate, c. 1580, cit. in Brand, Lowry, 1985:13)

From his indifference to everything that is worldly, His Majesty prefers and wears woollen stuffs, especially shawls...
(Abul Fazl, Ain-i Akbari, vol. I:96)

When the Khan Khanan was going to the court of the Emperor, a painter came to him and handed over to him one of his pictures. The scene depicted therein was of a lady who was taking her bath and that a maid-servant was rubbing the sole of her foot with a pumice-stone. The Khan Khanan looked at the picture for a moment and then, putting it in his palanquin, went away to pay homage to the Emperor. When he returned, the painter reappeared. He ordered that a sum of rupees five thousand be paid to him. The painter said, 'My picture is hardly worth more than five rupees, but there is one artistic skill which I have employed in it. If your Honour has marked that, then I shall be glad to accept your reward, for then I shall have the satisfaction that your Honour has really appreciated my work.' The Khan Khanan said, 'Your skill lies in that you have expressed in the lady's face the feeling which is produced by the rubbing of the sole with a pumice-stone.' The painter was much delighted and he went round the palki of that connoisseur.
(Kalimat-ush-Shuara, fol. 22b, transl. M. M. Haq, 1931: 622f)

VI

One ordinarily thinks of Mughal painting in the context of the imperial court, for the kind of painting that set standards of excellence in workmanship for virtually the entire country was indeed produced within the imperial ambit, in the ateliers attached to the court. This is precisely the reason why, when one thinks of Mughal painting, the names of the Mughal emperors come to one's mind: one speaks naturally of painting done for Humayun or Akbar, for Jahangir or Shahjahan. But this is not to say that all painting belonging to the Mughal period is 'imperial'. Clearly, in this period there was painting that was patronised by others than the emperor himself; painting was even aimed at satisfying a different kind of taste. Within the imperial household, there were princes of the blood royal who took deep interest in painting, the most distinguished example being that of Jahangir who, when he was still a prince and known as Salim, maintained a studio of his own during the lifetime of his father. Other princes with like interests are known: Mirza Hindal, Humayun's brother for instance, or Khurram, the future Shahjahan, who had independent contacts with painters before he ascended the throne.

Even outside the imperial circle, there were serious patrons of painting among the grandees of the court: the most distinguished name that comes to mind is that of Abdul Rahim Khan Khanan who had a remarkable group of painters and calligraphers and librarians working for him. Not too many colophons have survived, but sometimes an occasional one turns up to provide useful evidence of powerful nobles commissioning illustrated works and surrounding themselves with small circles of distinguished artists and poets. The *Kitab-i-Saat* (from which no. 84 is taken) was produced for Mirza Aziz Koka at Hajipur; likewise, the literary and artistic leanings of Zafar Khan who served for some time as governor of Kashmir and evidently maintained an atelier, are known. It would seem as if artists would, and occasionally did, find employment with less than imperial patrons; quite possibly, their work did eventually reach imperial hands, for it was a custom for grandees to present books, including illustrated ones, to their sovereign. There is not enough evidence available as yet about how entry to the imperial atelier was gained by artists, something that many artists for obvious reasons must have aspired to doing. Artists who made small beginnings with for sub-imperial patrons possibly hoped in this manner to be noticed by the emperor and perhaps to be asked to present themselves at the court, and eventually to work in the imperial atelier. This movement of artists could also have been in the opposite direction, and it is not difficult to envisage a situation in which an artist who had, for one reason or another, fallen out of favour at the imperial court then sought patronage at the sub-imperial level.

One also speaks of 'provincial Mughal' works, the term signifying work done at distant, regional centres, but also carrying a somewhat inferior ring, of work that was somewhat behind times, out of the main-stream. The connotation is not necessarily fair, for occasionally fine work was produced away from the centre of imperial power, the artist often adding to his native skills the freedom to experiment, to mingle styles, and to undertake essays that might have been frowned upon by the more exacting masters at the imperial atelier. Apart from 'provin-cial', the designation 'popular Mughal' is often used, a term applied to a great deal of work produced during the Mughal period, frequently stemming from a different tradi-tion, like the Rajput, but visibly showing the impact of the Mughal style, at a slight re-move of time. This can perhaps be best de-scribed as work that tries to get out of its own skin and assume a different persona, in the awareness of the highly prestigious imperial style. 'Popular' Mughal work tends some-times also to be 'folkish' and retains a cer-tain artlessness about itself. At yet another level, one speaks of 'bazaar Mughal' paint-ings: inexpensively priced, quickly and off-handedly tossed off, possessed of more pre-tence than integrity, true predecessors of those dry and repetitive works which were to figure so largely in the output of the 'Company' period.

VIII

The essentials of the technique followed by the Mughal painters remained the same over a considerable period of time and at various levels. The medium has often been described as 'gouache', sometimes even as 'tempera', but neither of these terms is wholly appropriate. While tempera suggests a 'medium composed of egg-yolk', gouache means watercolours to which an opacifier such as zinc white has been added. The Mughal painters did not add, as will be seen a little later, an opaque agent to their pig-ments, and used basically a watercolour technique while adding gum arabic as a binder. Also, the process of laying pig-ments and burnishing them distinguishes their work from the usual gouache. Their technique thus remains their own.

Miyan Nadim. He was ... a slave of this Commander-in-Chief ... He was so skilled in drawing and paint-ing that, since the days of Mani and Bihzad, none has been born who can rival him. He acquired this proficiency in the library, and in the service, of this Commander-in-Chief. In fact, the exalted Khan Khanan himself instructed and raised him to this high level. Thus, under the training of the Khan Khanan, he became a peerless master in his art. He breathed his last in the service of his master. He led a comfortable and care-free life, as he was handsomely paid by the Khan Khanan.

Bahbud ... was a slave of Mirza Baqir, the illustrious son of ... Mir Ali, the famous calligraphist. The afore-said Mirza (Baqir) was skilled in calligraphy and wrote such beautiful nastaliq, after the style of his father, that his writings find a place in the Albums of the connoisseurs, and excite much admiration. When he came to India and joined the service of the Khan Khanan, he handed over Bahbud, who is unrivalled in painting and nastaliq calligraphy, to the Khan Khanan. He is still alive and passes his time in the Library. He is engaged in adorning, embel-lishing and copying the manuscript of the Khan Khanan. In fact, he is peerless in these two arts, in his age. The writer has seen specimens of his paint-ing and calligraphy and is of opinion that undoubt-edly he is a 'Marvel of the Age'.

...

Madhu. He is a Hindu painter. In portraiture, draw-ing, painting and arabesque-design (tarrahi) he is the Mani and the Bihzad of his age. He has illus-trated most of the manuscripts of this court; he has drawn several court-scenes and painted excellent miniatures. He is employed in the library and holds, besides an allowance, Jagirs also. The writer has met him and has also seen his pictures in the pres-ence of this Commander-in-Chief. Verily, he is peer-less (in his art).

Mawlana Ibrahim ... was unrivalled in calligraphy, gilding, book-binding and was skilled as engraver on precious stones. He was much skilled in various arts, and was proficient and unsurpassed in other branches as well. He met the Commander-in-Chief at Ahmadnagar, in the Deccan, and entered his service there. He held the post of a librarian for a number of years. There are many specimens of his painting and gilding in this 'school of wise men' i.e. the library ... At times, he composed verses also. He had a good aptitude for poetry and was unri-valled among the exponents of this art in India. For reasons, which are not known to the writer, he was deprived of the honour of the service of the Khan Khanan. He travelled, during the remaining period of his life, throughout India, in search of a master and patron like the Khan Khanan, but he did not get any. He was always sorry, and regretted his mistake. At last the messenger of Death rolled the carpet of his existence ...

(Maathir-i-Rahimi, transl. M.M. Haq, 1931:625ff)

As a matter of rule, the ground or support consisted of hand-made paper, although there are distinguished exceptions including the great *Hamzanama,* illustrations of which were on cotton. In paper, several refinements were introduced in the Mughal times. Paper had been late in coming to India, and it would seem as if it was only from the 14th century onwards that it became a reasonably com-mon commodity. During the Mughal period, however, great fillip was given to its produc-tion, and major centres sprung up, each using perhaps slightly different basic mate-rials. The true nature of each kind of paper was only too well known to the painters, and they obviously knew exactly how paper made at Sialkot for instance differed from that made in Kashmir or what advantages paper made from cotton rag possessed over that made from grass or rice husk. Sheets of ordinarily thin paper were often pasted together to form the thickness of a thin card-board, this then being termed a *'wasli'.* The preparation of paper appropriate for a painting to be finished on was obviously a specialised task, and when one sees in the margins of some Jahangir period albums brief renderings of the various processes involved in painting, one finds the paper-maker always bending forward, burnishing sheets of paper with force, using a smooth stone burnisher, against a thick wooden board for taking out wrinkles and imparting to the paper that smoothness of surface on which the painter's brush would flow, en-countering no more than the resistance exactly desired.

The process of painting was highly refined and painstaking. A sheet thus prepared was placed on a wooden board which the painter kept on his knees as he sat on the ground to work. As a first step, a quick, fluent drawing was made with a brush in black or, some-times, ochre. This was then lightly covered with a flat layer of white, so thin that through it the underdrawing was visible. At this stage the outline of the original drawing was firmed up and, wherever necessary, corrections or emendations were made. Then followed the laying of pigments, one at a time; these were all laid flat to begin with, with no shades or tones. However, each time that a layer of pigments was applied in this manner, the painting would be placed face down on a smooth, flat surface, like a slab of ivory, and burnished from the back with a smooth rounded piece of stone, generally an agate. The binding medium being gum arabic, and the priming having been done in a flatly-laid white, the pigments possessed initially a certain body, some thickness. The process of vigorous burnishing from the back served two distinct purposes: first, of smoothening out the pigments and, secondly, of giving the surface a very pleasant sheen. This was followed by the patient filling in of finer details, and yet another reinforcing of outlines. It is at this stage that those superbly detailed eyes and hair etc. were put in, and that light modelling called *pardaz* that gave the figures a sense of volume, were done. In the terminology of the painters, this is when a painting was 'opened up', and started bearing a finished look. But much needed yet to be done: gold and silver, wherever decided upon, were applied: on thrones and draperies, on utensils and jewellery, in the sky or in the patterns of carpets and architectural decoration. Also carefully added were details in the jewellery, and those 'pearls' and 'emeralds' that one sees in finely crafted pictures were put in with somewhat thick pigments so that they stood out ever so slightly. As a rule, it was the figures that were finished first, and then came the background: architecture or landscape and the like. The outer rules on the page had been drawn early on, at the stage of the initial drawing itself; but margins, plain or decorative, were added at this stage. These in turn were expanded by the addition of elaborate floral or figurative borders that one sees so often in the great albums produced for Jahangir and Shahjahan.

Mughal painters, especially those attached to the imperial atelier, had access to a wide range of pigments, drawn both from mineral and vegetable sources. Traditional sources mention that the range of white came from lead white, kaolin and crushed conch-shell; black was obtained from lamp black. Blue of different hues and textures was obtained primarily from lapis lazuli, but also from indigo and azurite; yellow from orpiment (the *peori*-yellow obtained from cow's urine, a "magnesium or calcium salt of euxanthic acid", so common in Rajput work, was only infrequently used in Mughal painting); red from vermilion, minium and the kermes insect; green not only from the mixing of blue and yellow, but also from malachite and terra verde. The technique of using gold and silver was highly sophisticated, with gold powder mixed with gum arabic being generally preferred to the application of gold leaf, which tended to develop cracks after a period of time. Brushes were made by the painters themselves, with hair ordinarily taken from the tail of a squirrel, but also from the inside of the ear of a calf. The making of brushes was a process that required the highest concentration, and an almost mystical note enters the Persian painter Sadiq Beg's words when he describes the making of a brush. The fabled 'single haired' brush may not have been a reality, but brushes capable of extremely fine drawing were evidently in use.

Painter at work, Akbar period, c. 1600
Staatsbibliothek Preussischer Kulturbesitz, Berlin

The entire process of painting was, in fact, highly refined and complex, and one gets very little idea of how much was involved in the act of painting from those simple shells scattered around the painters when we see them at work in an occasional painting, or from those relatively austere-looking pen-boxes in which the famous '*qalams*' of the great masters were ordinarily kept and carried.

The transferring of designs from one drawing or painting to another was very much a part of the Mughal painter's craft. One of the favourite methods was the use of a pounce, a kind of stencil that consisted of extremely finely pricked holes along outlines: this pounce was then placed on a sheet and lightly daubed with a small cotton bag filled with fine ashes; this left a faint outline on the sheet below; this was then firmed up with a burnt-charcoal 'pencil' or brush and turned into a full-fledged design to be worked on. The other method of transferring a design was the *charba*, a fine, film-like sheet taken from the lining of a deerskin which could be placed over a painting for a tracing to be made from it.

The use of pounces and *charbas* helps explain the occasionally bewildering phenomenon of chancing upon paintings that look almost exactly alike. The making of copies was common, and the intention behind these was most often not dishonest. One can think of many circumstances under which copies were needed or made: an artist pitting his skills against those of another; gaining acquaintance through the making of copies with totally different techniques and conventions, as in the case of Mughal copies of European works; the sheer display of virtuosity, as in the famous instance of Jahangir having his painters copy a work brought by Sir Thomas Roe; the success of a certain work and consequent demand for its copies, as in the case of a portrait of the emperor or a prince. Somewhat distinct from copies is the matter of 'versions' in which the painter stays very close to an original or a model, but introduces minor variations of his own. A hunting scene of the Akbar period could be made in a different version in the Jahangir period, with very slight changes in the minor characters and the principal figure being substituted by another. One can also think, in the context of 'versions', of different artists trying their hands at the same subject like a bird or an animal, or the same scene illustrating an episode from a historical narrative with an established iconography of its own; of an artist bringing up to date, in his own version, a celebrated work by a great master of the past; and the like. All this makes the whole matter of originals and versions and copies in Mughal India far more complex than it initially appears.

Evidently, a very large number of paintings produced for the Mughals are now lost, and our judgments, necessarily based on survivals, might be erroneous. But one clearly gets the impression that throughout this period painting was a major activity at the court and at other levels. It fulfilled many needs, served many functions. When it centred on dynastic histories and contemporary chronicles, it linked itself with pride in the past and a mixture of pride and concern with the present; when it took portraits as its theme, it at once recorded appearances, preserved them for posterity, enabled an emperor to acquaint himself with the visages of all those whom he had to deal with, even serving as visual reports on the state of men (as evidenced by the case of Aurangzeb wanting to see for himself how his son whom he had imprisoned was doing); when it documented state occasions and showed ceremonial meetings, it served almost as an instrument of policy, and projected the royal image as in those grand allegorical pictures made for Jahangir and the magnificent *darbars* for him and his son; when it adorned the walls of Mughal palaces and chambers, it proclaimed imperial taste and breadth of outlook (as when Christian subjects were prominently displayed about the throne or in significant corners); when it became the object of exchanges of gifts, it addressed statements about the levels of skill and taste from one court to another. Above all, however, it fulfilled a genuine, inner need of the greatest of the Mughals, for there was in them remarkable passion for the art. Its worldly 'functions' apart, painting seems to have fed and sustained them: it was something related to the spirit, a life-enhancing force.

VIII

Unfortunately one knows all too little about the painters themselves. We have a long list of names, longer perhaps than from any other period of Indian history; we even have some information on a few of them in contemporary accounts like those of Abul Fazl and Badauni, and in the memoirs of the Emperor Jahangir himself; we have some signatures and many inscriptional attributions; and we can guess darkly at the personal preferences, apart from sheer skills, of some of the painters. But, with all this, our information remains poor. We have no accounts of their lives, no knowledge of what truly moved them, what their inner-most thoughts were. We know remarkably little

Want of genius, therefore, is not the reason why works of superior art are not exhibited in the capital. If the artists and manufacturers were encouraged, the useful and fine arts would flourish; but these unhappy men are contemned, treated with harshness, and inadequately remunerated for their labour. The rich will have every article at a cheap rate.
(François Bernier, Travels in the Mogul Empire, *1656–68, vol. I:255f)*

Keshavdas being kept from approaching the Emperor Akbar, Akbar period, c. 1590, from the Jahangir album
Staatsbibliothek Preussischer Kulturbesitz, Berlin

On this day Abu-l-Hasan, the painter, who has been honoured with the title of Nadiru-z-zaman, drew the picture of my accession as the frontispiece to the Jahangir-nama, and brought it to me. As it was worthy of all praise, he received endless favours. His work was perfect, and his picture is one of the chefs d'oeuvre of the age. At the present time he has no rival or equal. If at this day the masters Abdu-l-Hayy and Bihzad were alive, they would have done him justice. His father, Aqa Riza, of Herat, at the time when I was Prince, joined my service. He (Abu-l-Hasan) was a khanazad of my Court. There is, however, no comparison between his work and that of his father (i.e., he is far better than his father). One cannot put them into the same category. My connection was based on my having reared him. From his earliest years up to the present time I have always looked after him, till his art has arrived at this rank. Truly he has become Nadira-i-zaman ("the wonder of the age"). Also, Ustad Mansur has become such a master in painting that he has the title of Nadiru-l-Asr, and in the art of drawing is unique in his generation. In the time of my father's reign and my own these two have had no third.
(Jahangir, Tuzuk-i-Jahangiri, *vol. II:20)*

even about what they were paid, and what their true status was. True that some of them are referred to in greatly laudatory terms; we know of poetic and fine-sounding honorifics by which some of them were designated – 'Wonder of the Age', 'Rarity of the Realm' – and we read about master painters and calligraphers wielding pens that were 'sweet' or 'golden' or 'fragrant' and receiving on occasions grand rewards. But, on the other side of the coin, we have evidence like that of Bernier about the harsh treatment meted out to craftsmen, of painters routinely referring to themselves in terms of the greatest humility and signing their names under the feet of their patrons in portraits, thus mingling with 'golden dust', and constantly importuning their masters for a specific favour or an increase in emoluments. It is possible to attach exaggerated importance to these things, and some of this might only reflect courtly form, not the substance of a situation. But when a painter of the genius of Kesu (Keshav Das), bent with age and infirm of step, carries a humble petition to his emperor and is driven away by a stick-wielding minor court functionary who does not even allow him to approach the monarch, some disturbing thoughts do arise.

Absorption

1 Two folios from a dispersed *Quran*-manuscript

28.5 x 18.5 cm
Sultanate, 15th century or earlier; Delhi (?)
Rietberg Museum, Zurich
(Acquisition funded by Lucy Rudolph)

Several elements come together in this majestic *Quran,* the leaves of which remarkably combine boldness and elegance. The principal writing is in fine *raihani* with only three lines to a page, and between the lines appears a translation of the Arabic original in Persian in small *naskh* characters. But there is more, for through the finely rendered gold arabesques along the borders of the page run words in an austerely elegant *kufic* in blue and red. The corners are marked by tight, interlocking geometric designs in blue, gold, and red, imparting to the otherwise sparse page a sumptuous look.

The Persian interlinear translation fulfils a need, for in India Persian was much more familiar than Arabic to most Muslims settled there. But the mixing of the diverse elements, the flamboyance of the *raihani,* the precision of the *naskh,* the stateliness of the *kufic,* and the discreet yet elegant patterning also foreshadow, in some measure, the way in which different elements were to combine and later become absorbed in the course of the formation of the Mughal style of painting and writing. Marked sensitivity is visible in the way in which the Persian translation in *naskh* is introduced: it is placed directly below the Arabic lines, at an angle, so as not to impose a flatness upon the page. It is this very kind of sensitivity that one would encounter in Mughal painting in respect to the manner in which seemingly divergent streams are sought to be reconciled.

To determine the exact centre at which this *Quran* might have been produced in India is difficult: apart from Delhi, the seat of Islamic authority in pre-Mughal India, local sultanates at Jaunpur in the east, Malwa in central India, Gujarat in the west or the Deccani sultanates in the south come into mind as possible sources. It is increasingly clear that there was 'Islamic' painting in an Indo-Persian style in India, apart from the mainstream of Jaina and Rajput painting, before the coming of the Mughals. But it is not unlikely that it was into the calligraphy of the holy *Quran,* in which a "ray of God's knowledge falls on man's soul", that most energies were directed in Islamic India, especially considering the disfavour with which figural painting was viewed by many of the Delhi sultans who saw themselves obliged to uphold the orthodox authority of their faith in the land that they now ruled.

On the verso side of this double-page (Sura V, 12), a broad golden strip with *kufic* appears along the vertical border. Several leaves of this *Quran* have been published recently, thus: Arberry (1967:no.48), Falk (1985:no.116) and most recently Losty (1986:10). The style of the main script has been called both *raihani* as well as *muhaqqaq.*

Publ.: Raeuber, 1979, no. 34 (only verso).

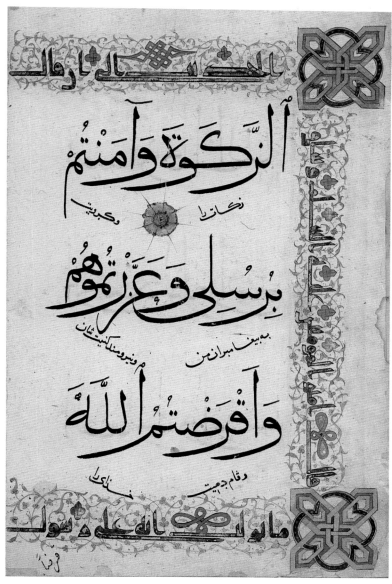

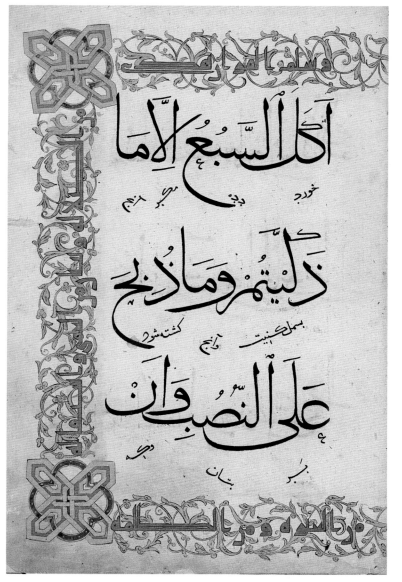

2 The chaste wife

Illustrated folio from a dispersed *Khamsa*-manuscript of Amir Khusraw Dehlavi
9.8 x 20 cm; page: 34 x 26.5 cm
Possibly Sultanate, c.1450 or earlier
Collection of Prince Sadruddin Aga Khan

The spanning of cultures that one sees in Amir Khusraw of Delhi (c.1253–1325), author of the *Khamsa* (Quintet) in Persian from which this folio comes but also a poet in Hindi and one deeply immersed in Indian music, is to an extent reflected also in the illustrations to this dispersed manuscript. In the style of its paintings so much is reminiscent of Egyptian Mamluk work or of small illustrations in Central Asian Inju manuscripts; but it is possible also to discern in the work distinct elements of 'Indian-ness'. In the paintings is to be seen a tantalizing presence of diverse elements, which has led to a sustained, lively argument among scholars about their origin.

The figures throughout the known leaves from this group remain recognizably of Islamic or foreign origin. The dresses, the high boots, the turbans, and the aspect of the female figures are clearly 'non-Hindu'; also, features like architectural details, the flat red backgrounds, the oversized flowering plants and bouquets introduced as part of the decorative scheme, can be traced back to non-Indian Islamic prototypes of the 14th century and earlier. But there is, at the same time, something in the general look of naiveté in these works, in some of the gestures (like the husband's pronounced gesture of wonder here at the proven constancy of his wife) and in an occasional attempt at rendering the transparency of garments that suggests an acquaintance with Indian work. What one thinks of as the nearest Indian source is Western Indian painting with its insistent lack of depth, attention to decorative detail, the spacing of figures to avoid overlapping, and the use of consistently flat backgrounds, even if the wiry strength of the drawing and the intricate patterning of Jaina works are not seen here.

If this *Khamsa* was indeed produced at some Muslim centre in northern India, it would represent one of the many extant styles which could have been drawn upon by the painter at the Mughal court.

For all its seeming coarseness of execution and obvious patchwork, the painting is possessed of much charm and through its directness, it captures some of the flavour of Amir Khusraw's verses. The silent exchange across a flowering plant between the embarrassed, wondering husband and his innocent but self-assured, chaste wife is skilfully established. The high horizon may be clichéd, but the half-open inner door shows a move towards innovation.

Ettinghausen (1961) and Khandalavala and Chandra (1969) draw detailed attention to this and other pre-Mughal Indo-Persian works. Beach (1981:42ff) attributes this *Khamsa*-manuscript to a date earlier than 1450.

The present page represents something of a patchwork, strips from other leaves and bits of paintings having been pieced together to 'compose' it.

Unpublished.

3 Queen Trishala with the newly born Tirthankara

Illustrated folio from a dispersed *Kalpasutra*-manuscript
11.6 x 27.9 cm
Western India, c.1450
Rietberg Museum, Zurich
(Acquisition funded by the Dr. Carlo Fleischmann Foundation)

Hieratic and innately deeply conservative, Jaina painting retained for close to 400 years the kind of general look that this leaf bears. The work is startlingly stylised and its elements are at first not easy to absorb, but then one is struck by its remarkable clarity.

To a contemporary viewer, especially to a devout Jaina, the written part of the page would have already established the context of the painting which illustrates the narrative. It is Queen Trishala who, lying on her couch, fondly holds the newborn Tirthankara (one of the 24 saviours of mankind) in the crook of her right arm as she gazes at him. The palace setting with elaborate architectural features above, the luxurious couch, the appurtenances on the floor by the side of the bed, delicacies placed in receptacles suspended from the ceiling all help quickly to establish the kingly setting; the queen's status is emphasized as much by the tiara she wears as by the nimbus behind her head. But nothing is fully worked out and there are features that need to be seen as purely conceptual, being in clear, insistent defiance of natural appearances. The projecting further eye and the angular treatment of the drapery, that seems to float in defiance of the laws of gravitation, the combination of points of view in the depiction of the body or the furniture, the dominant frontality, are all parts of the style that had been carefully worked out over a long period of time. Upon a basic linear structure made with a wiry, taut line, colours are imposed decoratively as are sumptuous patterns in the drapery, the jewellery and the architecture. The background stays flat, in this case a deep indigo-blue, for from the

point of view of telling the story in the sacred text it holds no interest. The range of colours remains limited, but its distribution shows great skill. The leaf is essentially small, vestigially following the format of the palm leaf, but combining as it does fine calligraphy with a small illustration; it is, like others of its kind, possessed of a distinct presence.

It is entirely likely that a number of painters brought to the imperial court of the Mughals, while the Mughal style was still being formed, a clear awareness of the 'Gujarati' style of painting, for it was not only widespread in northern India; some of the painters, judging from their Gujarati affiliations, might actually have been drawn from the very region in which this kind of work was most widely seen and practised. Once at the court, however, they clearly would have had to drop 'unnatural' elements like the projecting eye and the simple, unfinished frontality of view used in the rendering of objects. But something of the interest in patterning and of combining different points of view is likely to have stayed with them even when they were working in a different setting under the direction of different masters. That some changes occurred in time within the strict conservatism of the Jaina style is evident from a leaf like the present one, for it already departs in some ways from earlier Jaina paintings. As usual the format remains horizontal, associated in the Indian mind with sacred scriptures, and the relationship of the picture to the written part of the text stays much the same. But the decorative panels above and below, the vertical panels with the figures of other Tirthankaras at the side, as

well as the highly inventive central square with a figure of a horse instead of the usual circular dot to mark the place where originally a hole was formed for the binding string to pass through, all represent moves away from continuity and in the direction of change.

Publ: Czuma, 1975, no. 56.

4 Nanda, his kinsmen, and the child Krishna

Folio from a dispersed *Bhagavata Purana*-manuscript
17.7 x 23.8 cm
Early Rajput, c.1540
Rietberg Museum, Zurich
(Acquisition funded by Fritz and Monika von Schulthess)

The fondness with which the exploits of Krishna as a child, and later as a lover are celebrated in Hindu India is best reflected perhaps in that great text, the *Bhagavata Purana,* which served the Rajput painters as a perennial source of delight and inspiration. The story is nearly always told with passion and immediacy. In the episode seen here, the child Krishna, ever imperilled by dangers, has just killed the powerful demoness, Putana, sent by his evil uncle, Kamsa. The contest was unequal, but Krishna survives and, finding him safe, his foster father Nanda picks him up, holds him affectionately in his lap, "smells his forehead", as the text says, in the midst of a general sense of relief and joyousness. The women in Nanda's family and the other kinsmen gather at Nanda's house to celebrate the occasion. Quiet jubilation mingles with a sense of disbelief at Krishna's marvellous exploits.

There is great verve in this and other leaves of this *Bhagavata Purana* series. The drawing is vigorous, the compositions bold, the colours rich and warm and saturated. A bounding energy seems to run through the series. Even though the present leaf has virtually no action, one senses vibrancy in the work. With remarkable skill, the Rajput painter, drawing upon the antecedents of the style in which he is working, manages to impart with simple means an air of sumptuousness to the leaves. The palette is rather limited but is used with great intelligence; great variety seems to belong to the characters even though the figures look basically similar and clear formulas for types have been employed. Many elements of style remain constant in the series: the strong preference for flat background colours, the spacing out of figures, the presentation of objects and architectural features and trees from their most characteristic aspect, the clarity with which gestures are set forth, the rhythm that animates garments as they trace curvilinear patterns across space, the playful manner in which the horizon is treated and, above all, the sheer warmth of the palette and the passion with which the narrative is presented. In a work like this there is at once condensation and elaboration, economy of means and expansion of feeling.

At first sight, the work of the Mughal painter seems to bear little relationship to this vigorous, conceptual Rajput kind of work, but it is evident that elements of this style were absorbed into early projects like the Cleveland *Tutinama* and the *Hamzanama.* On occasions, one even finds small 'Rajput' passages inducted into larger early Mughal compositions. The avidity with which figures glance at each other, the firmness of their gestures are all toned down in Mughal work, but connections are still visible.

This series, which bears two names, Mitharam and Nana, possibly artists, is so widely dispersed that it is only recently that an attempt has been made to bring it together (Ehnbom, in press). There is no agreement among scholars about the centre where it could have been produced or the date to which it belongs. Both Rajasthan and the Delhi/Agra region are, however, most seriously regarded as possible centres, and the second quarter of the sixteenth century is considered the most likely date, making the series contemporary with so much other work in the derived Persian style and the Jaina style, both of which are 'pre-Mughal'.

Unpublished.

5 Zahhak slays the cow Birmayeh

Folio (30v) of Shah Tahmasp's *Shahnama,* mounted as an album page
47 x 31.8 cm
Iran, c. 1525
Private Collection

Not Persian of descent themselves, the Mughals brought with them to India a keen awareness of the splendours of Persian culture, especially as reflected in its painting and calligraphy. The passion that nearly all of them had for books, the loving care with which they assembled and looked after their libraries, could only have come from a deep attachment to learning. Fortunately, the learning at that point in time was often contained in fine, illustrated volumes that count among the treasures of the most cultivated princes of the Islamic world.

The *Shahnama,* from which this folio comes, was put together for Shah Tahmasp of Iran, and is justly celebrated as being among the finest surviving works of its kind in the world. The names of the greatest masters of the age, working in the awareness of the tradition of the great Bihzad, are associated with this enterprise: two of its folios bear the names of artists, Mir Musavvir and Dust Muhammad, but other masters at Shah Tahmasp's court like Aqa Mirak, Sultan Muhammad and Mir Sayyid Ali are believed to have been associated with it, too. The names are of significance, for at least two of these masters, Mir Sayyid Ali and Dust Muhammad, were later to be linked with India, having entered Humayun's service before he returned to India to reclaim his lost kingdom in 1555.

The hands within this great *Shahnama* vary a great deal, but the present folio serves well to illustrate the Iranian style of painting at its most splendid. The scene is that of the slaying of the cow Birmayeh by King Zahhak who lived in fear of a prophecy foretelling that his death would be at the hands of young Faridun who was being fed in exile on the milk of an extraordinary cow, Birmayeh. Here Zahhak arrives with his retainers and a hunt ensues in which he himself slays the cow while his companions embark upon widespread carnage. The quality of the work is dazzling and the many concerns of the Iranian artist of this time are reflected in a folio like this. The composition is very tightly controlled; the principal action is placed in the centre of the painting, but nothing, not even the dying goat at the left bottom corner or the balcony of the palace at the very top, is slurred over; there is remarkable observation in the rendering of animals who appear in all conceivable attitudes and states; the minutiae of detail in the tilework on the palace or the floral sprigs and the lush foliage are possessed of a virtuoso quality; the lower part of the work is presented as if seen from a height; the figures remain constant in size despite variations in distance. Through the painting runs a superb, finely nuanced sense of colour.

Clearly, this kind of work is radically different from that in the Jaina or Rajput styles which prevailed in the non-Islamic north-Indian setting prior to the coming of the Mughals, and it was to serve as a major source for the painters of Mughal India. But it was not to be duplicated: like much else, it simply flowed into it.

This folio has been attributed by S.C. Welch to the painter Sultan Muhammad, assisted by Mir Sayyid Ali (see Falk, 1985, no. 44 with extensive introduction by S.C. Welch). The leaves of this great *Shahnama,* known for some time as the "Houghton *Shahnama*" after its more recent owner, are now dispersed.

Publ.: Dickson, Welch, 1981, no. 17; Falk, 1985, no. 44.

6 Portrait of Shah Abul Maali

Leaf mounted as an album page, inscribed to Dust Muhammad; on verso, calligraphy
in *nastaliq* by Muhammad Reza
14.5 x 17.2 cm; page: 25 x 39 cm
Iran or Kabul, c. 1550
Collection of Prince Sadruddin Aga Khan

This portrait of an elegantly attired young man, sporting an elaborate Humayun-style turban with a flower tucked in it and a cloak loosely draped around the shoulders, shows him bending forward intently, in the act of writing on a sheet of paper with a slim reed pen. The sheet is supported by a wooden tablet that is held in place by the writer's left hand. The Persian writing on the sheet identifies this to be the likeness of "Shah Abul Maali of Kashghar", and states that it is the work of "Ustad Dust Musavvir".

The mould of portraiture in which the figure of this handsome youth is cast is familiar from Iranian work of this genre in the early 16th century. There one sees greater emphasis on the pattern and the abstract elegance of the form than on the study of individual character. Any personal traits one can read into the portrait come mostly from the posture or from a generalized expression of concentration; the setting in which the figure is placed contributes a great deal. Mughal portraiture was, however, to develop in a different direction, for the Mughal painter became far more interested in penetration of character than his Persian counterpart ever was; at the very least the Mughal painter chose different means for achieving this. In large, early compositions, general likenesses seemed to suffice, but whenever he came close to a character, isolating him against a flat background and focusing on him sharply, he seemed from very early on to be intent on touching the inner spirit while capturing outer appearance with marked faithfulness.

The painter Dust Muhammad, referred to in the inscription as 'Ustad Dust Musavvir', is likely to have brought to the Mughal court of Humayun the kind of 'Persian' approach to portraiture that we see in this work. Unfortunately nothing else of his work in India seems to have survived, and there is little that one can compare with the present work. But it is certain that it is on this kind of ground on which the Mughal painter at the court of Akbar built as far as portraiture was concerned.

The inscription on the sheet of paper held by Abul Maali is believed to be contemporary with the painting, but there is perhaps room for discussion of this. It is entirely likely that the work is by Dust Muhammad, but it is difficult to see him referring to himself as "Ustad Dust Muhammad". This is out of character, for ordinarily a painter refers to himself in far more humble terms. Also, in keeping with the convention of formal documents, the words "Jannat Ashiyani", meaning "nesting in Paradise", a posthumous title for Humayun used from the Akbar period onwards, has been respectfully set apart and should be read after the word "Hazrat" in the second line of the inscription where a short, blank space has been left. Of interest also is the fact that the invocatory words *'Allah-u Akbar'* are inscribed clearly at a different angle than the remaining part of the inscription. When one notices these details, the inscription takes on a different tone and character. It is possible that the inscription records, at a slightly later point in time, the facts relevant to the painting without necessarily being contemporary with it.

Publ.: S. C. Welch, 1979, no. 75; A. Welch, S. C. Welch, 1982, no. 49; Brand, Lowry, 1985, no. 81; Falk, 1985, no. 118.

34

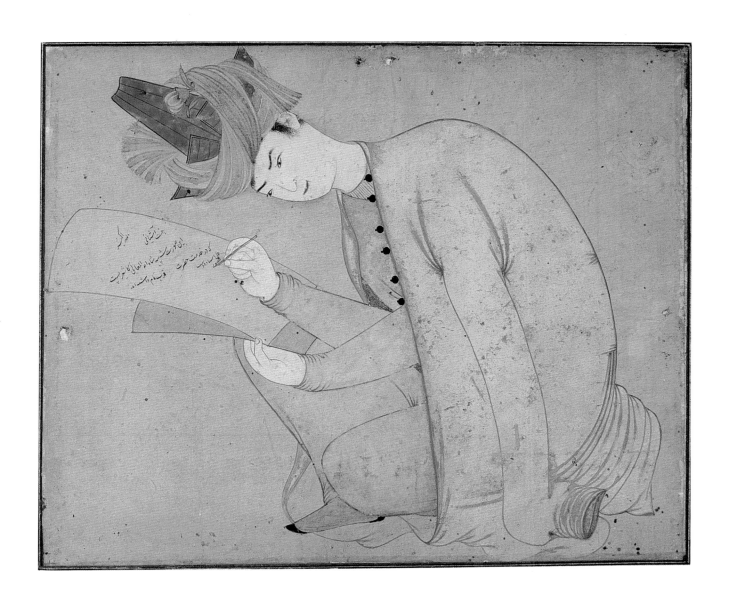

7 Amir Hamza fights the demons

Folio on cotton from a dispersed *Hamzanama*-manuscript
64 x 55.5 cm
Akbar period, 1562/77
Private Collection

There is nothing quite like the *Hamzanama* in the entire history of Indian painting; certainly nothing else in Mughal painting matches it either in scale or energy. The story of Amir Hamza, uncle of the prophet Muhammad, who as a hero of Islam sets out to carry its message throughout the world and encounters the strangest of adventures in distant and alien lands, was a favourite in India even before the coming of the Mughals and at least one illustrated pre-Mughal manuscript of it is known. But the Emperor Akbar, fascinated since his young years by its myriad tales of sorcerers and heroes, fairies and demons, scheming spies and hapless victims, tales that he himself was fond of reciting aloud to the ladies of the imperial household, commissioned the imperial atelier to work on a project of extraordinary proportions, a series of illustrations numbering 1400, to be completed in fourteen 'volumes' of one hundred works each. Our information is scanty and there are conflicting versions of the history of the enterprise, but it undoubtedly remains among the very earliest of Mughal painting.

The names of great masters are associated with it, first Mir Sayyid Ali and then Khwaja Abd-al Samad, the Iranian *ustads* who had accompanied Humayun to India and under whose supervision many Indian painters coming from diverse backgrounds began this stupendous task. Among the painters believed to have been associated with the project were the famous Daswant and Basawan.

This coming together of Persian masters and their Indian pupils or collaborators yielded spectacular results. It is easy to envisage how the entire project was seen as a major challenge and a remarkable opportunity. Not only did the tale with all its intricate ramifications of unlikely happenings and fantastic creatures spur the imagination and in some ways free it from pre-existing models: the sheer scale on which the paintings were made and the ground – cotton instead of the usual paper – also had few precedents. The painters drew whatever they could from their experience, but had to dip much more into their imagination to create pages full of great, bustling energy like the present one.

Close observation of the *Hamzanama* pages (see also no. 95) reveals elements that come from different sources: very Persian-looking trees and rocks and flowering plants, horned demons with gnarled bodies and serrated eyes who seem to come from Central Asia, renderings of architecture at once rich and massive for which there was virtually no precedent. But delicacy and energy, observation and imagination are so thoroughly worked in that the project seems at first sight to be completely unified. However, closer examination reveals different strands. Thus, if the plane tree, the flowering bush and the pattern on the dread mace carried by the demon are instantly recognizable as being Persian, the viewing from so close and the vividness of action in the leaf can be seen as being the Indian contribution to this work.

Publ.: Falk, 1985, no. 120.

8 Shiva, Vishnu, and a demon

Leaf from an unidentified series, mounted as an album page; on verso, calligraphy
in *nastaliq* by Muhammad Said al-Kashmiri
19.8 x 13.1 cm; page: 39.7 x 28.7 cm
Akbar-Jahangir period, 1600/10
Collection of Prince Sadruddin Aga Khan

In the warp and weft of the fabric of Mughal India, especially under Akbar, the Hindu thread stays strong and resilient. A clear pattern emerges from the policies and preferences of the emperor himself. When he takes Hindu princesses in marriage and chooses Hindu brides for his sons, this fits in well with his raising Hindu generals and administrators to the highest rank, the forming of alliances with Rajput princes and the blunting of the edge of Muslim orthodoxy and hostility towards Hinduism. The translation of the greatest of the Hindu classics into Persian, having ones like the *Ramayana* and the *Mahabharata* (as the *Razmnama*) painted by the finest of his artists, as well as employing a large number of Hindu painters in the imperial ateliers, were all meaningful acts.

In the process of rendering some of these pronounced Hindu themes by a mixed group of artists, however, the flavour of the illustrated myths changes appreciably, even if it is clear that much attention was paid to small iconographic details as on this leaf. The episode rendered by the Mughal painter here is not easy to identify. It is likely that the story told here is of the discomfort of Shiva at having bestowed an extravagant boon on a demon or *asura* who formerly was his devotee. Endowed with the power of burning anyone by placing his head over that person, the demon decided to test his powers against Shiva himself. Shiva then turned for aid to Vishnu who, according to one version of the story, "made him stand at the edge of a river" and proceeded to trick the demon into placing his hand above his own head and thus destroying himself. If this indeed is the story depicted here, all its elements are not present, for in the story Vishnu took the form of a woman, Mohini, the temptress, to entice the demon. This we do not see, but the presence of Shiva and Vishnu together on the bank of the river and the demon gesturing as if smitten by the beauty of Vishnu seem to serve as fair pointers.

What is of interest in this fine leaf is that the mythical figures are placed in the midst of what would be easy to recognize as a Persian-style rock-and-running-water-landscape. Such details as the ibex perched at the top of a cloud-like cliff, and faces hidden inside rocks (as in the top part of the rock cumulus in the middle of the painting) bear a very Persian look as modified in the Mughal style. The demon, dressed in a short skirt with a bell-girdle, is of the kind that one would encounter in a *Hamzanama* page, even if less hairy and less fierce here. Noticeable is the accuracy of iconographical detail in the figures both of Shiva and Vishnu,

the former with his crescent moon, trident, snake ornament, tiger skin and fair complexion; and the latter shown appropriately clad in a yellow lower garment, four-armed, carrying the conch-shell, discus, mace and lotus emblems, dark of complexion and wearing a three-pointed crown topped by flowers. Obvious help from Hindu sources seems to have been taken if the work was not in fact done by a Hindu painter who knew the iconography well. The style and the subject remain distanced from each other, but such was the very nature of the approaches that were worked out in the Mughal atelier.

Unpublished.

9 A sage-like king in his audience hall

Leaf from an unidentified series, mounted as an album page
15.8 x 8 cm; page: 30.5 x 19 cm
Akbar period, c. 1590
(Acquisition funded by Balthasar and Nanni Reinhart)

At first sight the setting appears wholly Mughal, with courtiers and other subjects standing and making gestures of obeisance and supplication in the courtyard of a palace, where a ruler is seated with his consort. But then one sees that the seated, dark-skinned, light-bearded figure wearing a crown is a figure from Hindu mythology. Not only is the manner of sitting, cross-legged with the sole of one foot clearly visible in the lap, so markedly Hindu; the figure can be seen wearing a *tilak* or caste mark on the forehead and holding *tulsi*-prayer beads in the right hand; but the truly eloquent detail is the spread-out lotus flower on which the sage-like figure is seated, for this denotes, in iconographical terms, a 'deity'. The long garland of flowers around the neck, the three-pointed crown with floral finials, and the manner in which a scarf is wrapped around the body add further emphasis to this identification. Also significant is the full-bosomed lady seated next to him. She is the very type of Rajput or Hindu woman seen so often in north Indian work.

Clearly the context of the painting is Hindu, but it is not easy to determine the legend or myth it draws upon. It is possible that the principal figure is none other than Dasharatha, father of Rama, hero of the great Hindu epic *Ramayana*, seated here with his favourite queen, Kaikeyi; the cause of the agitation on the part of the populace gathered in the courtyard may be the announcement of the exile of Rama to the forest for fourteen years. If this is so, we might have here a leaf from a *Ramayana* series now lost. Other *Ramayana* illustrated manuscripts are, of course, known from the Akbar period, but this one might then come from a small, delicately rendered *Ramayana*-manuscript of a pocket-book size.

It is interesting to observe that apart from the two principal figures, the setting and the temper of the entire work is characteristically Mughal. The architectural setting, the well-established range of characters among the courtiers and subjects, the manner in which the outer wall of the palace has been 'lowered' to afford a view of the happenings inside, the delicate colouring especially on the floor of the courtyard and on the chamber wall and the roof make the work rank with precise, highly finished works of the Mughal ateliers in this period. At the same time one notices that when the painter gets into the 'Hindu' element of the composition, as here, it is as if he slips into a different mode. The posture of the lady, with her right arm coming across the body and held against the chest, the careful 'iconic' manner of sitting of the princely figure, and the fluttering scarf behind him all hint at different connections, if not different origins.

Unpublished.

10 Crucifixion

Single leaf mounted as an album page; on verso, a flowering plant
14.4 x 8.6 cm; page: 30 x 21.1 cm
Akbar-Jahangir period, 1600/10
Collection of Prince Sadruddin Aga Khan

The marked liberality of spirit entertained by Akbar and a deep interest in the 'rarities' of other cultures, especially artefacts like paintings and icons, underlie one of the more absorbing aspects of Mughal India: the coming of Christianity and, through it, of European paintings and prints in the 16th century. The whole chapter is full of extraordinary colour and flavour, and contemporary accounts, both Mughal and Christian, are filled with fascinating details. Neither Europeans nor their artefacts were completely unknown before the middle of the 16th century, but the contact takes on a different aspect when the emperor himself shows great curiosity in this matter. A Jesuit mission from Portuguese Goa is welcomed to Fathepur Sikri and is allotted space within the confines of the imperial complex; the emperor himself pays visits together with his sons to the shrine set up by the Fathers; and all this leads to the Fathers' hope that Akbar himself might convert to Christianity.

This does not happen of course, but the emperor retains an attitude of deference and curiosity. In the process, as part of exchanges and gifts, European prints, frequently with Christian themes, come into the hands of the emperor and his painters. This leads to quite uncommon developments. The emperor himself encourages his painters to go and see altar-pieces and paintings with which the Christian fathers had adorned their places of worship. Some of the painters, notably Basawan and Kesu (Keshavdas), very quickly pick up the externals of the European style, showing great fascination not only for the subject matter but for the European treatment of anatomy, textiles and draperies, for distant views of cities in the background, for some kind of perspective, both linear and aerial, and for material objects like furniture and ceramics. It begins with making 'exact' copies of European works newly arrived in India, but soon the artists play with elements of style, and even try their hand at pastiches, in which passages from different paintings are combined, not necessarily with great logic or faithfulness, but as if playfully.

This scene of crucifixion, based probably on a Flemish painting, shows both marked accuracy of detail in copying, but also some variations. For the Mughal painter, rendering the human anatomy, as in the undraped body of Christ here, the swirls and folds of drapery, as seen around the loins of Jesus and in the cloak of the Virgin, must have posed a challenge. Some details are only imperfectly understood, but the attempt at veracity is quite remarkable, for one sees it in such details as the inscription at the head

of the cross, or the 'memento mori' at its foot. But the painter also introduces between the foreground and the distant town in the background low rolling hills that stand out as awkward; these he picks up again in the craggy mountains at the far back. Where St. John should be, at left, the painter introduces a figure with covered head and elaborate drapery that could easily be seen as a woman, but one cannot be certain about this. At any rate, this figure stands out as the least convincing in this otherwise fine rendering.

An inscription in Persian on the top border identifies the scene as representing "the Lord Jesus, Spirit of God", but it is in a much later hand and uses corrupt spellings.

On verso, a painting of a blooming plant with butterflies and birds is described as a *gul abbasi*-tree in an inscription.

Unpublished.

Innovation and Conservatism

11   A mother's love

Folio from an illustrated manuscript of the *Akhlaq-i Nasiri* ("The Nasirean Ethics")
Inscribed to Dhanraj
19.9 x 10.9 cm; page: 23.6 x 14.1 cm
Akbar period, 1590/95
Collection of Prince Sadruddin Aga Khan

The text to which this painting relates, along with a group of sixteen others, the *Akhlaq-i Nasiri*, was celebrated throughout the Islamic world, and remains "the best known ethical digest to be composed in medieval Persia, if not in all medieval Islam" (Wickens, 1964). For all its popularity, however, and its obvious authority, not many illustrated versions of the work are available and the present manuscript is certainly the only one from Mughal India that has come to light. It is possible that the text was all too rarely illustrated, for its contents do not lend themselves easily to visualisation in the manner that histories and chronicles and romantic poetry do. The text, as its author Nasir-ud Din (13th century) says in his preamble, was "devised for the correction of dispositions". Consisting of three major discourses, the first on ethics including principles and ends, the second on economics, and the third on politics, it addresses itself to moral and philosophical questions and embodies a code of practical conduct for a man of the world, especially a prince.

There is no narrative in the work, no story, no established characters or iconography that the painters could have drawn upon when illustrating this treatise. Clearly then they had to think for themselves, to select the passages to illustrate and to innovate while painting. This circumstance alone imparts to the present manuscript remarkable freshness in the context of Mughal painting.

The present leaf is taken from the third discourse, much of which centres around various kinds of love. Of love in the human species, referred to in the fragment of text on the painted page, the author Nasir-ud Din says there are two kinds: natural and voluntary. "An example of natural love is that of the mother for the child: if this class of love were not innate in the mother's nature, she would not give nurture to the child, and the survival of the species could not conceivably be effected." From the painter's point of view, this is an unpromising passage, but Dhanraj, the painter of this leaf, seems to have decided to conjure up here different images of motherly love. He sets, in the centre of the painting, just outside a tent, a mother seated suckling an infant in her lap: as she feeds him, she gazes fondly at his face. Slightly older children frolic around and rush towards their parents; another mother, in her tent, looks with affection at the pranks of her own little boys. But while much attention goes to the central part of the painting, where mothers' natural love is in abundant evidence, the painter introduces love also in the animal world. A foal is suckled by a mare who turns her long neck also to gaze at her offspring;

at the bottom, a pair of sheep seems to be moving towards two lambs, perhaps their offspring. Directly behind the tent in the middle of the painting, an old man is seen in earnest conversation with a young boy, perhaps the representation of a father and son, love between whom, as Nasir-ud Din points out, has a different character and flavour than that of a mother for her child.

In the composition, which incorporates two 'floating panels' of text in the approved tradition of illustrated manuscripts, there are passages which come from familiar sources like the formalized treatment of the bare rock, the tree in the middle, the structure atop a hillock in the far distance, and the shepherd moving away from the centre of the painting. But the summoning of consistent images of motherly love in the painting is different, and in its own way very affecting. A Hindu himself, the painter Dhanraj could easily have drawn upon those wonderfully poetic images of motherly love in Hindi poetry, where Yashoda dotes over young Krishna, or Kaushalya, in the *Ramayana*, pines for Rama, "like a cow for her calf". But while the intensity of the love seen here comes possibly from these or similar images, the scene is set out differently so that there is no confusion. In fact, the painter chooses to show here some kind of 'tribal' or nomadic setting so that the love focused on is truly "natural", not tainted by the possibilities of future gain, as one might imagine in an urban or palace setting. There is no formality in the atmosphere, no obvious restriction of any kind. A natural, easy air pervades the work.

The Nasirean Ethics is available in an excellent translation by Wickens (1964). Only one illustrated manuscript from the Mughal-period is known, to which the present as well as a number of other paintings (nos. 13, 22, 55, 56, 57, 58) belong. Formerly in the Bibliotheca Phillippica (Sotheby's, November 27, 1974:no.684), the manuscript has 17 illustrations. Two significant works are published by A. Welch (1982:no.58). Apart from Dhanraj, six other painters' names figure on the illustrations in this manuscript, all of them Hindus, and each known to have been associated with the imperial workshop. Unfortunately the colophon of this fine manuscript has not survived, leaving us with no clear date or name of the patron.

Unpublished.

12   The poet Sadi with his patron

Folio (91a) from an illustrated manuscript of the *Kulliyat* ("Complete works") of Sadi
27.6 x 15.1 cm; page: 41.7 x 26.4 cm
Akbar-Jahangir period, 1600/05
Collection of Prince Sadruddin Aga Khan

Shaikh Musleh-ud-din Sadi, that "nightingale of a thousand songs", ranks among the most celebrated poets of Persia, and few works have ever attained, in the Islamic world, the popularity of his famed *Gulistan* (Garden of Flowers) or *Bustan* (Garden of Fragrance). The charm of these works is immense, for they combine not only great beauty of meaning with simplicity of style, but have those 'pleasing alternations of prose and verse, of wit and gravity' that have led generations in the Persian-speaking world to commit long passages from them to memory. From his work Sadi himself emerges as a man of deep, genuine piety, full of warm friendships and charity for fellow-beings. Manuscripts of Sadi's works, including some of his *Kulliyat* ('Complete Works') which include his *ghazals,* apart from the *Gulistan* and *Bustan,* were as popular in Mughal India as they were in Persia, and several illustrated versions are known. The present folio comes from a complete manuscript of the *Kulliyat,* calligraphed by the celebrated penman, Abdul Rahim al-Haravi; unfortunately, however, the colophon gives neither the name of the patron nor the date of its completion.

Within the twenty-three illustrations of this manuscript, there are stylistic variations. Several painters seem to have worked on the manuscript, although only a few names, including those of Dharamdas and Hiranand, figure on the works themselves. But it would seem as if two parallel approaches to illustration were visible here. The subject could not possibly have been unfamiliar to the painters who collaborated on this enterprise, and behind some illustrations stand clear Persian models, while others bear a more decidedly 'Mughal' look.

This page relates to the early section of the work, the preamble, in which the *shaikh* pays tribute to his patron in approved oriental fashion. Designating him as "the lord of the earth, the axis of fortune's wheel, the successor of Solomon, the defender of the faithful," Sadi speaks in humility of himself being simply a piece of clay that has become perfumed 'because of its association with the rose'. In the illustration a little more than the coming-together of poet and patron is rendered, and there is possibly a reference to a popular story according to which the *shaikh* was sent fifty thousand dinars with the request that he accept them and build a house in Shiraz for the benefit of those who come and go. We see the *shaikh* dressed in a relatively simple, striped robe with a book, a scroll, a pair of scissors, an ink pot – all part of the iconography of a writer or poet – seated on a simple rush mat in front of an octagonal, domed chamber. Facing him is a princely figure dressed in a feathered Mongol hat, and between them is a tray filled with glittering pieces of gold. Attendants and grooms stand at respectful distance, and a horse, suggesting recent arrival, is introduced at the bottom left corner.

This splendid leaf has been attributed by A. Welch (1982:no.64) to Aqa Riza, the painter who arrived from Iran in the late 1580s and worked principally for Jahangir who was then a prince but whose deep passion for painting had led him to gather gifted men around him even during the lifetime of his father, Akbar. Aqa Riza, unlike his famous son Abul Hasan, retained in his work strong elements of conservatism, unable to shake off his adherence to the Persian idiom and atmosphere. This painting is recognizably Mughal (notice, for instance, the treatment of the interior of the pavilion), but much in it retains a firm link with its Persian source: the treatment of the plane tree that grows by the side of the octagonal chamber, the dark tonality and the structure of the rocks, the occasional plant and the flowering shrub that springs up in the foreground, behind the platform the dazzling glow in the sky, the retainers' and attendants' manner of standing, above all the extreme fineness of the intricate texture of the rush mat or the pile of gold coins in the tray. The conservatism of this leaf becomes more evident when one compares it with other illustrations from this fine manuscript (see no. 88). In its own way it is an affecting work; it harks back to the past, preserving a memory which in the hands of other Mughal artists had begun to dim at this point in time.

The manuscript consists of 195 leaves; 57 pages are left blank but have a finished gold margin. On this early folio appears a Shahjahani seal, signifying that the volume was once in the imperial library. The blank pages and the missing section headings, however, indicate that some work still remained to be done on the manuscript.

For further paintings from the same manuscript, see nos. 15, 61, 77, 86, 88, 99.

Publ.: A. Welch, S.C. Welch, 1982, no. 64.

13 "Like a torrent, difficult to contain"

Folio from the same *Akhlaq-i Nasiri* as no. 11
Inscribed to Nand Gwaliori (the word 'Gwaliori' in very faint characters)
18.3 x 10.1 cm; page: 23.6 x 13.8 cm
Akbar period, 1590/95
Collection of Prince Sadruddin Aga Khan

Much as in the preceding work from the same illustrated manuscript (no. 11), the painter here must have had to draw upon his own resources while visualising a passage from the fifth section of the third discourse of Nasir-ud Din's text which is "on the government of retainers and the manners of kings' followers." The section opens with much useful advice on how to "converse with kings and leaders", and it comes to the specific problem of an individual like a minister or counsellor who has to "manage his master". The writer says that if it be the obligation of such a man to make known to his master what is proper for him to do, "he should recognize that kings and leaders are like a torrent coming down from the mountain top; whoever tries all at once to divert it from one course to another will perish, but if a man first accommodates himself there too, gently and subtly raising one bank with earth and waste matter, he will be able to lead it in any other direction he wishes."

Availing himself of Nasir-ud Din's metaphor, the painter Nand, associated with many a fine page from Akbari manuscripts, here decides to go beyond the context of kings and counsellors, and takes the opportunity to depict a scene that might have been close to his own heart, and one he might not have had much occasion to render in the course of normal work in the Mughal atelier: a cloud burst and the resulting rush of a torrential stream. When one comes to think of it, there is remarkably little representation of rain in Mughal painting: in general the skies tend to be clear or inhabited by formalised clouds, Chinese or Indian. This makes it quite different from the situation in Rajput painting where, in the context of the telling of myths, of the rendering of a cycle of seasons like the *Barahmasa*, or of the situations of lovers who meet despite natural obstructions and long for each other when the monsoon breaks, there is much joyous celebration of rain. Nand decides here, then, to indulge himself, and creates a landscape that is green and lush and charged with moisture, in which peacocks prance on rocktops while thundering clouds rage in the sky and a great torrent rushes down from the mountains. He avails himself of the convention of piled-up rocks for the mountains and the distant view of a palace; he also makes a clear reference to a man at the point of perishing in the swift flow of water, while another stretches a hapless hand towards him, something that the text briefly refers to. But, for the rest, the painting remains a personal statement. These clouds are also somewhat formalised, but they are palpably charged with water, and the torrent here is not like the discreet, orderly streams

of Persian work or some formalised rivers across which bridges are thrown in Mughal painting. This torrent is noisy and impetuous, as well-observed as the miniscule rendering of a peasant at the back: he brings out his pair of oxen for tilling the field (while rain, rendered here in remarkably fine streaks, softens the ground), much like an Indian peasant even today would do.

Unpublished.

14 A prince visiting a hermit

Leaf mounted as an album page; on verso, unsigned calligraphy in *nastaliq*
34.2 x 23 cm; page: 39.6 x 31.3 cm
Akbar period, 1585/90
Collection of Prince Sadruddin Aga Khan

The theme of this painting, the meeting of a high aristocrat and a humble dervish is, as A. Welch and S.C. Welch aptly point out (1982:160), "resonant in Iranian literature and art." This "fleeting juxtaposition and distant affinity of temporal and spiritual authority" has always held a strong appeal both in Iran and India. The prince whom we see here is an Indian, as are his followers and retainers, judging from their appearance and their dresses, and their outsized, dappled horses. But much else here retains a 'foreign flavour.'

The painting has been attributed by S.C. Welch to the great Iranian master, Khwaja Abd-al Samad, who had come from Shiraz to India, having entered Humayun's service. The *khwaja* ('man of distinction') was a man of many parts, a painter, a calligrapher, also an able administrator, and he rose to considerable eminence under Akbar, not only superintending work in the imperial atelier but also being appointed Master of the Mint and given charge of the administration of Multan in the Panjab. His is one of the few careers of Mughal artists that one can trace, and he finds mention on more than one occasion in Abul Fazl's pages who records that the *khwaja* had the honorific *Shirin qalam,* 'Sweet Pen', a title that we encounter on paintings bearing his name more than once. Under Abd-al Samad's tutelage, many a painter of Indian origin was trained and great projects like the *Hamzanama* were carried out.

Clearly, much was seen by Abd-al Samad in his long career in India by way of change and innovation, but it would seem as if he himself remained innately conservative. As Beach (1981:20) points out, his work in general "shows none of the interest in liveliness of colour, originality of composition, or European techniques of modelling and perspective that were imbedded in the general vocabulary of Mughal painting by the 1580s." The remarkable master of the brush that he was, Abd-al Samad continued to retain a distinct preference for the fineness of the Iranian style that he had grown up with. This becomes clear from a comparison of his early signed works with those that he did quite late in his life, roughly dateable to the nineties of the 16th century. One sees it in his preference, as here, for this wonderfully laid out landscape of rocks and running water and plane trees which is so reminiscent of Iranian work; his interest remains strong in surface design with little real involvement in questions of weight and mass and space, questions that were exciting the imagination of younger artists whom he himself was training at the time.

The colours are rather thinly applied, but the details in this painting are exquisitely done: the lean but eager frame of the hermit who holds his hand out in exposition, the slightly downward inclined head of the prince who humbly receives words of advice or enlightenment, the peacefully seated doe and fawn next to the hermit, the derelict dervish-like character sitting at some distance listening to the conversation, and the fine crisp details in the rendering of foliage and rock and dresses. At the same time, things are viewed from a distance, with an air of detachment that runs counter to the strain of passion that had started coursing through Mughal painting at this time.

Publ.: A. Welch, S.C. Welch, 1982, no. 55; Brand, Lowry, 1985, no. 68.

15 King Dara and the herdsman

Folio (28b) from the same *Kulliyat* of Sadi as no. 12
27.9 x 15.8 cm; page: 41.7 x 26.4 cm
Akbar-Jahangir period, 1600/05
Collection of Prince Sadruddin Aga Khan

Among the many moral tales in the *Bustan,* a decided favourite is that of the Emperor Dara and the herdsman. Commanding great glory and wealth, the emperor once finds himself in a position of disadvantage when he is separated from his hunting party and comes to a wilderness where he meets a herdsman who approaches him. Suddenly feeling insecure, the emperor readies himself for defence when the herdsman speaks words not of hostility but of gentle reproach. In Sadi's poetic words, the herdsman reminds the emperor:

"It's neither laudable provision nor good judgment
When the emperor knows not enemy from friend!
It is in high station a condition of living
That you should know who each inferior is."

The herdsman points out with great rustic simplicity that he at least knows each animal in his own herd well.

As a sober and useful reminder of the need on the part of the mighty to pay greater attention to the humble ones around them, the tale was widely known and recited and figures prominently in illustrated manuscripts of Sadi's works both from Persia and from India.

The painter of this unsigned leaf of the fine *Kulliyat,* being thoroughly familiar with the Persian iconography and models of the same episode, slips into a mode of painting which, in the context of what was happening in Mughal painting around 1600, can only be called conservative: the entire scene is viewed from a certain distance and a given height; at the same time the rocks of variegated hues that mushroom all over the painting and reach as far as the eye can see, the herd of horses painted with great delight in varying colours and sizes and attitudes, the encampment in the distance, and the rim of gold in the sky, all stand out as different from what one might describe at this point in time as the mainstream of Mughal painting. If one makes the effort, almost exact prototypes of the manner in which the horses are treated here or the men perch atop rocks can be traced back to sources outside of India and, highly accomplished as this work is, it comes as a stylistic surprise at this time.

It is of interest to compare this page with a Persian painting of the same theme (Binyon, 1965:no.37) to see how much of the iconography of the scene is taken from the earlier rendering.

Publ.: A. Welch, S.C. Welch, 1982, no. 64.

نصیحت ز منعم شنید نگفت | گهبان مرعی بخندید وگفت
که دشمن بد اندیش نشر دوست | نه تندبی محمود و رای نکوست
بیند نیم از بد اندیش باز | کنون تا بهر دم پش باز
تو هم کله خویش داری بجای | مرا کله بانی بتعقلبست وای

چه آیست در مهتری شرط نیست | نصیحت ز منعم شنید نگفت
مرا بارها در حصنه دیده | نه تند محمود و رای نکوست
تو نم من بامور سهد یار | کنون تا بهر دم پش باز
جو دارا شنید این حکایت فزد | تو هم کله خویش داری بجای

که که تیر بر ابدانی که کبست | چه آیست در مهتری شرط نیست
ز خیل و چرا کاه پرسیده | مرا بارها در حصنه دیده
که اسپی برون آورم از غبار | تو نم من بامور سهد یار
بکوبش کفت وکوبش کرد | جو دارا شنید این حکایت فزد

49

16 Rustam rescues Bihzan from the dungeon

Folio from a dispersed illustrated *Shahnama*-manuscript
19 x 15.5 cm; page: 32 x 20.7 cm
Shahjahan period, c. 1640
Rietberg Museum, Zurich
(Eugen Fritz Bequest)

For close to nine hundred years, the *Shah-nama* of Firdausi has held powerful sway in the Islamic world. It was admired in India as much as in Persia and other countries as the embodiment "of the whole national legend of an ancient and imaginative race", for "its majestic breadth and range", and its "sonorous sweep of language." The epic was, as Wilkinson says, "inspired by a deep sense of the greatness of Providence and the impermanence of mortal things."

The narrative is exceedingly long and involved, but full of those 'weird glimpses of strange and terrible things' that hold the reader's attention, and because it combines a deep love of beauty and valor and strength, the perennial appeal of the work is understandable. For the illustrators the work held a special interest, for the narrative is full of extraordinary happenings. Across the centuries, a whole iconography of celebrated episodes from the *Shahnama* had emerged, an iconography that was drawn upon as much by the painters of the Timurid world and of Persia as by those of India.

The quality of work in the illustrated *Shahnama* manuscripts that have survived from Mughal India is greatly varied but it is interesting to see how, again and again, the painter turns to iconography and models as seen and remembered from a long time back. This leaf from a dispersed manuscript shows a celebrated episode in the epic in which the great hero Rustam rescues Bihzan from the dungeon into which he had been thrown by king Afrasiyab for the crime of being in love with his daugher Manizah. But Rustam survived for a long time with the help of Manizah who had been exiled by her father. When it was discovered that Bihzan was alive and not lost as first reported, the hero Rustam was entrusted with the task of locating him with the help of Manizah, who lit a wood fire at night to guide him. Rustam found the dungeon but its mouth had been blocked by a great boulder, all but impossible to move. But Rustam, as always equal to the task, lifted the stone, flung it far away and drew Bihzan out of the pit with a rope, thus freeing him of his fetters.

The painter of this leaf, working in a competent workman-like manner, shows very clear awareness of earlier models. The iconography of Rustam with his animal-skin headgear, and his golden mace with an animal head, is accurate; the entire setting, that of a wilderness, the pit, the number of companions with whom Rustam arrives, the figure of Manizah, the heavy stone which Rustam has flung away from the top of the pit, the blaze of fire, are all instantly recognizable.

What is of uncommon interest is that while the artist tries to introduce variations, as in the rendering of the pit which is different from the way in which it is usually rendered in standard Persian works, or by introducing two horses which stand out awkwardly towards the top right of the painting, he continues noticeably to draw upon Persian conventions. It is as if the moment the thought of a rocky landscape in a Persian setting arises, well-used pictorial conventions present themselves. The formula for the piled-up rocks, the characteristically isolated Persian tree, are all related to the tendency to keep alive a whole series of conventions.

Unpublished.

17 Rustam slays the white demon

Folio from a *Shahnama*-manuscript, mounted as an album page
20 x 14 cm; page: 34.5 x 26.5 cm
Shahjahan period, c.1650
Rietberg Museum, Zurich

Of the celebrated exploits of the great war-rior-hero Rustam, narrated with such verve in the *Shahnama,* the 'seven courses of Rustam' always remained great favourites with illustrators, single album leaves some-times centering on one or the other of these exploits. Among these seven courses, in which the incomparable hero on his way to rescuing Kai Kaus encounters a fresh dan-ger each of the seven days that the journey takes him, overcoming them all, his bout of strength with the terrible white *div* or demon who had taken captive the Shah of Iran held special fascination. In the story, Rustam over-powers the demon after a fierce struggle and, piercing his heart, takes blood out to pour it into the eyes of the captured Shah Kai Kaus and his companions so that their blindness can be cured.

The slaying of the White Demon is the sub-ject of this inventive and, in its own way, rather delicately-worked leaf. The painter plays here with many elements, principally with the awesome figure of the *div* which is made up as a composite of many animal and human heads. This clever and playful device, so much a favourite of Persian and Indian artists alike, is generally seen in fig-ures of animals like elephants and camels with riders (see no. 24); it is not often that a *div*'s body is shown as comprising of many figures. The painter thus draws upon a source established in a different context for introducing this innovation. Belonging to the times that he did, he also does not eschew the temptation of bringing in a view of a city in the distance, although some-where in the middle and not at the furthest point in the painting. But the painter's obvi-ous favourite is the rocky Persian landscape in which he lets himself go in the fantastic play of colours and shapes. The large group of boulders that looms so prominently in the background, and the bare, curving piled rocks towards the left of the two combatants, have received uncommon attention from the painter. The way he handles all these ele-ments is of interest, for even though many of the features like the diminutive trees in the distance and the feeling for atmosphere are attempts at innovation, these, being a stylistic throwback, represent a kind of 'new conservatism' that seems to come into being at this time in Mughal India.

Unpublished.

18 Princely lovers in a pavilion

Lightly tinted drawing, mounted as an album page
20.5 x 12.5 cm; page: 39 x 28.5 cm
Akbar-Jahangir period, 1600/10
Collection of Prince Sadruddin Aga Khan

The constant interplay between conservatism and change remains a continuing feature of Mughal painting. This does not result, as one might fear, in awkward works in which the elements are never reconciled. It is with singular success in fact that elements are often mingled. From the point of view of analysing the style, the task of isolating different strains, to the extent possible, retains a certain fascination, as in this delicate drawing.

In its general look, the work is unmistakably Mughal: apart from such details as the views of the city and the shrine with the walking *sadhu* in the background, the figure of the lady, the act of offering *pan* – spiced betel-leaf – by the prince to his beloved, the details of architecture, etc., the whole sense of space and the manner in which the drawing is laid out can be quickly perceived as Mughal. The exchange between the lovers, as he holds her extended left arm with his own even as she lightly resists his advance, is thoroughly Rajput in feeling, and the prominent placing of two cages in the courtyard with two different kinds of birds makes one wonder if these commonly-seen birds, the parrot and the mynah, have not been brought in to tell a tale. The intimacy of feeling introduced in the form of an old lady who converses with a conspicuously Muslim-looking younger woman with a 'Safavid' child at her side, is again the kind of detail that a Rajput painter would render with natural delight. There are other elements in the drawing, especially the drapery of the two women in the courtyard, that might be taken from European sources as already absorbed in Mughal work. But the manner in which the superbly rendered tree, which more or less dominates the composition and certainly balances its straight architectural lines, and the crisp, precise delineation of flowering trees and plants (which are interestingly combined with a thoroughly Indian plantain-tree), bespeak of other connections, in part Iranian, in part Deccani. But all this said, the drawing which has been attributed to the early years of Abul Hasan (c.1601) by A. Welch and S.C. Welch (1982:182) remains itself not an uneasy pastiche.

Publ.: A. Welch, S.C. Welch, 1982, no. 61.

Virtuosity

19 Two camels fighting

Single leaf inscribed with four lines in *nastaliq* at the top
By Abd-al Samad
18.8 x 22.4 cm
Akbar period, c. 1590
Private Collection

A passage from a letter written by Humayun to Rashid Khan, the ruler of Kashghar, helps illumine our understanding of some of the qualities in painting held in high esteem by the early Mughals. In the letter, which was accompanied by a gift of works of art, Humayun speaks with pride of some of the more important craftsmen who had joined his court just before he returned to India: "From among those matchless artists who had presented themselves before me in Iraq and Khurasan and were generously rewarded, a group came and joined my service in Shawwal A.H. 959 September / October 1552. One of them is the painter Mir Sayyid Ali, the *nadir al-asr* ('Wonder of the Times'), who is matchless in painting *(taswir)*. He has painted on a grain of rice a polo scene – two horsemen stand within the field, a third comes galloping from one corner, while a fourth horseman stands at one end, receiving a mallet from a footman; at each end of the field are two goal posts; ..."
"Another is the painter Maulana Abd al-Samad, the unique one of the time *(farid al-dahr),* the *shirin-qalam,* who has surpassed his contemporaries. He has made on a grain of rice a large field on which a group is playing polo ..."

Much was to happen in Mughal painting later, and many other qualities were to be incorporated and admired in it. But somewhere within himself, the Mughal painter never quite lost either interest in or admiration for fine workmanship of the kind described here. Sheer technical brilliance and virtuoso effects remained significant values, and whenever he got the opportunity, a master painter went into passages that could be held up to his peers and patron as proof of his incomparable skills.

In the early years of the 16th century, the great Persian master Bihzad (after whom Khwaja Abd-al Samad named one of his two sons) had painted a picture of two fighting dromedaries with such dazzling display of brushwork that it was to linger long in the memory of painters. Some Mughal versions of his work were made, among them this superbly painted leaf by Abd-al Samad. The painting carries the master's signature in a very minute hand in the lower corner of the top left panel. The entire inscription of four lines is in fact of deep interest, for it adds to the whole scene an air of poignancy: in it Abd-al Samad speaks of his sending to his "knowledgeable, witty, and astute son, Sharif Khan" this painting as a 'reminder' of himself. But he prefaces the note by stating that he is painting it at a time when "his faculties have stopped working, his brush moves but sluggishly, and his remarkable sight has grown dim at the infirm age of 85 that he has now reached." One cannot accurately guess at what lies behind the writing of this epistle but it is evident that, even at this advanced age, the master sets out here to adduce proof of his remarkable control of brush and colour. The idea and the composition has clearly been taken from the Persian master (although he reverses the design), but the execution is his own, calling for a display of breathtaking virtuosity. The rocky landscape with trees, gnarled with age and swiftly being denuded of leaves, is impressive enough, but in the fighting dromedaries one sees that attention to detail and that combination of vigour and delicacy which was a painter's dream to achieve: the minutely twisted and braided ropes and bands of the harnesses of the dromedaries, the bristly hair on their bodies, each singly painted, the light foam at their mouths as they snarl and bite, the hairless patches on their thigh and knee-joints. Likewise are the knitted eye-brows of the keepers who try to bring the fighting beasts within control, the motionless spindle of the old man at the top right observing this fight from a distance, the knots of the ropes which the keepers pull at and the stricken look in the eye of the darker, hairier dromedary who is having the worst of the fight.

Seeing the quality of this exquisitely coloured work in the hand of a master at the age of 85, one almost begins to believe in the rice grains on which polo games in progress were painted, and on which whole couplets in Persian were inscribed.

The inscription on this painting contains possibly a little more information than hitherto seen. The first few words, including the very rubbed one at the very beginning, almost certainly mention the painter's age *(haftad-wa-panj)* rather than make a reference to him as *Ustad-wa-Shaikh.* In the second line, again, there is possibly a mention of this painting being sent "as a reminder and a lamp for the sight", a reference perhaps to the style and workmanship that needs to be held up as a model. If this suggestion is correct, it would seem as if Abd-al Samad here is intent upon calling his son's attention to the kind of art from which theirs has sprung; to their roots, in other words.

It is noteworthy that Bihzad too was old, seventy years of age, when he painted the famous dromedaries (Binyon, Gray, 1971:no.87a; Das, 1978:no.31a).

Publ.: Falk, 1985, no. 21; Brand, Lowry, 1985, no. 58.

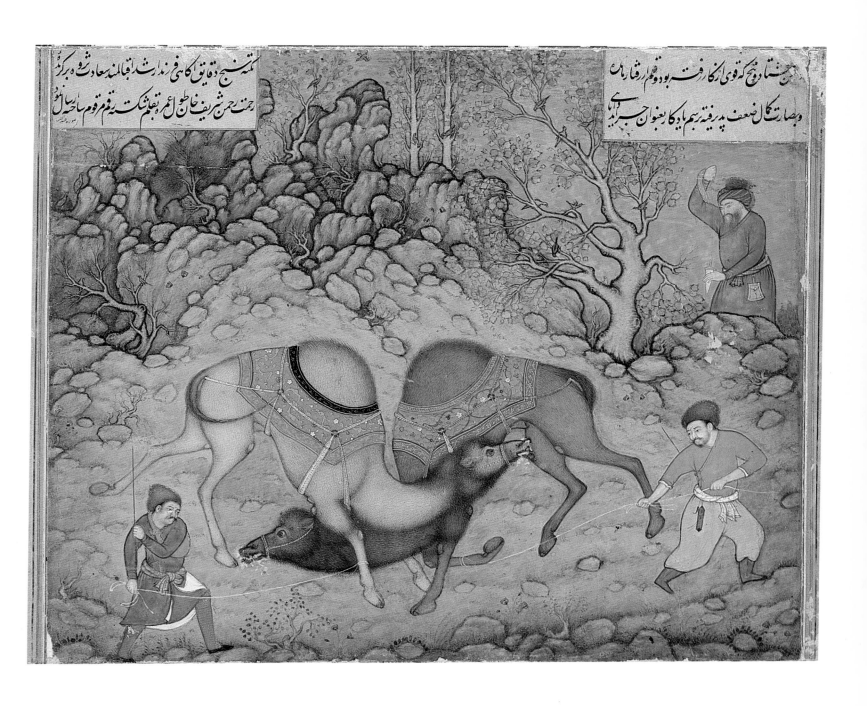

20 Bathing women

Single leaf mounted as an album page
15.4 x 6.9 cm; page: 23.4 x 14.7 cm
Akbar period, c. 1590
Rietberg Museum, Zurich
(Acquisition funded by Lucy Rudolph)

The context remains unclear. The subject of women bathing is by no means unknown either to Persian or to Mughal painting, but the situation here is not the usual one: that of a hero espying a young maiden bathing in the open, or princesses frolicking to keep themselves cool and entertained. The feeling in this singularly small painting is one of some anxiety judging from stances and looks. As three well-formed women bathe in a cistern of water fed by a Persian wheel, a young woman carrying a child in her arms arrives. The bathing women turn to look at her, questions in their eyes, a slight sense of unease, even impatience being communicated by their gestures. Perhaps an episode from a tale is being told on this page, an unexpected happening in which a princess and her child are involved. But this remains a guess at best.

Clearly, however, the intention of the painter here is to go considerably beyond the telling of a tale for, having established the elements of the episode and the characters in it, he becomes utterly absorbed in delicacy of craftsmanship. This is not something that we would expect in the treatment of a subject like this – the situation can be rendered with clarity even without this painstaking effort – but it seems as if it is the nature of this painter to give his very best in this respect. The first impression the painting makes is that of a straight-forward human situation; it is when one starts taking in the exquisite detailing that one becomes aware of its qualities. Almost everything in the painting needs a second look in order for its subtleties to be properly taken in. The architectural detail with the raised well towards the right, the channel of water leading from it to the cistern and the wall with two alcoves, one with a regular pattern of interstices in it, like the trees both inside the small courtyard and outside beyond the wall, are handled with firmness; but they are also deliberately played down and somewhat thinly coloured so as to throw the figures of the women into sharper relief. The women themselves, full-bosomed and broadly built, unlike those nearly evanescent maidens in Persian painting, are exquisitely drawn, bodies supple and resilient, complexions smooth but earthy, faces remarkably expressive; the arch of the eyebrow, the corner of the mouth, the tilt of the head make eloquent statements about states of mind. But nearly as much delicacy of treatment is reserved by the painter for seemingly insignificant details, and one has to be very alert so as not to miss any of them. One needs to notice, for instance, the delicate manner in which the fingers of the left hand of the fairest complexioned of them all, the one in the middle, rest on the left shoulder of the maiden at the extreme right; the left hand, with which the fully clothed woman holds the child against herself, partially under the diaphanous, nearly invisible muslin wrap of the child; the wisps of hair that, slightly wet and looking like down, cling lovingly to the forms of the bathing women; the strands of necklaces made up of fine lustrous pearls, each singly articulated; the pattern of the golden shoes worn by the woman at left that picks up the upward rhythm of the front end of her garment; two thin roots sprouting out of the plastered wall where the water channel joins the parapet of the well. One also takes in the fine moss at one edge of the trunk of the tree at the back, directly below the neatly hung drying cloth; the arrangement of wooden stakes on which a climber has been trained at the bottom right, and blades of grass in the foreground that feel as if in rendering them the brush had barely touched the surface of the paper. It would seem as if the true subject of the painting is its preciousness, not the episode that it illustrates.

The painting has been trimmed on all sides, but it is unlikely that it was very much larger in its original state than it is now. A narrow geometric border, strips taken from some illuminated manuscript, and an outer border were once placed around it. None of these is in any way related to the work, and nothing in them matches either its refinement of workmanship or delicacy of feeling.

Publ.: Octagon, vol. 23,3:23.

21 The flight of a *simurgh*

Leaf from an unidentified series; on verso, calligraphy in *nastaliq* by Muhammad Hussain
Inscribed to Basawan
33.1 x 21 cm; page: 39 x 25.2 cm
Painting: Akbar period, c. 1590; calligraphy: c. 1635 or later
Collection of Prince Sadruddin Aga Khan

For Basawan, whose name appears in a small inscription at the very top of the page, Abul Fazl, Akbar's biographer, had the very highest of praise: "In backgrounding, drawing of features, distribution of colours, portrait painting and several other branches, he is most excellent, so much so that many critics prefer him to Daswant." Several remarkable works by Basawan have survived, some of them very early ones, and discussing the present page, A. Welch (1982:no.57) speaks of "the sense of tangible volume, the prevailing softness of figures and receding landscape, and the sensitive and the sympathetic observation" that one sees in it.

To identify this scene is not easy: it possibly makes a reference to an episode from the poet Nizami's work, *Haft Paykar,* in which a story is told of a prince arriving in a paradise-like land by clinging to the feet of a *simurgh.* There are some elements of the story in the painting, and even if this is not the precise tale being told here, a world of myth is certainly being referred to: a small craggy piece of land surrounded by a great ocean; a little temple nestling in the midst of trees at the right, the only sign of habitation on this stretch of land; the wonderfully wrought *simurgh,* that resplendent creature of fancy in Islamic painting; the princely figure suspended in the air, clinging to the bird's claws; two other figures, perhaps the prince's companions, on the point of being swallowed by the giant creature's mouth; the fearsome creatures of the deep that look curiously upwards at the strange happenings in the sky. There is a wonderful sense of fantasy in the work that comes not only from the giant bird soaring above but also from the total stillness of this lush piece of land, a sense of isolation and danger emphasized by the presence of water on both sides of the land; in this setting, even the presence of the soaring rocky mass at left is meant to be seen perhaps as part of a fantasy, everything else below looking so real and earthbound in its own way.

Very delicately coloured and softly drawn, the painting is full of virtuoso passages. The *simurgh* demands attention for all its dread appearance, its flashing eyes and its tail flailing the sky, but it has been painted almost affectionately. One notices also the five principal trees on the island, each of them worked on with painstaking care and deliberately shown possessing of a personality or profile distinguishable from all others; there is playfulness in the rendering of the flowering tree with small pink flowers as it is placed against the towering rock with its dominant pinks that combine greens and greys; the vertical edge of the stretch of land seems to be full of creases and folds like some curtain suspended inside a chamber; the great expanse of water that rises so high even at the back holds many a mystery in its womb, the painter seems to say. It is these elements, not necessarily the human figures, though finely sketched, that seem to have yielded possibly the greatest satisfaction to the painter.

The fine calligraphy in the hand of Muhammad Hussain on the other side is mounted on an album page associated with the Shahjahan period.

Publ.: A. Welch, S.C. Welch, 1982, no. 57.

59

22 A feat of horsemanship

Folio from the same *Akhlaq-i Nasiri* as no. 11
Inscribed to Kanak Sing (Gang Singh?)
19.2 x 10.4 cm; page: 23.6 x 14 cm
Akbar period, 1590/95
Collection of Prince Sadruddin Aga Khan

The two floating panels of calligraphy are from the text in the "Second Discourse" of Nasir-ud Din, in which he discusses pursuits of different kinds, noble, base, and intermediate. He lists the pursuits that are to be associated with three classes of liberal men: those devoted to intelligence, those who make letters and culture their concern and those who depend upon strength and courage. The latter concern themselves with "horsemanship, military command, the control of frontiers, and the repulsion of enemies", all of these being part of 'chivalry'.

Much like his colleagues who worked on this fine illustrated manuscript, the painter, Gang Singh, must have had his share of problems in deciding what passage to pick from Nasir-ud Din's text for illustration – virtually all of them are devoid of narrative interest and refer to no specific personalities – and how best to render it. He decides upon "*sawari wa sipahagari*", in essence "horsemanship and soldiering", and turns to focus on a kind of feat that he might have personally witnessed. Choosing a princely figure as his model, he shows him followed by companions and retainers, most of them also on horseback, as they reach a small flat piece of land surrounded by a craggy landscape. The suggestion here is that the prince comes on full gallop and suddenly reins the horse in; the horse stops in his tracks, rises on his hind-feet, front legs pawing the air, while the prince throws his spear high into the air, only to catch it in his extended right arm as it falls; both horse and rider have at this moment achieved total motionlessness. It is a virtuoso feat, eliciting admiration from the prince's companions who look on intently, wondering fingers raised to their lips, their eyes glued to the extended arm and the spear high in the air.

As if matching this virtuoso display, the painter decides to show off his own considerable skills in this very 'painterly' page. Setting the scene in the midst of a rocky landscape, he delicately and playfully renders the conventionalized rocks in an extraordinary range of colours. As they sprout and spread and expand over virtually the entire painting from the bottom to the very top, he explores all kinds of possibilities of combining colours and shapes in them, especially creating a dark patch behind the prince's lightly coloured form to throw it into relief. He seems to be so involved with rocks, in fact, that the conventional distant view of a city, so common in Mughal paintings of this period, is pushed back to the point of negligence, the range of grey, blue, and brown rocks taking precedence at the very top of the painting.

The other elements, part of the iconography of a 'wild landscape' – the birds, the narrow courses of water, the animals running around – receive no more than the necessary attention. The painter, on the other hand, turns to the forms of the horses: the prince's dappled grey animal apart, the seven other horses are rendered in carefully variegated colours, no two horses being of the same hue or pattern. The painter also tries out some other things, like the foreshortened horse ridden by the old courtier at the top right and the unusual *dhoti*-clad Hindu courtier at the bottom of this arc.

The painter's name has been generally taken to be 'Kanak Sing'. It is more likely that the name is 'Gang Singh'; this reading is equally justified from the way the words are formed, and this Hindu name rings more authentic in this form than as 'Kanak Sing'.

Publ.: Sotheby's, November 27, 1974, (Bibliotheca Phillippica), no. 684; A. Welch, S.C. Welch, 1982, no. 58.

23　Visitation: the Virgin meets Elisabeth

Single leaf mounted as an album page; on verso, calligraphic exercise in *nastaliq*
13 x 10.4 cm
Akbar-Jahangir period, 1600/10
Rietberg Museum, Zurich
(Acquisition funded by Balthasar and Nanni Reinhart)

The exact European work upon which this Mughal copy or version is based remains as yet unidentified, but the scene is easily determined. After the Angel Gabriel has brought to the Virgin strange but blessed tidings, she leaves her home to visit Elisabeth, her relative, who has also conceived despite her and her husband Zachariah's advanced years. The Virgin's visit and the meeting of the two ladies, each blessed in her own way, is the subject of many a Christian work, and evidently a European version of this scene, among others, reached the Mughal court, where it was picked up by a Mughal painter to work from.

Seen initially perhaps merely as curiosities, European works excited the imagination of many a Mughal painter: Basawan, Kesu, Abul Hasan among them. Making copies of these 'alien-looking' works or inducting passages from them in their own work, turned with time into a matter of pride, for the exercise demanded skills that were unusual for the painter. Soon figures in all kinds of attitudes, in dress or undress, clothed in strangely heavy and creased garments appeared in Mughal albums as close copies or integrated into larger, more Indian-looking compositions. Elements of achitecture and receding landscapes were played with, atmospheric effects were sought to be established, and an awareness of cast shadows or given sources of light flickered in many a Mughal work.

It is likely that the painter of this refined, deeply felt work had access only to an engraving, not a coloured original, and he seems to have filled in the colours from his own imagination. But the moment rendered in the work must have been painstakingly explained to him, for without this he could not have captured that marked feeling of tenderness. Three of the four figures, the two ladies and Zachariah who is rendered dumb by divine command for these months, are remarkably convincing: the young Virgin, with a delicate halo over her head, is shown with a smile hovering lightly around her lips, as she holds her arm softly against her discreetly covered belly; the older Elisabeth solicitously takes the Virgin's hand and moves her face close to her as if whispering a confidence; the balding Zachariah, who holds Joseph's hand, appears humble but contented, with his eyes nearly closed and his hat held against his chest. Only the incoming figure of Joseph, long-haired and bearded, falls short of the other three. But where the painter truly seeks to show off his virtuosity is in the rendering of the garments and the softly articulated features of the principal figures. The weight of the garments, their intricate folds and curves painted with extremely fine shading and the sense of real movement and rustling in the clothes must all have placed real demands upon his skill. But he handles these details with self-assurance and delight and perhaps goes even beyond the strict demands of the original engraving. One senses this especially in the garments around the heads of the two ladies and the manner in which the white shawl falls around the neck of Elisabeth.

The painter also essays an attempt at depth in the scene: here his manner of handling space is, like much else, from a borrowed source. Not everything comes off well: there is some inexplicable awkwardness in the figure of Joseph and the perspective of the prominent building in the background, with the play of shadows upon it, shows areas of imperfect understanding. But in essence, the work remains remarkable for the skills it employs and for the feeling it evokes. The warmth of the human exchange in it glows somewhat like the gold in the sky.

On verso the exercise in *nastaliq* calligraphy shows some letters repeated over and over again. Among the few words clearly discernible, the names of Ali, Hasan and Hussain occur several times, apart from the name of the prophet. The word 'Miskin' also figures on this page, but it is difficult to determine if any importance needs to be attached to it.

Another 'Visitation'-scene, dated 1678, is published in Martin, 1912, no. 173a.

Unpublished.

24 A composite elephant

Single leaf mounted as an album page; on verso, calligraphy in *nastaliq*
by Abdulla al-Hussaini
13.4 x 20 cm; page: 25 x 28.8 cm
Painting: Akbar period, c. 1600; borders and calligraphy: Shahjahan period, c. 1640
Collection of Prince Sadruddin Aga Khan

There is both playfulness and meaning in the numerous composite figures that one encounters in the art of widely varying cultures over long periods of time. S.C. Welch cites (1976:40) among the many antecedents of composite works the 'animal style' of art in the first millennium before Christ, 12th century stone sculpture from Seljuk Anatolia and paintings and drawings of the 15th and 16th century both from Persia and India. The significance, the hidden meaning in these works, is not easy to guess at and images of this complexity, Welch says, possibly "encouraged the artist – and still encourage the viewer – to explore his subconscious responses."

Within the Indian tradition, which also has its riches in composite figures and arrangements, one sees once again this very mixture of meaning and playfulness. The myriad women whose bodies interlock to form a palanquin in which Krishna rides, the *nari kunjara,* an elephant made up of the bodies of women, the *nava gunjara* composed of nine different creatures that represent the cosmic form of Vishnu, especially in the pictorial tradition of Orissa, all partake of this mixing of elements. It is likely (A. Welch, S.C. Welch, 1982:186ff) that in the Islamic tradition the figure shown riding an elephant is often Sulaiman (Solomon) who holds sway over all kinds of creatures, and upon whom attend fairies, demons and dread animals of all description.

Whatever the origins of the idea, the making of a composite image like the one seen here seems to have turned into a test of skills, a proof alike of liveliness of imagination and control of line and colour on the part of the painter. Not all composite figures succeed equally well, for often much is slurred over and repetition of the same form leads to deadening effects. There is exuberance in this elephant which is being ridden by a kingly figure whose Babur-like head is topped by a golden crown, from which tongues of fire leap into the air at the back, in simulation of the fluttering loose ends of a turban. Within the body of the elephant are contained an incredible number of animals, birds and men who are more onlookers than actors in this drama. The creatures are tightly packed into the pachydermic frame, most of them ill-at-ease with each other. Unmindful of the fierce conflict raging within it, the elephant moves with a stately gait, in its trunk a serpent coiled in simulation of the iron chains that many an elephant carries in Mughal and Rajput painting. The background is lightly tinted, generally sparse with a soft rendering of rocks and trees. These and the uncoloured figure of the man walking in front serve to emphasize the richness of effect created by the fine colouring of the various creatures forming the body of the elephant.

The painting is in a horizontal format but is mounted on a vertical album leaf. This leads to a somewhat awkward and unusual effect, but the painting must have been valued enough to risk this arrangement. As is common, the delicately coloured borders filled with figures manage to take a cue from the painting: animals and birds are sprinkled all over, each finely studied, possibly making a reference to its counterpart within the elephant's body.

The other side of the leaf has borders that are equally delicate but purely floral. They surround a panel of calligraphy signed by Abdulla al-Hussaini, who was among the prominent at the court of Shahjahan. The lines are a citation from the sayings of Ali, 'leader of the believers', held in great esteem among the Shiites.

A. Welch remarks that the calligraphy is written in *taliq* and should be dated around 1640.

Publ.: A. Welch, S.C. Welch, 1982, no. 62; Falk, 1985, no. 132.

25 The court of Solomon

Folio from an unidentified manuscript, mounted as an album page
27.3 x 15.4 cm; page: 34.5 x 22.7 cm
Akbar-Jahangir period, 1600/05
Collection of Prince Sadruddin Aga Khan

The two brief panels of calligraphy at the top are in praise of someone, perhaps a ruler or a patron, whom one cannot identify because the second half of the verse is missing. The person is lauded as being a veritable Yaqub (Jacob) in his sympathy, a Yusuf (Joseph) in beauty of appearance, a Yahya (John) in piety and a Sulaiman (Solomon) in the command of his dominions. It is of interest to see that out of these four legendary figures, to whom allusion is made, the painter picks the figure of Sulaiman for this 'illustration'. It would seem as if he were going slightly off-course, but painting the court of Solomon was clearly an idea difficult to resist. With Sulaiman, a fantastic range of beings is associated over whom he had control, *jinns* and *divs,* fairies and demons, things supernatural and subdivine and animals of all ilk and species. Wind was in his power and there was no language, human or animal, that Sulaiman did not speak. The court of Sulaiman then is where one can indulge one's fantasy.

In this striking rendition, in which the seated figure of Sulaiman occupies the centre of the picture, a feast of some kind is in progress, and those that stand nearest the sovereign are winged fairies and demons in servile positions. Here the *peris* stand still, their wings rising above them and their feathered bodies unclothed. One also sees demons, ordinarily so fierce and awesome, in a state of total subjugation, scurrying around like court servants, carrying trays of food or gifts. There is more to be seen in the lowest part and at the very top of the page. For here the painter presents a whole menagerie of animals and birds. We see them in pairs, as if it were not the court of Sulaiman but some Noah's ark that were the subject, but the play with the idea is meaningful, for the painter can thus display to advantage his ability to set off male against female of the same species and thus present a remarkably well observed range. Here on the right, standing in a phalanx at the foot of the hexagonal parapet on which Sulaiman sits on his throne, are the leopard and lion, tiger, hyena, *cheetah,* a pair of jackals, stags, goats, antelopes and sheep; on the left are cranes, rhinoceroses, dromedaries, water buffaloes, asses and hares, all in pairs, only the horse and elephant single. This is by no means all, for above in the sky are the denizens of the air, most prominently the mythical *simurgh* with his brilliant plumage, but also peacocks and ducks, parakeets and falcons and the like. One knows of Mughal pages in which birds of different feather are presented in all their dazzling brilliance; there are, of course, also those distinguished studies of single animals or birds;

but wherever he could, in the scenes of Majnun in the wilderness, a hunt in the forest, or as here in the court of Sulaiman, the artist seems to have seized the occasion with eagerness to render birds and animals in great profusion.

This painting has been attributed by S.C. Welch (1959:140) to the painter Madhu Khanazad. A. Welch and S.C. Welch (1982:190) believe that this leaf was part of a now dispersed *Divan* of Hafiz and see in it "an ideal image of Mughal kingship", in which the sovereign binds a remarkably diverse society together with the help of a sound administrative structure. He also indicates that this painting could only have been painted for Akbar. It may be added that only this emperor – like the figure of Solomon – sat cross-legged while giving audience.

Publ.: Grousset, 1930, no. 218; Strzygowski, 1933, no. 216; S.C. Welch, 1959, no. 11; Welch, Beach, 1965, no. 6; A. Welch, S.C. Welch, 1982, no. 63; Falk, 1985, no. 131.

26 Princely figure on horseback

Single leaf mounted as an album page
19 x 16.2 cm; page: 36.5 x 24.9 cm
Painting: Jahangir period, c. 1610; borders: Shahjahan period, c. 1640
Collection of Prince Sadruddin Aga Khan

It is unlikely that this painting was intended as a portrait of a specific person: it does not easily fit into one's idea of portraiture in Mughal India at this point in time. The painter was, on the other hand, possibly drawing upon his awareness of images of those elegant young men of almost effeminate beauty that flit through Persian painting so often. Here he does not show the youth standing under a tree or seated in a garden with a cup of wine, reading verses; he places him on horseback, fits him out with the paraphernalia of a hunter, a bow, a quiver and arrow held decoratively in his hand, but no object of hunt is indicated unless it be that it is "hearts" that the youth is out to hunt.

Everything in this painting is carefully orchestrated towards building up a feeling of refinement and elegance. The youth himself is finely drawn and limpidly coloured, wearing an orange *jama* set off by an elaborate brocaded girdle in gold and a rich, full turban into which are stuck lightly swaying *sarpesh*-like feathers; the horse which seems to be prancing in one spot rather than moving forward, is coloured a spotted grey, which is set off by the henna-dyed legs and tail and has gold pieces attached to its fetlocks, pieces that one can imagine making a tinkling sound with each movement; the saddlery and other accoutrements of the horse consist of embroidered finery that partakes of the quality of precise illumination on album pages. The setting is full of wonderfully crisp details, too: a slender plane-like tree, an old trunk (meaningfully?) yielding to a new one, bends gently inwards at the right as shoots from another plant curve in the opposite direction at the other end; the ground is packed with flowering plants painted with great preciousness of feeling. Among them are narcissi blooming in all their beauty and poppies that sit lightly on stems and leaves with a dull jade-green sheen; even simple blades of grass, bending and curving with their own weight, acquire a life in the hand of the painter. The background with a high horizon is a flat, bluish mauve that admirably helps to set off these exquisite details of the prince and the horse, the trees and the plants.

The short, calligraphed panels above and below the painted part of the page are late additions to extend the painting in either direction to conform to the album format. But little of the elegance of the painting is reflected in them, for they are not only picked up arbitrarily from some calligraphed *divan;* they are even pasted in random order on the page. The outer borders reveal, however, the sensitivity that one associates with many an album border from the Shahjahan period.

The painting shows some marked Deccani characteristics. First Ettinghausen (1961:no.9), then Beach (1978:144) and A. Welch, S.C. Welch (1982:198ff) have attributed this painting to Muhammad Ali. His oeuvre includes a painting of an elegant standing girl in the Binney collection, signed with the words 'Muhammad Ali Jahangir Shahi', which points to his being a Mughal artist.

Publ.: Stchoukine, 1935, no. 69; Skelton, 1957, no. 9; A. Welch, S.C. Welch, 1982, no. 65; S.C. Welch, 1985, no. 151.

27 "A lamp hard to extinguish"

Calligraphy in *nastaliq* by Mir Ali, mounted as an album page; on verso,
calligraphy by Muhammad Salih
16.1 x 7.6 cm; page: 39 x 25.4 cm
Calligraphy: Jahangir period, c. 1620; borders: Shahjahan period, c. 1640
Collection of Prince Sadruddin Aga Khan

The passion for calligraphy in Islam, its almost reverential attitude towards it, is reflected in Abul Fazl's fine chapter in the *Ain-i Akbari* on 'the arts of writing and painting'. Conceding the excellence of many paintings, he goes on to say: "Yet pictures are much inferior to the written letter, in as much as the letter may embody the wisdom of bygone ages, and become a means to intellectual progress." He goes on to speak of the great attention that the art of writing had received under Akbar, an art that he himself clearly cites as "the more important of the two." As he puts it: "The letter, a magical power, is spiritual geometry emanating from the pen of invention; a heavenly writ from the hand of fate; it contains the secret word, and is the tongue of the hand. The spoken word goes to the hearts of such as are present to hear it; the letter gives wisdom to those that are near and far."

Great calligraphers find mention in the records of Mughal India, some of them being honored with the kinds of titles and honorifics that the painters received from the emperors. The great Muhammad Hussain of Kashmir was designated *Zarrin qalam,* 'one who wields a golden pen', and Abdul Rahim received the honorific *Ambarin qalam*, 'he of the amber-like pen', the world of colour and fragrance wrought by these master calligraphers being invoked in their titles. This calligraphed sheet is in the hand of Mir Ali who pens here a *qata* in four lines, composed in a spirit of humble homage to the Almighty:

"Oh God, should wind seize all the world
Thy glorious lamp could never be extinguished
And should water submerge all the world
The stains on this sinner's soul would never be scrubbed clean."

The tone is one of deep humility, contrasting the brightness of the eternity of God's light with the dim hopelessness of the sinner's state, precisely the kind of exalted thought that gives 'magical power' to the written word. The calligraphy is in a finely controlled and poetic hand and is set against a floral, illuminated ground on which a pair of goats is painted with extreme fineness; in the triangular panels at the top right and the bottom left of the *qata* is again some more painting showing a *simurgh* chasing a duck and two small birds. In this there is remarkable sensitivity, for the mythical *simurgh* bird stands often for the divine essence in Islamic thought (see A. Welch, 1979:191). There are other, smaller panels that are arranged around the principal *qata,* also in *nastaliq,* continuing the mystical tone set in the centre of the page.

The written part with its fine combination of painting and illumination and calligraphy is surrounded in turn by a floral illuminated border of gold against a dark ground; around this, however, is a far more accomplished outer border associated with the Shahjahan period with finely delineated animals and birds in a floral landscape of great beauty.

On verso is another calligraphed and illuminated page in the hand of Muhammad Salih, possibly the same calligrapher who is recommended to the emperor in a petition by Muhammad Hussain, now in the Rietberg Museum.

A. Welch (1979:191f) discusses the calligrapher Mir Ali al-Harawi ('of Herat') who worked in Mughal India and is to be distinguished from the famous master of the 14th/15th century, Mir Ali Tabrizi, who is assumed to be the inventor of *nastaliq*. On the outer border of the recto side there is a small presentation inscription mentioning the year 12 and the name of a *nawab*.

Publ.: A. Welch, 1979, no. 83.

28 "The pain that love inflicts"

Calligraphy in *nastaliq*, mounted as an album page; signed by Faqir Ali
18.2 x 10 cm; page: 37.8 x 25.6 cm
Calligraphy: c. 1540 or later; border: Shahjahan period, c. 1640
Collection of Prince Sadruddin Aga Khan

The elegantly scripted *rubai* (quatrain) speaks of the pain that love inflicts:

"It was that quicksilver charm that robbed me of my life
And left my heart desolate, as if in ruins
Such is my pain that no words avail to describe it,
And such my state that no eloquence can convey it."

What made these four lines worthy of being included in a royal album clearly is not the quality of poetry in them, but the elegant manner in which they are calligraphed. It takes the most trained of eyes to discern differences in the qualities of calligraphy, but the greatest of calligraphers spoke of themselves with humility. The words of Maulana Mir Ali of Herat, to whom many distinguished specimens of calligraphy are attributed, illustrate how famous calligraphers themselves held the hand of others in reverence. Abul Fazl reports that when Mir Ali was asked about the difference between his writing and that of Maulana Sultan Ali of Meshed, the great master whom he had tried to follow, the calligrapher is reported to have said: "I also have brought writing to perfection; but yet, his method has a peculiar charm."

The *nastaliq*-script in four diagonally placed lines on this page seems to float in marbled clouds which even intrude into the two corner triangles. Otherwise the background shows small flowers strewn equally on the golden background. The great beauty of the calligraphy here is enhanced by decorated margins in the hand of the 'Master of the Borders'. The distinctive elements of this master's style, in A. Welch's words (1982:222), are clear: "Individual petals, leaves, and stems are bordered with shiny gold, like jewels in a precious setting... an arabesque that seems to swirl with utter natural ease obeys instead a strict geometry and moves with principled precision; deer rest at measured intervals, and some birds perch attentively while others poise about to land or fly. It is a world closely observed in all its natural details but set in an order too obvious and too exact for nature." The jewel-like glow of the borders does not always go with every work mounted on a Shahjahani album, but here it seems to underscore, even enhance, the cool precision of the calligraphy. It is possible that there is some meaning in the scheme of the birds and animals distributed over the borders of this album page, for one can see them as pairs, possibly stricken by the kind of love that the poem speaks of. At least the two birds with eager, open beaks looking at each other from a distance in the lower right half of the border seem to catch the mood of the poem admirably.

A. Welch (1982:222) attributes the calligraphy to Mir Ali, identifying him as Mir Ali al-Harawi, the great master who died about 1544. The signatory inscription here, however, reads '(al-)Faqir Ali'. While it is possible that the word 'Faqir' in this name is used simply to denote humility, the absence of the word 'Mir', ordinarily found in specimens of calligraphy bearing the name of Mir Ali, raises the possibility that the calligrapher of this panel may have been one Faqir Ali, a name that is not by any means uncommon in India.

Publ.: A. Welch, S.C. Welch, 1982, no. 73; Falk, 1985, no. 146.

29 Two tulips and an iris

Single leaf possibly intended to be mounted as an album page
26.3 x 15.9 cm; page: 32.1 x 20.1 cm
Shahjahan period, c. 1645
Collection of Prince Sadruddin Aga Khan

"Tulips of many colours cover these foothills [around Kabul]; I once counted them up; it came out at 32 or 33 different sorts. We named one the rose-scented, because its perfume was a little like that of the red rose; it grows by itself on Shaikh's plain, here and nowhere else. The hundred-leaved tulip is another..." Thus wrote Babur, the first of the great Mughals in India. His passion and his sensitivity towards the shapes and colours of flowers clearly passed down a whole line of kings, and with Jahangir and Shahjahan flowers became an obsession, a matter of the spirit.

Precise observation had always marked the Mughals. Notice, for instance, this description of an Indian flower, the *jasun,* once again by Babur: "It is not a grass; its plant is in stems like the bush of the red rose. The flower of the *jasun* is fuller in colour than the pomegranate, and maybe of the size of the red rose, but the red rose, when its bud has grown, opens simply, whereas when the *jasun* bud opens, a stem on which other petals grow, is seen like a heart amongst its expanded petals. Though the two are parts of the one flower, yet the outcome of the lengthening and thinning of that stem-like heart of the first opened petals gives the semblance of two flowers. It is not a common matter."

Here one finds the emperor observing like a miniaturist. The artists working for Jahangir and Shahjahan, possessed of the same keen eye, sometimes imparted to the flowers that they painted an unearthly air of lyricism, combining in an evanescent fashion the natural and the ideal.

A. Welch and S.C. Welch (1982:217ff), upon whose fine description one can draw, attribute the painting to the same 'Master of the Borders' who was responsible for those exquisite borders of Shahjahan-period albums (as no. 28). This master painter clearly wants us to see how finely he has observed the flowers: the erect stalk of the central tulip undulating slightly, its single leaf of rich and subtly variegated green curving about the stalk and inclining its tip 'as if in a slow and measured dance around the centre.' The fine shading of the pinks and the streaks of yellow in the flower, the crispness with which the petals curve 'and just open enough to reveal the depth of pink along their inner surfaces' are at once subtle and precise, as are the cupped petals of the iris, 'slightly parted to reveal pollen like the softest powder.' The other tulip to the left receives a little less attention, as it is done on a smaller scale.

The rose apart, it is the tulip under the name *lala* that figures most commonly in Persian and Urdu poetry. One gets exquisitely poetic names for different kinds of tulips: the Tulip of the Desert, the Tulip with a Burnt Heart, the Tulip with a Head Bent in Sorrow and the like, descriptions that suit the poet's purpose well, for he likens the tulip often to the beauty of the face of the beloved. The greatest poet of the Urdu language, Ghalib, writing in the middle of the 19th century, was to use the rose and the tulip in a different context when he said: *Sab kahan kuchh lala-o gul men numayan ho gayin Khak men kya suraten hongi ki pinhan ho gayin.* "Not all, just a few of them have taken the form of these tulips and these roses / oh, what beauteous faces, and how many, must be lying covered by this dust."

Publ.: A. Welch, S.C. Welch, 1982, no. 72; S.C. Welch, 1985, no. 161.

30 The nightingale and the rose

Calligraphy in *nastaliq* mounted as an album page, signed by Faqir Ali
37.5 x 25.5 cm
Calligraphy: 16th century; border: Shahjahan period, c. 1640
Private Collection

The love of the nightingale for the rose is spoken of with such eloquence and delicacy in Persian and Urdu poetry, that it seldom fails to touch the heart, even when through excessive use it came, with time, to belong to the twilight world of literary clichés. But each time a gifted calligrapher wrote out the words, as here in this *rubai* or quatrain in which the nightingale speaks to the cool morning breeze of her hopeless, unrequited love for the rose, it seems as if they received a fresh lease of life.

The floral decoration that serves as the background for this panel of calligraphy in very discreet gold and sparsely-used blue and red is appropriate to the content of the elegantly calligraphed *rubai*. At the same time it would seem as if, using his incomparable skills, the master artist who painted the borders of this and many another distinguished leaf of Shahjahan albums decides here to leave out all animals from his figural, decorative scheme and to limit himself to birds, apart from floral arabesques, for this would somehow go better with the meaning of the verse calligraphed here. The birds are elegantly paired, rendered with such delicacy that they seem in places to be indistinguishable from the floral patterns, and though not all of them are associated with flowers in Persian poetry, they seem to be gazing intently at the flowers laid out on the page, rather than wheeling about in the air as they do so often. They stand or perch lightly and direct their eyes not so much at each other as at these incredibly elegant flowers and stems that seem to 'dance a visual minuet'.

The name of the calligrapher, Faqir Ali, appears also on the similarly mounted calligraphy, no. 28, around which the borders seem to be by the same 'Master of the Borders'.

Unpublished.

31 A Page from a *Bustan*-manuscript

Calligraphy in *nastaliq,* mounted as an album page
16.2 x 7.8 cm; page: 38.5 x 26.6 cm
Shahjahan period, c.1650
Private Collection

The manuscript from which this leaf comes must have borne an unusually fine, if slightly subdued look, for the calligraphy is in very small, well-formed characters. The verses are carefully separated down the middle by a narrow, decorative, vertically introduced illuminated panel; the entire ground is filled with little floral decorations in red and light yellow against gold. One can imagine the impression that must have been made by page after page filled with such delicacy and precision in one manuscript.

The page, published as from an "unidentified Persian heroic poem", belongs to Sadi's classic work, *Bustan,* and the verses are in general praise of the poet's patron.

The page is mounted on one of those highly refined Shahjahan-period album leaves, executed with great crispness and precision of detail. The master painter of the borders seems here to have decided to introduce, instead of animals and birds in a scheme of floral decoration, only flowering plants that all look wonderfully alive, even if highly stylized. Of interest is to notice how symmetrical the entire arrangement is, one plant alternating with another with singular regularity. When one sees the plants closely, one discovers how identical those of the same kind look, as if a stencil had been used with remarkable rigour, each flower and bud and stem and leaf exactly duplicated from one to the other of the same kind. But a deadening repetitive effect is very skilfully avoided by introducing variety, at least on this page, through the much smaller plants that fill the background without demanding the viewer's immediate attention. There are a number of them and the manner in which they are playfully sprinkled over the entire page makes sure that the total effect is not as if the same metre were used over and over again in a poem; suddenly there is a change of pace and rhythm.

It has been remarked that Shahjahan, for whom this album was possibly mounted, had a passion for clean, precise lines and for orderliness of the kind that one sees in the great buildings he raised. The architectural decoration on those buildings matches the calculated precision of their design; it is this very quality that one sees in the superbly controlled decorative schemes of his album pages.

The text belongs to the *Bustan,* verses 145–158. Falk has attributed the magnificent border to the 'Master of the Borders' of the Shahjahan period.

Publ.: Falk, 1985, no. 150.

32 A *Qazi's* debauchery exposed

Folio from a dispersed *Gulistan*-manuscript of Sadi, mounted as an album page
9.6 x 12.8 cm; page: 33.5 x 21 cm
Shahjahan period, c. 1640
Private Collection

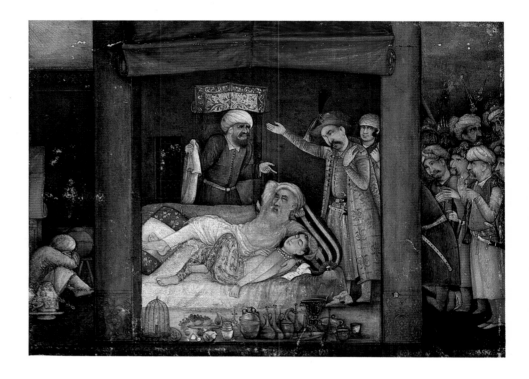

It is with relish that the Persian poet Sadi tells in his celebrated *Gulistan* many a tale of honorable men in compromising situations, always ending his stories on a note of wit or morality. Here it is a judicial officer, a *qazi*, whose consuming passion for a young boy, a farrier's son, landed him in this predicament. His heart 'aflame and restless', the *qazi* was able to gain his desire after much effort. Finally, when the young boy responded to the *qazi*'s advances supported by promise of gold, the *qazi* spent a whole night with him "with wine in his head, and his love in his embrace." But the *qazi*'s enemies carried the news of his debauchery to the king who had always held the judicial officer in high esteem for his piety. The king finally arrived on the spot, followed by a whole retinue of men, to discover the truth for himself and he saw the boy in slumber "and wine spilled, and the goblet broken and the *qazi* in a drunken sleep unconscious of all existence." The story finally ends with the *qazi* being able to extricate himself from this situation using his wit and his eloquence, the king winding the case up by asking those that had brought the complaint against the *qazi* to him to look within themselves, for "when you are burdened with faults of your own, how can you reproach others with their faults?"

The elements of the story are clearly laid out: the venerable looking *qazi*, drunk but relaxed, the young boy around whose shoulders he wraps his left arm, the man who sneaks up on the *qazi* pulling the wrap off the lovers, the crowd of retainers at the right, the king bending over slightly and pointing with his right arm to the rising sun, the wine and fruit on the floor, the candle in its glass cover and the *qazi*'s servant asleep at the extreme left, unmindful of all these happenings. The tale has often been told and illustrated, but the painter of this fine leaf, which explores a whole range of emotions and reactions, is interested principally in the interplay of light and darkness, using the device of the candle to establish European chiaroscuro-like effects. The flickering light that gradually diminishes away from the brightly lit middle with the loving pair on the bed, the dark wall of the chamber against which the king and the *qazi*'s enemies catch some of the light, the crowd of puzzled and intrigued retainers on the right slowly melting into the dark, the especially sensitively rendered figure of the sleeping servant at the extreme left, are all painted with great delicacy. One also takes in the small but significant detail of the sky lit with the morning rays of the sun at left, for in the story the *qazi* asks the King whether the sun was still rising in the East because if it was, all sins

were liable to be forgiven, in the words of the *Quran*!

Night effects like those seen are not usual in India, neither in Mughal nor in Rajput painting, the time of day or night more often than not being suggested through a telling sign or detail like a lamp suspended from the ceiling, a candle-stand in a corner, lotuses beginning to open in a pond or peacocks moving around on house tops. Darkness is not unknown, but after the time of evening or night has been established, everything tends to be viewed in an even, abstract light. Some night effects are known, but they stand out more or less as exceptions. One Mughal painter, whose career spans the period from Akbar to Shahjahan and who had a strong interest in night scenes, is Payag, brother of Balchand. It is to him that this painting has been attributed by A. Welch.

The miniature possibly comes from a complete manuscript of the *Gulistan* of the Shahjahan period. Originally, it might have formed the middle part of a page with writing both at the top and bottom. In its present state, it has been turned into an album page with an illuminated panel added on top and a calligraphed and illuminated panel at the bottom. The whole page is then mounted on a large sheet with a prominent flower painted at the top looking much more Iranian than Indian.

It might be observed that the name of the painter Payag, a small portrait of whom has also survived, might perhaps be more reasonably read as 'Bhag'. The way the name is now read, 'Payag', rings somewhat odd in the Indian context. On the other hand, 'Bhag', which written in Persian would appear almost exactly like 'Payag', is a well-known Hindu name and would fit this painter whose brother, Balchand, was evidently a Hindu.

Publ.: Falk, 1985, no. 144.

33 A floral fantasy

Single leaf mounted as an album page
20.5 x 13.1 cm; page: 23.5 x 16.6 cm
Mughal or Deccani, c. 1650
Collection of Prince Sadruddin Aga Khan

In a joyous, exuberant manner the painter seems here to play a game with the viewer. At first, the page is seen as 'a floral fantasy', an unlikely mélange of a whole range of flowers and garden insects: roses, plum blossoms, violets, irises, butterflies that hover delicately over blossoms and bees that approach them with a purpose and also, prominently, a pair of birds. But everything is made to appear inextricably mixed up, and if one does not read the principal plants carefully, one might even think that from the point above the bird in the middle of the painting the rose and the plum blossoms are growing on different branches of the same plant, the point where the two 'merge' being artfully concealed by the body of the bird. One is asked, thus, to disentangle elements that intertwine and mix, a little like the tendrils of the small flowering plant which grows between the two plants and clings to them insistently. The painter's playfulness extends further, for he brings so many stylistic elements into the same work that one is kept guessing; one sees features that are Persian, European, Mughal, and Deccani but no single strain clearly dominates over the others: the painting remains tantalizingly itself.

If the painting bears a general look of fantasy, it is because the sum of the parts gives it that character rather than the individual parts themselves. Marked closeness of observation can be seen in practically all that the painter brings in: it is not often that one sees tiny little thorns on Indian rose stems or leaves as carefully serrated as they are here; again, the sight of petals lightly drifting down, just fallen from a fully open rose, is not common, nor is the little lady-bug at the extreme left. To be sure, there are conventions that the painter draws upon in many matters, but his eye is clear and his aim is a celebration of the many forms and colours of nature.

A. Welch (1982:227) has ascribed this work to 'a Deccani master whose style is less decorative than the Persian, "less naturalistic than the Mughal, less factual and less moralizing than the Dutch." He believes the painter to have had been active in Golkunda before Aurangzeb conquered that commercially significant centre.

Publ.: A. Welch, S.C. Welch, 1982, no. 75; Falk, 1985, no. 151.

The Imperial Image

34   Babur lays out a garden at Istalif
35

Double-page illustration from a dispersed *Baburnama*-manuscript
Inscribed at the right: 'Drawing by Miskina, painting by Sanwalah';
left: 'Drawing by Miskina, painting by Nand Gwaliori'
34   24.5 x 13.8 cm; page: 41.2 x 26.3 cm
35   25 x 14 cm;   page: 41.2 x 25.8 cm
Akbar period, c.1589
Private Collection

Emperor Akbar, who evidently commissioned the manuscript from which these two folios come, held his grandfather Babur not only in esteem and reverence, but in deep affection. That the memoirs of this remarkable man who founded the Mughal dynasty in India, among the most engaging autobiographies of their kind, should be translated from its original Turkish into Persian more than once, thus, comes as no surprise. When Abul Fazl refers to Babur as "king of the four quarters and of the seven heavens; celestial sovereign; diadem of the sublime throne; great of genius and greatness conferring; ... searcher after knowledge; a saintly sovereign; enthroned in the kingdom of reality and spirituality", he is only reflecting Akbar's own views. Certainly, for the painters at the imperial court Babur was a figure to be recollected and celebrated.

But it is of interest to see how not only the great military exploits of Babur and his many adventures and conquests figure in the illustrated versions of the *Baburnama*. He is presented more or less as he emerges from his own words, a man intrepid in action, but deeply involved in much else; a keen observer of nature, interested not only in himself but in others; entirely capable of enjoying himself in the brief bouts of leisure between tumultuous action; and indulging, as here, in his favourite pursuit of bringing order and symmetry into things, something that he, in his own words, found so wanting in 'Hindustan'.

Here we find the emperor supervising the laying out of the garden at Istalif in the neighbourhood of Kabul. Here, at a place that he much admired, with its vineyards and fine orchards on both sides of a great torrent, "with waters needing no ice, cold and, mostly, pure", he found the great garden that another Timurid prince, Ulugh Beg Mirza, had laid at an earlier point in time. Babur acquired the ground and proceeded to 'set it right'. In his own words: "There is a pleasant halting place outside it under great planes, green, shady, and beautiful. A one-mill stream, trees on both banks, flows constantly through the middle of the garden; formerly its course was zig-zag and irregular; I had it made straight and orderly; so the place became very beautiful." Babur did much else in the neighbourhood. He found a spring nearby, around which three sorts of trees grew, trees that he got to be very fond of. Finding a spring there, "I ordered that the spring should be enclosed in mortared stonework, 10 by 10, and that a symmetrical, right-angled platform should be built on each of its sides so as to overlook the whole field of Judas trees. If, the world over, there

is a place to match this when the *arghawan*-plants are in full bloom, I do not know it."

This passage in the *Baburnama* is completely devoid of dramatic interest: there is no spirited action, nothing through which the superiority or greatness of Babur can be established; no historical or genealogical information is communicated. If it is regarded as a fit subject for 'illustration' in the *Baburnama,* not only in the present manuscript but in other versions of it, the choice is meaningful, like the surprising inclusion of studies of animals and fruit trees at a later point in time among the 'illustrations' of the work. Clearly there is a concern with bringing out an important aspect of Babur's personality, making a pointed reference to this passionate facet of his, as part of his total image as a man. We do know from Babur's own writings that he was involved in the laying or modification of countless gardens, some of them outside of India; what is remarkable is that, as part of the imperial image of the founder of the Mughal dynasty in India, this aspect is thus sought to be visually underscored.

The scene is not confined to one page, but extends to two. The talents of three of the most gifted artists in the Akbari workshops come together here, and the pages possess that certain ease, that maturity that had come to painting in Mughal India at this point. Babur's delight in this cultivated activity is mirrored in the sense of excitement on these pages and in the way in which colours seem to bloom like flowers in them. The activities are well observed: the emperor issuing instructions, the architect or superintendent taking them in and passing them on to the workers, the digging of pits, the cleaning of the water courses with spades, the measuring of geometrically-laid parterres, the transferring of plants from one spot to the other. These mark the page at left, where there is the kind of order and symmetry that Babur longed for; at the same time, in the right half of the double-page painting things are seen as they exist in nature, seemingly disorderly like the stream that rushes down the side of the cliffs and moves leftwards. Here, the atmosphere is one of a joyous gathering: a musician perches on a rock playing his lute, and others go about their ordinary business, while three men at the extreme left move towards the 'orderly', constructed part of the garden in the left half. A subtle connection is established between the two halves through the figure of the man (at the extreme right of the left half) turning his head to look out of the painting, obviously at what is going on in the right half of the scene.

It is of interest to observe that the painter shows Babur here quite young and unbearded, unlike the way we see him in later pictures where a decided 'iconography' of his has been established. Clearly in this detail there is an awareness of the fact that the event referred to here goes back to the year 1504, 22 full years before the invasion of India took place. The scene may in fact bear no visual relationship to Istalif at all, but this kind of licence was always understood to be part of the business of illustration. Only pointers like the rock and the stream are provided; the rest of it has to be brought out by the text. The introduction of the plantain tree in the left half of the painting and the date palms in the right half are not to be seen as renderings of 'observed detail': they belong to the different sets of motifs for orderly gardens and wild growths.

Four major manuscripts of the *Baburnama* and paintings of a fifth, now in Istanbul, are known, the earliest of them believed to be the one in the Victoria and Albert Museum. As E. Smart points out, there is a broadly common pictorial scheme in these manuscripts even though they differ stylistically, and it is possible to conclude that the later ones were made in the awareness of the one that is now regarded as the earliest of these.

Another version of the left page, now in the National Gallery of Canada in Ottawa (Heeramaneck, 1984: no.161) depicts masons constructing the fountain.

Publ.: Soustiel, 1973, nos.16 and 17; Soustiel, 1974, nos.1 and 2; Pinder-Wilson, 1976, no.24; Falk, 1978, nos.93 and 94; Falk, 1985, no.126; Brand, Lowry, 1985, no.33; Soustiel, 1986, p.12.

36 The Emperor Akbar in a flotilla of barges

Folio from a dispersed *Akbarnama*-manuscript
21.5 x 12.1 cm; page: 28.1 x 18.5 cm
Akbar period, c. 1604
Private Collection

In his account of the rich and turbulent life of Emperor Akbar, Abul Fazl at one point speaks of an expedition by water to the eastern provinces in the middle of the year 1574. A campaign lies ahead in the regions of Hajipur and Patna; pressing business of state cannot be set aside and throughout the campaign the emperor keeps receiving news and issuing orders to the armies he had dispatched in other directions. But it is characteristic of Akbar's energy that in the midst of all this, the fitting out of the expedition by river receives "the personal attention of His Majesty". Abul Fazl continues: "Such wonderfully fashioned boats were made under his directions as to be beyond the powers of description. There were various delightful quarters and decks, and there were gardens such as clever craftsmen could not make on land. The bows, too, of everyone of those waterhouses were made in the shape of animals, so as to astonish spectators. The clerks arranged large boats for every office which is required for administrative purposes, and all the courtiers had boats suitable to their degree. There were wonderful instances of architecture, and various canopies and extraordinary decorations etc., so that if this writer should proceed to describe them he would be thought to be exaggerating.

"T'was a wonderous device of the master sage,
A moving house while the inmates stood still."

Abul Fazl provides further details in the course of his description. He lists as many as nineteen 'renowned companions' who went with the emperor on this expedition, including some of the most famous names of the times like Raja Mansingh, Zain Khan Koka, Raja Birbal; he also mentions a group of learned men who went on the expedition to keep the emperor company. Two 'mountain-like, swift-as-the-wind elephants' are mentioned, the first one being put 'into one boat with two female elephants'. We also hear of 'an orchestra' that eventually got damaged in a hurricane. But when it set out, "the spectacle was an astonishing one".

In the manner that the painter of this delightful, remarkably detailed page lays it out, we see it all: the emperor himself, seated Hindu-fashion with legs crossed in the pavilion atop the central barge with a ram's head at its bow; the grandees of the state receiving instructions; the courtiers and men of lesser rank in the lower part of the barge; two barges with closed structures in red, presumably housing the 'veiled ladies of the household'; the learned men, one of them prominently carrying a book in his hand, possibly Abul Fazl himself, in a smaller barge in the foreground; the two elephants, one with two female companions on one boat and the other seemingly amused by the bow shaped in the form of an elephant much like himself; an orchestra of musicians and "sweet, heart-entrancing minstrels" in a boat towards the top left.

In doing all this, the painter is clearly not simply providing a visual inventory that corresponds with Abul Fazl's description of the flotilla of barges; he is evoking in his own fashion a novel, majestic occasion. In the process he does not neglect his own painterly concerns, as one would notice from the superb rendering of the elephants, and the fine treatment of water that combines convention with sharp observation. The faces in the painting do not possess the same penetration of character that one finds in several other Mughal works, and no one is named, no one identified by minutely written inscriptions as was to become common in the Jahangir period. It is a generalized picture of a rich, variegated court on the move.

This page comes from the 'second' *Akbarnama* that is generally dated to c. 1604 and referred to as the 'Chester Beatty' *Akbarnama* after a volume with 61 illustrations in the Chester Beatty Library in Dublin. The work consisted of other volumes; one of them is in the British Library, and several pages are dispersed over public and private collections.

For a comparable work, see Kramrisch, 1986, no. 19.

Publ.: Blochet, 1928, no. 27,4; Falk, 1985, no. 135.

37 The Emperor Jahangir giving audience

Folio from a dispersed *Jahangirnama*-manuscript, inscribed to *Nadir-al Zaman* (Abul Hasan), later mounted as an album page; on verso, four lines of calligraphy signed by Muhammad Husayn al-Kashmiri, called *Zarrin Qalam* ('Golden Pen')
31.5 x 20.5 cm; page: 55.7 x 35 cm
Jahangir period, c. 1620
Collection of Prince Sadruddin Aga Khan

It is not easy to think of a court that was more penetrated by etiquette and governed by the strictest codes of conduct than the Mughal. As early as the times of Babur and Humayun much had been laid down by way of these codes, and one is made aware at each step of how complex the whole system of ranking at court was. But information about the court of Akbar, provided by the tireless Abul Fazl, is far fuller and richer in detail and, apart from ceremony, we get a picture of a solid, dense structure of administrative machinery, procedure, rules and regulations at all possible levels.

In his *Ain* or institute 73, for example, Abul Fazl speaks of 'regulations for admission to court', prefacing what is to follow by stating that "admittance is a distinction conferred on the nation at large", and stating that it is proper that this be so, for such admittance "is for the success of a government what irrigation is for a flowerbed; it is the field on which the hopes of the nation ripen into fruit." Of Akbar he says that he receives twice in the course of the day, "when people of all classes can satisfy their eyes and hearts with the light of his countenance. First, after performing his morning devotions, he is visible from outside the awning to people of all ranks, whether they be given to worldly pursuits or to a life of solitary contemplation without any molestation from the mace-bearers. This mode of showing himself is called, in the language of the country, *darshan* (view); and it frequently happens that business is transacted at this time." The emperor also "frequently appears at the window, which opens into the state hall, for the transaction of business; or he dispenses there justice calmly and serenely, or examines into the dispensation of justice ... every officer of government then presents various reports, or explains his several wants, and is instructed by His Majesty how to proceed."

The custom of appearing at a window, giving a *darshan* from a *jharokha*, the Hindi word for a balcony-window, seems to have been taken over by the emperor from the world of Rajput princes who showed themselves every day, as in Mewar, to their subjects; the practice served not only Akbar well, but also his son and successor, Jahangir, who refers to his *jharokha* appearances several times in his memoirs and whom we see in this exquisitely detailed painting. Here he appears in a *jharokha* at the very top, a marble window above the easily recognizable red sandstone structure of the fort at Agra. Above, where the emperor gazes down surrounded by a nearly divine aura, there are only two other heads, those of princes, visible in subsidiary windows on either side. It is below,

arranged very precisely on the raised marble structure and then in the vast courtyard, that one sees the rank and file of the Mughal empire gathered together to gain a 'sacred' view of the emperor and, hopefully, to have petitions heard. Prominently visible is the golden chain towards the left which had been installed at the emperor's orders with the idea that the humblest of his subjects could resort to him in the final analysis, if grievances remained unattended to: the petitioner could pull this golden chain with bells and hope for the emperor's attention.

Here, men of high rank, grandees of the empire, most of them identified through tiny inscriptions on the collars or the girdles of the dresses they wear, stand in serried order, appropriately in proximity to the font of all authority, the emperor himself. The scene in the courtyard is not as orderly but infinitely more colourful, for here it is 'common' people of every conceivable type and station that have gathered. One sees Hindus and Muslims, Turks and Afghans, Persians and Abyssinians; one sees also petty officials and petitioners, minstrels and account-keepers, elephant-*mahouts* and plain onlookers. One also sees, as if detached from all this bustle and activity around him, a venerable-looking bearded figure of a man of God behind a door in the middle of the painting.

It is not a specific occasion that the painter is recording here, no precise moment that one can identify. What we see is an evocation of the grandeur of the court held in public, its colour and its variety, a combination of order and tumult, while the air is heavy with smug satisfaction and hope of redress. The principal figures are portrayed, as is often the case with paintings of this period, on the basis of close observation and there are some remarkable portraits here; the painter never loses contact with reality, for even when he gets down to lowly subjects, trumpet players and singers and petitioners, he seems to catch real life characters participating in a situation, presenting in his own way a kind of microcosm of the great diversity of India.

The painting is inscribed with the words: "The work of the lowliest (of the low), *Nadir-al Zaman*" in a faint hand directly below the door behind which the recluse-like character sits. It is not unlikely that this is a late inscription made in the awareness of several signed works by Abul Hasan for Jahangir. Another inscription just above this and now blurred, might however, instead of referring to the bearded figure inside, have contained a different name, possibly that of a painter other than *Nadir-al Zaman*.

Among the inscriptions identifying the many grandees and courtiers in the painting are the names of (in the group at top) Itimad-ud Daulah, Murtaza Khan, Asif Khan, Khankhanan, and Mahabat Khan; (to the left) Itiqad Khan, Habsh Khan, and Rai Man; (at right) Sadiq, Khwaja Abul Hasan, and Rai Maluk. Also identified are two attendants: Shafqat Chela, and Qasim Ali Kotwal.

The present page has margins which were probably added for turning it into an album page. On verso is a fine calligraphy in *nastaliq* with lines by the Iranian mystical poet Ayn al-Qadat Hamadani.

Publ.: A. Welch, S.C. Welch, 1982, no. 70; S.C. Welch, 1985, no. 116.

38   The Emperor Jahangir's lion hunt
39

38   Single leaf
Inscribed on verso to
'Farrukh Khurd Chela'
26 x 19.3 cm
Jahangir period, c.1610
Collection of Prince Sadruddin Aga Khan

39   Single leaf
Inscribed in *devanagari* on verso
26 x 17 cm
Jahangir period, c.1615
Collection of Prince Sadruddin Aga Khan

"Superficial, wordly observers see in killing an animal a sort of pleasure, and in their ignorance stride about... on the field of their passions. But deep inquirers see in hunting a means of acquisition of knowledge... this is the case with His Majesty." So begins a section on hunting in Abul Fazl's *Ain-i Akbari*. The emperor's use of royal hunts as 'a means of increasing his knowledge' of the people and their condition might well have moved Akbar; but in the case of Jahangir, his son, hunting had developed into a passion. This emperor's memoirs are densely sprinkled with mention of royal hunts, and every ten pages or so one comes upon fairly detailed notes on specific kills. That hunting was seen as an activity befitting a ruler, a test of his skills and his courage alike, is without doubt; but for Jahangir it was something of an obsession. At places in the memoirs an inventory is given of all the animals and game he had hunted in a given span of days. Thus: "At this time they represented that in 56 days 1'632 animals, quadrupeds and birds had been killed; the tigers were seven in number; *nilgais*, male and female, 70; black buck, 51; does and mountain goats and antelopes etc, 82..." There is a marked note of pride in this long passage, and it is not surprising that in the painter's mind, as indeed in that of many a companion and grandee of the emperor, the image of Jahangir as a great hunter should remain in sharp focus. When reference to this passion could be combined with the description of an actual incident, an excellent subject emerged for the painter's attention.

On occasions, the emperor narrates in some detail a hunting incident like the one of an encounter with a lion in which the Rajput ruler Anup Ray, the emperor's son, Prince Khurram (the future Shahjahan) and other companions of his became involved. The wounding of the chief huntsman by the lion, the taking of shots at him by the emperor, the savagery with which the lion mauled the retainers, the courage with which the Rajput took the lion's blows and struck him in turn, the prince's attack on the lion with his sword, are all narrated in great graphic detail. On another occasion a lion hunt is described by the emperor when the lion had charged the retainers and wounded ten or twelve of them, only to be finally killed by the emperor himself.

It is against this background and the stories that must have gained currency about the emperor's prowess, that these paintings need to be seen. Here, the emperor is on elephant-back, pinning down with his long spear the lion who has thrown a companion on the ground, while a prince comes charging on horseback and strikes the lion with his sword. While the centre of the painting is taken up with excited, animated action, towards the top right a lioness reaches for another hunter who clambers up a tree; one retainer, from the safety of his perch, throws his hands helplessly into the air; some companions, one of them with a hunting dog, look at the scene with nervousness; but also going on is normal activity associated with a hunt, like the retinue on horseback towards the top left, carrying royal insignia, and the retainer at bottom left, kneeling close to a horse and looking at a duck brought down by a falcon; they appear entirely unperturbed, even unaware of the dramatic happening in the middle of the painting. This last detail is vital, for it helps to establish the fact that the painting combines a memory of what could have been a real incident, or something very close to it, and the general iconography of a hunting scene as visualised by a Mughal painter. The incident might well have been trimmed to suit the imperial image: the introduction of the royal elephant, the emperor spearing the lion instead of shooting at him from a distance, the prince charging with an uncommonly long sword and so on. But, interestingly, even to those who had witnessed the scene – the painter almost certainly had not – the changes in its rendering would not make any difference: the painting would still be seen as 'real' in its own way, an authentic visual rendering.

The painting in its entirety is a take-off on a vigorous Akbar-period hunting scene with nearly all of these elements present in it. It is easy to imagine how popular a work like this was in Jahangir's time and how many versions of it could have been commissioned, some by the emperor himself, others possibly by his grandees. The second painting (no.39) is clearly yet another version, and comparing these two examples can be absorbing. Casually seen, the two paintings look identical, for nearly everything that is in the first is present in the second, making it difficult to decide which of the two was made first. The entire action, the environment, the details of the animals and human figures, are almost exactly duplicated: one notices this especially in the form of the elephant, the lion, the charging figure of the prince on horseback, the energetic movement on the emperor's part, the lioness springing towards a man climbing up a tree, the nervous character in the midst of the rocks throwing his hands in the air, the horse galloping away, even the group of retainers with the dog and the attendant kneeling on the ground. This uncanny resemblance can be explained only in terms of the fact that

a pricked pounce, a *charba* – tracing on a deerskin – must have been used. Through this technique, well-known to Mughal painters, nearly everything could be transferred from one work to another, but only in terms of outlines and general design. The colouring was apt to change, and minor details such as the form of the rocks here, the outline of the tree, the figures of some retainers in the background, might not even have been transferred in outline, for these were not 'significant' details and could easily be filled in by the second painter from imagination or from his general repertoire of pictures like this. One notices that certain colour details are indeed different: for example the caparison on the elephant, the colours of the dresses worn by the prince, the emperor's companion on elephant-back, the hunter near the ducks in the foreground, the man being mauled by the lion and so on. But the second of the two paintings (no.39) seems to be the later one, for in it one sees a certain tendency towards decorativeness that seems like an afterthought, details such as the jewellery worn by the emperor, missing in the first painting but prominently visible in the second, the coloured blue and pink rocks different from the more evenly coloured rocks in the first painting, the introduction of the monkey on the tree to complete the 'iconography' of a tree in the wilderness.

The first painting (no. 38) has inscriptions in Persian on the back, one of them stating that it is the work of "Farrukh Khurd, Chela", and the other, in *shikasta*, stating that it is a painting of the Emperor Jahangir with Sultan Parwiz, the prince drawing a sword from horseback, and Sohrab Khan sitting behind the emperor on the elephant. There are some notes with numbers indicating possibly the price paid by a late owner. The second painting (no. 39) has no inscriptions in Persian but two in Rajasthani in different hands, stating that this is a painting of the Emperor Jahangir hunting a lion, and adding, in a different hand, that the prince 'Shahjahan' is on the horse. The tone of these inscriptions is Rajasthani; it is likely that this painting entered a Rajput prince's collection, and these entries were made there for the sake of properly identifying the subject.

It may be of interest to note that of this subject there is an early drawing of the Akbar period (now in the Cleveland Museum of Art; published by Leach, 1986, no. 11); there is also a brilliant sketch showing Emperor Jahangir with a rifle and Prince Khurram with a sword attacking a lion to defend a companion (S.C. Welch, 1985:no.117). Some lion hunt paintings are discussed by Skelton (1969:33ff) and additional examples are reproduced in Falk, 1979, no. 15.

Publ.: Falk, 1978, no. 16; A. Welch, S.C. Welch, 1982, no. 66; Falk, 1985, no. 137; Leach 1986, no. 11a and b.

39

38

40 The noble house of Timur

Leaf from an album made for Shahjahan; signed by Hashim
27 x 19.2 cm; page: 37 x 25 cm
Shahjahan period, dated A.H. 1064 / c. 1653 A.D.
Private Collection

For the Mughals it always was a matter of the greatest pride to trace their descent from Amir Timur, one of the most remarkable figures in Asian history. One has only to examine a formal seal, like the one fixed on a *farman* or royal order, to realise what this connection meant to the Mughals: if the seal belonged to the reign of Jahangir, his name would figure at the heart of a large circle within which there are several smaller circles along the rim, each containing the name of an ancestor so that, properly interpreted, the seal would read: Nuruddin Jahangir Padishah son of Akbar Padishah son of Humayun Padishah son of Babur Padishah son of Umar Shaikh Mirza, son of Sultan Abu Said, son of Sultan Muhammad Mirza, son of Miran Shah, son of Amir Timur, Sahib Qiran, "Lord of the Astral Conjunction". This is where the sequence ends. On his part, Timur had taken a simple title, that of "Amir" or commander, and was happy to have himself known as 'Gurkan' meaning son-in-law, thereby establishing a relationship with yet another great conqueror, Chingiz Khan. But for his descendants to invoke his memory was to claim a decided place in history.

Again and again, these ancestral connections are visually rendered, and many distinguished Mughal works show within the frame of the same painting several generations of the house of Timur in simulation of a tree of genealogy, as it were. The point behind painting these 'family portraits' is not difficult to guess at, even if the precise occasion for doing so remains sometimes obscure. One clear meaning that one can read into these is their political significance, especially where succession had been in dispute: a painting is used to make a clear statement about legitimacy. The point made visually in such a 'portrait' is the symbolic transfer of authority from one generation to another through the presentation of a valued object like a *sarpesh* (an ornamental turban pin, which served as a symbol of royalty) or even a valuable jewel set in gold. The meaning of these statements was evidently not lost on the viewers, and while some works were undoubtedly commissioned by the emperors, there is every possibility that painters on their own sometimes conjured up these visions and took them for presentation to a patron.

In this superbly drawn and coloured work, which follows a 'genealogical tree' pattern and has the air of a tableau, Amir Timur sits in the middle of the picture, on a throne with a high, decorated back topped by a royal umbrella, holding a *sarpesh* in his extended right hand which Babur, also seated at left on a throne, is about to receive in his cupped hands. At right is yet another prince, likewise seated on a throne and holding in his extended right hand an instrument that looks like a compass. While the prince's appearance suggests that this is Humayun, the iconography of the 'compass' brings to mind Ulugh Beg, another Timurid prince, a great builder and astronomer. The two thrones of the rulers at the sides are also topped by royal umbrellas, and all three principal figures appear nimbate, their heads set against the tops of the thrones. In the foreground, standing at either end, are two other figures, the one at left looking very much like an Akbari character and the one at right, in his *Chaghatai*-cap marked prominently by an embroidered lion in gold, appearing very much as belonging to the Humayuni court. Both of them stand with hands lightly crossed against their waist, as if in humble attendance before the majestic trio seated on the thrones that are placed on an exquisitely patterned carpet. Behind Timur rises a *chinar* tree with pairs of birds nesting or perching on branches, possibly a reference to a tree the very root of which is Amir Timur. A high-pointed hillock in jade-green rises like the dome of a building at the back; gold and blue clouds float in the sky conventionally; elegantly painted poppies occupy the lower part of the painting at the edge of a body of water in which stand two ducks. The page is mounted on a superbly painted border with precise renderings of flowers and birds that one recognizes from several pages of the Shahjahan albums.

The painting is in the hand of Hashim whose beautifully calligraphed signature appears close to the standing Humayuni figure. Hashim, much of whose work is associated with finely observed and executed portraits from the Shahjahan period, clearly availed himself of pre-existing models to render the figures of Timur, Babur and the seated figure at the right. An iconographical detail linked with the figure of Babur is the book lying in his lap, most likely a copy of his famous memoirs, the *Baburnama*.

A further version – also signed by the painter Hashim, undated but possibly earlier – represents Timur in the centre, Humayun and Jahangir on the right, Babur and Akbar on the left. The figure of a poet, perhaps of Sadi, is added on the left (Falk and Archer, 1981, no. 83). Strikingly similar are the carpets in both paintings. The painter Hashim is discussed by Beach, 1978:127.

Publ.: Martin, 1912, no. 214; Falk, 1985, no. 152; Octagon, vol. 22,3, p. 9.

41 A Mughal tree of descent

Fragments, possibly from a scroll, later mounted as an album page
The Miran Shah-group inscribed with the words: 'Work of Dhanraj'
36.1 x 24.3 cm
Shahjahan period, c. 1630
Collection of Prince Sadruddin Aga Khan

Departing slightly from those remarkable 'family portraits' of the house of Timur, in which several generations of rulers are seen seated together, and a symbolic act of transfer of authority is the very point of the painting, this fragment sets the genealogical connections differently: it takes the form of a vertical table of descent, a statement of family connections from one generation to the other. The top part of this page, three vertical sections of illumination, did not originally form part of this composition and, even though earlier in date, these panels were incorporated into the page later, for the twin purpose of adding lustre and replacing what is now lost. What is now lost is a similar pictorial record of the generations preceding that of Jahangir who occupies here the centre of the painting in the large roundel. One has to read this painting, thus, in three parts: the uppermost consisting only of illumination; the middle with the Emperor Jahangir shown with his sons and grandsons in smaller roundels on either side of him; and the lowermost showing Mirza Miran Shah in the large roundel in the middle, also with his sons and grandsons, each of them identified through an inscription. (In the reproduction on the facing page, the segments have been rearranged.)

The arrangement, as one can see, is somewhat askew, for in the line of descent Jahangir is considerably lower than Mirza Miran Shah who was a son of Amir Timur. The Miran Shah group has visibly been taken from elsewhere, almost certainly from the upper part of the original painting or scroll, and joined to this page at a later point of time to extend it. This part is not unconnected to the house of Timur which this painting, in its original state, must have represented pictorially; it is simply out of place at the point where it is shown, for Miran Shah is not descended from Jahangir, but an ancestor of his from several generations back.

It is the middle part, of Jahangir and his sons and grandsons, that is most important. The monarch, he who succeeded to the throne, is shown in the middle of the page, linked by a thin vertical line above and below to the generations preceding and succeeding; connecting his image, in a roundel, are figures of his sons and grandsons, also in roundels but becoming increasingly smaller as they move away from the sovereign, all of them linked by lines to establish their connections clearly. All his sons are shown at the sides or a little below except the son who succeeded the ruler and became sovereign in the next generation. Thus, one can visualise that the line extending downwards from Jahangir would have ended in another roundel where the portrait of Shahjahan, shown as a ruling sovereign, would have been. Likewise, directly above Jahangir and connected with this line would have been the portrait of Akbar with his other sons except Jahangir who would be placed exactly where he is now, in the direct line of descent as sovereign. It must then have proceeded back to Amir Timur, "Sahib Qiran", from whom all the great Mughals claimed their proud and direct descent.

As one sees the painting now, the four sons of Jahangir represented in this segment are Khusrau, Parwiz, Shahriar and Jahandar, each identified by a neatly-placed inscription; three of Parwiz's sons, and four of Khusrau's sons also figure in this group. Likewise, Mirza Miran Shah in the other part of the painting is linked to his six sons, two of whom are represented here as having sons of their own.

In its original state, this kind of pictorial *shijra-i nisb,* 'genealogical tree', would have been seen as an artistic tour de force, for some of the 'portraits' are exceedingly tiny, and yet possessed of distinctive characteristics. It is not easy to guess at the source from which the painter took these likenesses, for they extend to several generations. But it is a safe guess that some were based on observation, and others on pre-existing models or visual conjecture.

The lower part of the page is inscribed to the painter Dhanraj whose name we know from some Akbar and Jahangir period paintings. It is difficult to make out, however, why his name should appear only on a fragment, that with the Miran Shah group.

Publ.: Stchoukine, 1930, no. 1; Das, 1978, no. 33; A. Welch, S. C. Welch, 1982, no. 70.

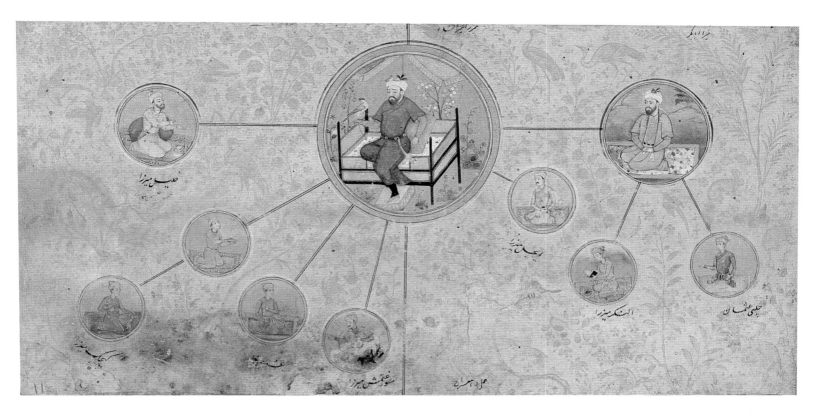

42　The Emperor Akbar standing

Leaf from an album with figurative borders
21.5 x 13 cm; page: 36.8 x 25 cm
Shahjahan period, c. 1645
Collection of Prince Sadruddin Aga Khan

It is not easy to recall another such portrait of the great emperor standing in splendid isolation as he is here, which has survived from his own times, rich as they were in portraiture. Nearly always, when we see him in his own lifetime, it is in warm, human contact with other people, engaged in every conceivable activity, seen as a part of history while shaping it. Here we see him differently – as he is meant to be seen – as the grand old figure from whom authority had descended to the next generations, and whose shadow still touched India in the age of Shahjahan who almost certainly commissioned this work. The portrait embodies a statement, like so many other portraits of Shahjahan himself: a statement that is about grandeur but also somehow about isolation. The splendid nimbus behind the emperor's aged head radiating light in all directions, the dramatic sun-streaked sky towards the top, the little segment of earth on which the emperor firmly stands as its master, the splendid dress that he wears, unlike any perhaps that he really wore in life (for he dressed far more simply), establish a magnificence which, as in so many Shahjahan period album pages, is also reflected in the secondary figures in the margins. Here, entirely appropriately, we see two putti appearing at the top of the page through the clouds carrying a baldachin in their hands, connoting divine grace that descends from on high to the emperor; the retainers and servitors on the left margin carry objects that Akbar's servants in his own lifetime would have done: a royal parasol or *chhatra,* a sword-wrap and a shield. Perhaps one can continue reading meaning into the lower part of the border where an antelope struts about like a leader of the herd, thus forming a counter-balance to the angels at the top.

Clearly, in having this kind of portrait painted and incorporated into an imperial album, Shahjahan was more than simply stating his deep affection for his grandfather: he was evoking the grandeur and the blessings of him who was now 'nesting in the sky', was *arsh-ashiyani,* as his posthumous title stated.

A similar portrait of Akbar from the Shahjahan period with a comparable border is published in Martin, 1912, no. 213.

Publ.: Brown, 1924, no. 26; S.C. Welch, 1963, no. 17; A. Welch, S.C. Welch, 1982, no. 74; Falk, 1985, no. 149.

43 Shahjahan examining the royal seal

Single leaf mounted as an album page
Shahjahan's portrait signed by *Nadir al-Zaman* (Abul Hasan);
above: small portrait of Jahangir, signed by Balchand. Mounted as an album page;
on verso, calligraphy in *nastaliq* signed by Muhammad Hussain
55.2 x 34.5 cm
Shahjahan period, c. 1628
Collection of Prince Sadruddin Aga Khan

The two portraits seen incorporated on this album page are quite unrelated (even though their subjects are not), and seem to have been brought together at the time when the album to which they belong was put together. Jahangir's small but warmly drawn portrait by one of his most gifted painters, Balchand, is likely to have been taken from a somewhat larger composition and placed here, possibly as an afterthought; it is the sumptuous, truly imperial-looking figure of Shahjahan that commands greater, more immediate attention. The emperor is seen nimbate, with fine rays radiating from the circle which is left uncoloured directly behind the emperor's head to throw it into sharper relief; in his left hand the emperor holds an engraved seal, much as he would hold a flower or a ruby in some state portraits; his right arm covers the hilt of the dagger that is stuck in his waistband, while the hand rests lightly on the sword. An air of true magnificence belongs to the image: the precious look, the noble sharply observed features, the superbly coloured mauve dress set off by the golden-yellow fastenings of the *jama* under the right arm, the strings of pearls, emeralds and rubies that bedeck the turban and the neck and the wrists of the emperor, is carefully worked in. The emperor does not appear to be in the act of gazing at the seal but looks far into the distance, the seal being held up simply as an emblem, delicately between forefinger and thumb. There is no great warmth in the face, but the point of the painting seems not to depict Shahjahan as a warm human being but as an emperor, in the nature of things possessed of majesty and grandeur as well as slightly aloof and distant.

The fine inscription along the curving edge of the oval frame of the portrait lends more meaning to the stance and the unusual detail of the seal: it records that the painting was made in the first year of the fortunate accession (to the throne), and that it was presented "to the sight of the most pure one" in the course of a hunt (?) by the 'humblest of the servants, Nadir-ul Zaman'. The seal also has an inscription, perfectly legible despite its miniscule size; on it appear the words *'Abul Muzaffar Muhammad Shihab ud-Din Shahjahan Padishah Ghazi, Sahib Qiran-i Sani'.* With very minor modifications, this is the very seal that Shahjahan struck in the first year of his reign: on these his titles include not only Shahjahan, 'Lord of the World', but in keeping with Mughal tradition, also as Padishah Ghazi, "King of Kings (ever) victorious", and the all important title, *Sahib Qaran-i Sani,* "Second Lord of the Astral Conjunction", a title clearly recalling that of Amir Timur who was referred to as

"Lord of the astral conjunction". The seal has also engraved on it the year '1'.

This series of inscriptions brings one close to the intention of the work: the portrait is made by Abul Hasan in celebration of the accession of the Emperor Shahjahan to the throne in the very first year and presented as an act of homage, much in the same manner as the grandees of the empire would bring their own offerings to him on that auspicious day. Through this, quite clearly, the painter also advances his claim upon the patronage of the emperor. Abul Hasan was by no means unknown to Shahjahan who 'inherited' him from his father's distinguished atelier when he succeeded to the throne; but a new relationship needed to be struck between patron and painter, and through this exquisitely detailed and fine picture, Abul Hasan is drawing the emperor's attention to his own remarkable gifts. One has to recall to one's mind Jahangir's words about Abul Hasan when he says: "On this day Abul Hasan the painter, who has been honoured with the title of Nadir-al Zaman, drew the picture of my accession as the frontispiece to the *Jahangirnama,* and brought it to me. As it was worthy of all praise, he received endless favours. His work was perfect, and his picture is one of the chefs-d'oeuvre of the age. At the present time he has no rival or equal..." In a sense, Abul Hasan, in making this portrait and presenting it to the emperor, is repeating what he had done for Jahangir: celebrating the royal accession symbolized by the newly engraved and struck seal that Shahjahan so daintily holds in his left hand.

A. Welch (1982:no. 71) draws sharp attention to the difference between Balchand's portrait of Jahangir and that of Shahjahan on the same leaf, referring to "the sense of volume in the father's portrait" which "has been reduced to flatness in the son's", the latter figure projecting "opulent display instead of depth of character." The emperor's portrait in this oval frame apparently gained a measure of popularity, for another portrait in this format showing Shahjahan holding the seal and even containing part of the very inscription on this painting, was earlier published by Basil Gray in Ashton, 1950, no. 753, pl. 136.

Publ.: A. Welch, S.C. Welch, 1982, no. 71; Falk, 1985, no. 143.

44 Shahjahan in *darbar*

Partly unfinished leaf intended for an album
29 x 19.5 cm
Shahjahan period, c. 1640
Private Collection

The atmosphere is one of great formality, the emperor seated on a raised throne, with the grandees of the state standing in orderly rows on either side, leaving the ground bare for the display of two rich, sumptuous carpets that cover the ground, the one directly below the throne more floral and decorative than the one in the foreground. Unlike in many Jahangir-period court scenes, the various characters here are not identified through inscriptions discreetly placed on their dress-collars or belts; there is also no specific business being transacted, like the presentation of a gift, the arrival of an embassy, the departure of a prince to head an expedition, etc. The point of the painting simply is to evoke the magnificence of the emperor surrounded by the choicest men of his kingdom.

The faces are all carefully, individually rendered and, if one were to make the effort, one might be able to identify them through comparison with a large number of Shahjahan period portraits; the picture, the moment, is however quite intentionally 'generalized'. The most that one can see in the occasion is the emperor raising his right hand as if to issue instructions which are being humbly received by the figure standing closest to him at the left, possibly a Hindu prince. If we are unable to reach further into the work, it is not for want of sufficient information: it is the intentionally generalized nature of the painting that keeps us from doing so.

The gravity of the court is, however, made immediately apparent by the emperor's own bearing, his sitting nimbate on his splendid throne, and the grandees standing in respectful attitudes and sumptuous dress. Even the petty functionaries, those carrying long staffs in their hands or holding the yak-tail fly-whisk, are touched by the same earnestness of bearing as the grandees themselves.

The impression made by the painting would have been even more sumptuous if it were finished. As it now stands, the throne, the canopy, the balustrade, the foot-stool, the bolster behind the emperor, and a dress or two need to be worked on for greater detailing. Some indication of what the throne might have looked like, if fully finished by the painter, is available from the front right leg which is studded with precious stones. The intention clearly was to fill the entire structure of the throne, perhaps also the footstool, with this very pattern. The delicate, elaborate top and the balustrade in front of the throne, clearly demarcating the area of 'closeness' to the emperor – grandees

45 Shahjahan in old age

Portrait in medallion-form
Diameter: 9.7 cm
Shahjahan period, c. 1655
Rietberg Museum, Zurich

were even addressed sometimes in formal Mughal documents as "being near the feet of the blessed throne" – also need more detailing.

A weighty, glittering statement is intended to be made by the work which, by the way it is cut off at the bottom, carries a suggestion of continuation beyond its confines to include an endless multitude of those that stay in attendance upon the emperor in all his majesty.

The throne approximates the famous 'peacock throne' made for Shahjahan. For an exquisite representation of Shahjahan on the peacock throne see S.C. Welch, 1985, no. 154.

Publ.: Gradmann, 1953, no. 1.

When one speaks of emperors in the context of Mughal splendour and ceremony, one thinks of the many ensigns of royalty that were charged with meaning, and served as part of the entire style and substance of the empire. Thus one thinks of the *aurang* or throne made in several forms, of the *chhatra* or umbrella, of the *sayaban* of an oval form held by an attendant to keep off the rays of the sun, and of the *kaukabs* hung before the assembly hall betokening the presence of the sovereign. One also thinks of other things like the standard, flags, drums to the beating of which only sovereigns were entitled, and so on. The *shamsa* – that "arch of royalty, a divine light which God directly transfers to kings without the assistance of men" – of which Abul Fazl speaks, might have been a picture of the sun affixed to the gates or walls of kingly palaces; but in royal portraits, the *shamsa* becomes the nimbus, a radiant halo of light behind the head that painters took delight in rendering with such precision and care. If 'the king of kings' was to be seen as 'the prop of the sky', as poets put it, as one "the umbrella of whose fortune is the sky's shadow", the nimbus was truly appropriate to kingly use.

Countless portraits of Mughal sovereigns were painted, showing them seated in state, embarking upon campaigns, conducting the affairs of state, receiving petitions and the like. In most of these, several details help in establishing the air of authority that surrounds the ruler; but when it came to painting a portrait on a truly miniature scale, in which even such details as the emperor standing imperiously with a sword in hand were left out, the painter's task was probably not easy. Providing the likeness of the sovereign offered no difficulty; what was challenging was to communicate the essence of his power and majesty.

Here in the case of Shahjahan, a large number of whose single portraits have survived, the painter goes about his task with marked intelligence. The nimbus behind the head, the decorative bolster at the back, the rich clothing including the *sarpesh,* the strands of pearls and precious stones serve an obvious purpose. But three significant, if relatively small, details are added: the flower that the emperor holds lightly between forefinger and thumb, the archer's ring worn on the thumb, and a little fly-whisk the handle of which is held in the left hand. Clearly, these contain suggestions that were not meant to be missed. The flower points evidently to the emperor's love of beauty, of the delicate and evanescent things of life; the archer's ring, always a great favourite of Shahjahan, hints at his prowess and his

soldierly skills; the small fly-whisk with a bunch of dark coloured hair (unlike the large yak's tail white fly-whisks which are an insignia of royalty) is almost certainly an object conferred by a holy man upon the emperor, which he here proudly carries to signify an awareness of the inner life, of devotion to men of God. This last is an object one sees in the hands of Shahjahan; and later in those of his son Aurangzeb who succeeded him and even of Farrukh Siyar; but it is not seen in the hands of the sovereigns who had preceded him on the throne of India. One sometimes sees these small fly-whisks lying by the side of dervishes; almost certainly, therefore, in the hands of the emperor a fly-whisk of this kind must have special significance, possibly betokening affiliation to a preceptor.

Through these three objects, pointedly included in this small a format, a great deal is said: perhaps the ideals of royalty are being proclaimed. These details apart, the work is highly refined, delicate alike in line and colouring. There is also much sympathy in the rendering, Shahjahan having lost here some of that distant and cold look that he bears in his portraits as a younger man. Evidently not only age but a certain richness of mind had come to him at this point, something which the painter captures with great deftness.

A strikingly similar portrait of Shahjahan, not in the circular but a squarish format, is now in the Bodleian Library, Oxford (see Gascoigne, 1972:207); a slightly earlier oval portrait is published in Heeramaneck Galleries catalogue (by A.C. Eastman, no. 48; information from J. Bautze).

The very small scale of imperial and princely portraits in 17th century India is often believed to have been inspired by the fashion that came to the Mughal court with English works of this type. Small, circular or oval medallion portraits served, in the Mughal context, the twin purpose of being a decoration and declaration of loyalty at the same time; they were also tucked in their turbans sometimes by courtiers.

Publ.: Brinker, Fischer, 1980, no. 17.

Concern with the Past

46 The court of Abaqa Khan, the Mongol

Folio from a *Chingiznama*-manuscript (a section of the *Jami-al Tavarikh* by Rashid-al Din)
Inscribed: 'Painting by Ali Quli, drawing and prominent faces by Farrukh'
33 x 20.9 cm; page: 36.2 x 24.6 cm
Akbar period, 1595/1600
Private Collection

Many pre-Mughal Muslim rulers of India had taken interest in histories and chronicles of their own reigns, but nothing truly compares with the intense interest taken by Akbar in the past. He was aware of the distinguished memoirs left by his grandfather; he personally asked Gulbadan Begam to record whatever she could of the times of Humayun, his father; concerning his own reign, history as it was being lived and shaped, he commissioned his companion and friend Abul Fazl "to write down with the pen of sincerity the account of glorious events". But really the emperor also wanted to reach much further back, and it is as part of this desire that he took interest in works like the history of the house of Timur *(Tawarikh-i Khandan-i Timuriya)*, and the *Chingiznama* which forms part of the *Jami-al Tawarikh* of Rashid-al Din, that extraordinary world history completed around 1307. The interest in the *Chingiznama* was entirely understandable, for the Mughals who traced their descent to Timur, also saw themselves as descended from Chingiz Khan.

Clearly, the task of 'illustrating' these histories was assigned by royal decree to the painters. But, once thus assigned, the painters must have decided to explore the past in their own manner, establishing images of what belonged to a different time and a different place. They were evidently not able to free themselves of an intense awareness of the present from these reconstructions of the past, but a decided effort was made. In the case of the writing of histories, one reads of the Emperor Akbar keeping close watch on the progress of the work commissioned by him, having segments regularly read to him from these histories and even asking for explanations of events that he thought were illogically recorded, all in the interest of veracity. Given this, and given our knowledge of the fact that the emperor "personally examined", every week, the work of the painters which was laid before him, one can easily visualise the situation in which little details were picked up and made the subject of discussion between Akbar and his painters. How it all exactly proceeded one may not be able to reconstruct, but that a lively interest in histories and the visualisation of events was taken, can safely be assumed.

This page represents no specific event; it contains an imaginary portrait of Abaqa Khan who is identified in the inscription, as "the son of Hulaku Khan, son of Tulawi Khan, son of Chingiz Khan." Abaqa Khan, the Mongol, ruled over Iran in the 13th century, building on the inheritance of the state that he had received from his father. Himself a Buddhist, he was in his own way a tolerant ruler. In the painters' reconstruction of his court, one sees him seated on a high throne, carrying on a discussion with two subordinates or visitors seated on benches a little outside his pavilion. Much is reminiscent of the contemporary Mughal setting with which the painters were familiar, but it is of interest to see how a clear effort is made to create a different atmosphere. The distinctive plumed Mongol head-gear, worn by all men in the painting, in itself gives to the scene a distinguishing air, but other details are brought in to suggest a different setting, a different kind of etiquette. The chairs on which at least four people are seated in the courtyard next to the ruler's pavilion are not usually seen in the standard Mughal paintings of this period; the manner in which drinks are laid out on a small parapet in the courtyard is again meant to be read as being different from the austere formality of the Mughal court under Akbar. The appearance of the women in the pavilion and, beyond that, in the doorway, are possibly other indications of this being a different time and a different place. One notices at the same time the unusual roof of the pavilion, unlike those that one sees in Mughal paintings proper of the Akbar period. Clearly, there are familiar passages like the grandees and the courtiers exchanging views, a hawk carried on a gloved hand, the retainers armed with swords and shields and standing respectfully behind the ruler; but these are stock details that in the painters' view would belong to any court, including Abaqa Khan's.

The illustrated manuscript of the *Chingiznama* is sometimes referred to as the *Jami-al Tawarikh*. As Brand and Lowry (1985:145) point out, however, the *Chingiznama* forms only part of the *Jami-al Tawarikh,* and focuses essentially on the life of Chingiz Khan and his immediate descendants.

Prof. W. Heissig, Bonn, remarked recently (private communication) upon the fact that the Mughal painter had picked up the details of the dress of the Mongols well since, from the Yuan-period onwards, the Mongols donned pheasant-feathers in their headgear and wore their long swords on their backs to be able to draw them with lightning swiftness over their heads when attacking.

Publ.: Falk, 1985, no. 130; Brand, Lowry, 1985, no. 36.

47 Mourning at the death of Abaqa Khan

Folio from the same *Chingiznama*-manuscript as no. 46
Inscribed: 'Drawing by Mukund, painting by Banwari the Elder'
31.1 x 20.1 cm; page: 36.5 x 24.6 cm
Akbar period, 1595/1600
Collection of Prince Sadruddin Aga Khan

The death of Ilkhan Abaqa Khan casts a pall over the Mongol domains, and there is great mourning. As his coffin bedecked by flower garlands lies in the courtyard of the palace, the late ruler's turban topped by a prominent plume, is ceremonially placed upon it in homage. It is not only members of the family or Mongol grandees who shed tears and cast their heads down in grief; all kinds of people have gathered around the coffin, the painter's way of drawing attention to Abaqa Khan's connections. Perhaps people of different faiths are represented here, for though a Buddhist himself, Abaqa Khan's tolerance in religious matters must have drawn various people towards him.

The happenings in the courtyard, where men alone are gathered, are carefully separated from the inner parts of the palace where uncontrollable grief seems to reign. Inside are the women's chambers and here the painter produces an uncommon study of women mourning the death of a loved one. Hands flail the air, breasts are beaten, veils are brought to cover the eyes in attitudes of utter despair while loud lamentations rise from the wives, the concubines, the women of the household in general. There is seemingly more control over emotion directly outside the palace, but here grief takes on a different character. As bakers arrive to deliver the usual basketfuls of loaves to the palace, they are turned away, for in mourning no food will be served or eaten. It is in this context that the gesture of the staff bearer and the Mongol servitors are to be understood. The routine of life comes to a halt.

One notices that the scale on which the painters render this event is limited, for strong and powerful as Abaqa Khan must have been, the painters know that his estate bore no comparison to the grandeur that belonged to the Mughal court under Akbar. There is therefore some indication of status in the manner in which the architecture is laid out, but none of the splendour of a Mughal palace. One notices, too, that the headgears that are sported by the various men in the painting do not include an Akbari turban proper, something which the painters would almost naturally bring in, were they referring to their own times. Through this kind of thought-out detail, a reference is being made to another time that lay long back in the past.

A. Welch (1982:160) points out that the depiction of mourning "seems to derive pictorially from 14th century Iranian painting" (see for instance illustrations of the Demotte *Shahnama*). Mourning scenes were also painted by other Persian painters, including Bihzad and his pupils, so highly esteemed in Mughal India (see Gray, 1961:122).

Publ.: A. Welch, S.C. Welch, 1982, no. 54.

48 A dispute is brought before Yahya Barmaki

Folio from a dispersed manuscript of the *Akhbar-i Barmakiyan*
25 x 16 cm; page: 39.3 x 27.5 cm
Akbar period, 1595/1600
Private Collection

The traditions of the Barmakis (Barmecides) go back even further than the *Chingiznama* does, for this celebrated family that stood in the Islamic mind for great munificence and sense of justice, met its end in the early years of the ninth century, in the times of the famous caliph, Harun-al Rashid (reigned 786–806). The account of the Barmakis had been penned by Ziya-ud Din Barani in Persian in the 14th century, and somehow came to attention in the 16th century when so much was being done at the imperial Mughal atelier under Akbar, and in the ateliers of his grandees like the Khankhanan and Mirza Aziz Koka. The manuscript of the illustrated *Akhbar-i Barmakiyan* is unfortunately now dispersed. It would seem as if the episodes picked from it for illustration are those which highlight the many virtues of the best of the Barmakis, including Jaffar and his father, the able Yahya, who was known in his own time throughout the Islamic world for his refined manner of speech and his remarkable mastery of points of Islamic law.

The passage that the present leaf illustrates concerns a family dispute brought before Yahya Barmaki who sits here listening to the case, consulting a *mufti,* hearing evidence from the *kotwal* of the city and the neighbours of the couple, between whom the dispute had risen. The husband, accused of breach of faith and malintent, is brought in tied-up by the *kotwal,* while his wife, who has brought charges, stands with a raised hand slightly towards the back. Animated discussion is in progress, views are being exchanged, and a sense of tension is in the air. Eventually, Yahya's compassion triumphs and the husband is released.

As in the case of early passages from the history of the Mongols in the *Chingiznama,* the painter of this leaf is intent upon 'faithfully' reconstructing a situation from which he was removed by more than seven hundred years. The general setting of the scene appears to be Mughal, but even here, realising that Yahya Barmaki was only a minister and no great potentate, the scale of grandeur is considerably toned down. The building in which Yahya sits is far less imposing than a Mughal palace which ordinarily the painter would have been most comfortable at rendering. The dresses of the principal characters and the citizens who appear as witnesses are very carefully picked so as not to duplicate the Mughal fashion either in *jamas* or in turbans; the turbans in particular are made heavy, suitable for the heads of *shaikhs,* or men who belonged to an earlier but distinctly Islamic setting. The tiny but significant detail of the attendant standing

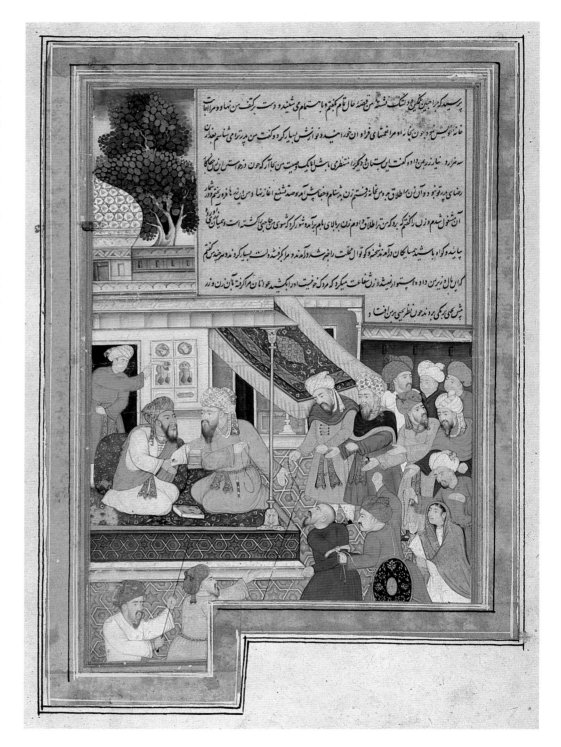

49　Alexander the Great in a tree pavilion

Folio from a dispersed *Iskandernama*-manuscript, mounted as an album page; on verso, calligraphy in Persian
17.1 x 11.9 cm; page: 44 x 28.6 cm
Jahangir period, c. 1620
Collection of Prince Sadruddin Aga Khan

behind the Yahya waving a simple piece of cloth over his patron's head is to be noted, for the painter shows sharp awareness of the convention concerning fly-whisks: the usually fly-whisks consist of a yak's tail, but only sovereigns are entitled to these, this being one of the recognizable, well-established ensigns of royalty. His own surroundings and his own experience still cling to the painter's brush, but he does make a clear effort to turn this encounter with the past into a different kind of work than what he would do while negotiating the present.

Binney has suggested (1973:39) that this manuscript which has "thin colours and a straight-forward, unadorned style" was possibly prepared for a patron other than the emperor himself. This view is supported by A. Welch and S.C. Welch (1982:157) who discuss this illustrated manuscript in detail, and by Ehnbom (1985:42).

Publ.: Falk, 1978, no. 7.

The magic of Alexander's name had clearly captured the Islamic world at a very early point of time, and he figures, as Sikander or Iskander, in many a tale and narrative poem including the famous *Iskandernama* of the great Persian poet Nizami. Countless stories are told of him in which he emerges not only as a great conqueror, a king of kings, but as a man truly in search of knowledge, seeking encounters with divines and holy men, and occasionally having wonderfully subtle verbal exchanges with them. Alexander's mastery of the world is equalled, in this apocryphal cycle of stories, by his awareness of the human condition. For poets and songsters to speak of Alexander, however, was one thing; portraying him, as painters had to do, was another. In what manner the image of Alexander was handed down is unknown, but it is not difficult to identify him in much Islamic work, for two major iconographical details are established: the golden helmet that he wears with an engraved image on it of his favourite horse, Bucephalus, and his dress which consists essentially of a tunic with a squarish neck. His auburn hair, as remembered in the eastern tradition, is sometimes added as a further refinement of this 'iconography', but it is not always seen in all representations of him.

Here, from an episode in Nizami's *Iskandernama,* one sees Alexander seated in a pavilion set in the midst of the forked branches of a great plane-tree, and reached from the ground by a flight of wooden steps. Next to him is a princely figure wearing a prominent *Chaghatai*-cap with a projecting *kulah* and a feather stuck in it, offering Alexander a gold platter from which he daintily picks up a goblet. At the foot of the tree, towards the left, another princely figure wearing the same kind of hat, has just arrived on horseback and dismounted, and is in the act of presenting a book to an attendant who will, undoubtedly, take it up to Alexander for his examination. On the ground at the right sits a group of musicians playing on a clarinet-like wind instrument, a tambourine, and a string instrument with a bow. Behind this trio of music-makers stands an attendant with hands folded prominently against his waist. In the background normal activity goes on, and one sees herdsmen in the midst of a group of horses, a wood-cutter carrying a load of dried wood on his head, and two other men, possibly foresters. An air of refinement belongs to the work, the figures being drawn with much care, the tree precisely articulated, the horses animated and spirited; the colouring like the line is delicate and rich at the same time.

What stands out in the painting, however, is the manner in which the painter sets about the task of reconstructing a segment of the remote past. Circumscribed as he is by the episode that he is illustrating, the majesty of Alexander cannot be communicated by a grand court or a campaign setting; rather, his many interests are hinted at by the book, the musicians, perhaps by an exchange of verses over a goblet of wine. Alexander's own appearance is unmistakably 'alien', with that helmet and dress; but the painter takes very special care in establishing two other points through his choice of the principal figures: the *Chaghatai* caps that two figures wear here hark back to a Turkish world, the kind of world that Humayun would feel comfortable in. Two other characters wear black hats with domed tops and split brims in the front and back, possibly a visualisation of European hats of some kind; two of the musicians are clad in *shaikh*-like heavy turbans with small projecting skull caps or *kulahs;* but also, quite significantly, the young musician with the tambourine and the attendant at the back wear no ordinary hats but what are clearly crowns. Quite possibly the suggestion here is that even kings are in an incomparably inferior position vis-à-vis Alexander, who is the *Shahenshah,* king of kings. In the context of Jahangir's times to which this painting belongs, the tree pavilion is in itself an innovation, and it reminds one of similar structures to be seen in some early representations of Humayun's times. All in all a pointed, elaborate effort is made by the painter to suggest, if not quite explore, a different age than his own.

Alexander's iconography is apparently followed consistently in other leaves of this *Iskandernama* manuscript, once part of the Warren Hastings album (see Binney, 1973:75). Even the connection with learned men and princes wearing crowns and plumes and standing in attendance seems to continue through one part of the work to another.

A tree pavilion and a celebration of poetry and wine remind one of another representation, on the border of a Jahangir album page (Goetz, 1958:no.1). A figure reminiscent of Humayun sits with a young companion with a crown-like hat; together they hold a book while at the foot of the tree pavilion a number of musicians, picnic-cooks and servants with drinks stand in attendance. The subject is known in Persian, but is rarely seen in Indian painting.

Publ.: Sotheby's, November 27, 1974 (Bibliotheca Phillippica), no. 797.

Concern with the Present

50 Babur races his horse with two companions

Folio from a dispersed *Baburnama*-manuscript
Inscribed to Mitra (Mathura?)
21.5 x 13.5 cm; page: 26.5 x 15.8 cm
Akbar period, c. 1590
Collection of Prince Sadruddin Aga Khan

There is remarkable acceleration of pace in the last twenty years of Akbar's reign in the production of illustrated manuscripts of 'histories' and chronicles. The recording of events had always been a major concern in Mughal India, but at this point the energies of the artists working in the imperial ateliers seem so clearly to be directed towards producing major extensive works that breathe the air of the times in which the artists themselves were living. A natural choice for an illustrated manuscript was the *Baburnama,* being the memoirs of Akbar's grandfather, Zahir-ud Din Muhammad Babur, founder of the Mughal power in India. Akbar himself had never known Babur, being born twelve years after his distinguished grandfather's death, but was deeply attached to his memory, seeing in him not only the intrepid adventurer and conqueror that he was, but a man of many parts. He commissioned a fresh rendering of the memoirs of Babur from the original Turkish into Persian, and this was completed in 1589 by the Khankhanan, Abdul Rahim.

This must have been deemed an appropriate moment to order the imperial atelier to turn out a copy of the work, illustrated by some of the best artists then available. Over the next ten years or so, starting in 1590, at least four copies of the *Baburnama* were prepared, not necessarily all of them in the imperial atelier or for the emperor's own use. But a kind of model was evolved in which episodes were selected for illustration, more or less precise text points were identified, and certain 'iconographies' established. What lay behind this process of selection is not easy to determine, but one can visualise long and serious discussions. The *Baburnama* is a long text that spreads over accounts of marches and battles, of celebrations and descriptions of the countryside, of references to the past and wonderful observations of the present. A remarkable section of this text written in a style characterized as "terse, word-thrifty, restrained, and lucid", is "an account of Hindustan" that Babur conquered but never truly liked. In this account, however, figure superb descriptions of people, their customs and manners, and the flora and fauna of India which were reserved for detailed attention by the painters. Quite clearly, the canvas was large and the choices difficult to make.

For the painters, however, as much as for the emperor for whom they were working, Babur's times were not really the past but the present, for he was not some figure wrapped in the mists of antiquity but a living name whose presence could be felt in the India of the 16th century. To render episodes

from the *Baburnama*, therefore, even when they belonged to a period of time when Babur had not yet conquered India in 1526, the painters seem to have decided to draw almost wholly upon their own experience of the kinds of events described by the emperor in his memoirs. In their view, it would seem, a hunt by Babur was much the same as a hunt in Akbar's times; the taking of a fortress must have partaken of the same tumult and gore in Babur's times as in Akbar's, and so on. One senses this in numerous leaves of the *Baburnama* as painted by Akbari artists. Some care is taken at times to make the world of Babur less grand than the world the painters saw around themselves, for this would conform to reality and reflect the honest spirit in which Babur wrote his journal; but a strong sense of the present can be felt in most of the illustrations.

There is much vigour in this page as we see Babur, dressed in an orange *jama* fastened with sets of buttons and loops in front and wearing the kind of Turkish turban that was to become part of his 'iconography', leading two other companions on horseback. The moment depicted is not chosen to show him in any grand light, for the reference in the narrative here is to how, in 1501, the energetic emperor was racing some of his companions on horseback; at one point he turned back to look how far they were behind him, for he was clearly leading them; right then, his saddle slipped a little and he was thrown to the ground. "Although I at once got up and remounted", the emperor says, "my brain did not steady till the evening; till then this world and what went on appeared to me like things felt and seen in a dream or fancy." The companions as we see them here are not far behind; the emperor has turned his head around, but is not falling to the ground; the region is not that of Samarkand as in the text, but far nearer home from the artists' point of view. The whole scene is truly set in the present, the outline of the town in the distance, the landscape, especially the flora including the tree in the distance, are all part of an immediate experience. But as always, one has to be alert about details, and while one takes in the delicate colouring, the combination of ease and complexity in the composition, the spirit of restless energy reflected in the emperor's figure and those of the three horses, one also does not miss the significant detail of the fluttering white cloth strip close to the stirrup of the emperor's horse, precisely the 'girth which had slackened' to cause the emperor's fall.

Of the four or five best known *Baburnama* illustrated manuscripts that have survived, this leaf seems to come from the first of the manuscripts, datable to circa 1590, a group of whose leaves is in the Victoria and Albert Museum. Further manuscripts or parts thereof are in the British Museum, the Walters Art Gallery in Baltimore, the Museum for Eastern Cultures in Moscow, and the National Museum in New Delhi (discussed in detail by Smart, 1978:111ff and Beach, 1981:77). According to A. Welch, (1982:151ff) "it cannot come from either the Moscow or the New Delhi manuscripts, since in both of them the same scene a moment later is illustrated, showing Babur already tumbled off his horse." Tyulayev (1960:no.10) reproduces from the Moscow *Baburnama* the exact counterpart to this leaf.

The name of the painter at the bottom of the page, in red ink, is generally read as 'Mitra'. It is possible, however, that the artist's name was Mathura, a far more likely Hindu name.

Publ.: A. Welch, S.C. Welch, 1982, no. 51.

من کذشت بجهت دیدن اسپان ایشان که چه مقدار

عقب مانده اند خم شده برگشته دیدم تک اسپ خود کنده

111

51 The Emperor Babur slays a wild ass

Folio from a dispersed *Baburnama*-manuscript, mounted as an album page
24.5 x 14.6 cm; page: 34.4 x 23 cm
Akbar period, c.1590
Private Collection

In the midst of marches and battles and conquest and despair, the Emperor Babur always found time for nearly all the things that were close to his heart: these certainly included hunting. The point at which the painter picks up the emperor's narrative is May 1507, long before the campaign that established the Mughal empire in India. In Babur's own words: "Next day, when we had ridden from that camp, a hunting circle was formed in the plain of Kattawaz where deer and wild asses are always plentiful and always fat. Masses went into the ring; masses were killed. During the hunt I galloped after a wild ass, on getting near shot one arrow, shot another but did not bring it down, it only running more slowly for the two wounds. Spurring forward and getting into position quite close to it, I chopped at the nape of its neck behind the ears and cut through the wind-pipe; it stopped, turned over and died. My sword cut well!... I shot another wild ass (later), most of the wild asses and deer brought down in that hunt were fat, but not one of them was so fat as the one I first killed. Turning back from that raid, we went to Kabul and there dismounted."

Mughal painters were to paint countless scenes of hunt, both under Akbar and later under Jahangir. A standard format of hunting scenes had been established, but this scene is possessed of a sense of immediacy. One would naturally expect the painter to depend much on imagination while rendering a scene that took place more than eighty years before his own time, and some of this one sees in the curious Kashmiri-looking pyramidal wooden structure behind the hill at right, and in the stylized rocks that mushroom at left from which a little stream of water descends to the bottom of the picture. But a strong sense of participation, of involved observation belong to the central part of the picture where Babur is just about to sheath his sword after having slain the fat wild ass of which he speaks. The last kick that the ass delivers as he is about to fall, the mixed feelings of uncertainty and triumph on the emperor's face, the frenetic speed with which other animals, antelopes and spotted deer and foxes flee from the spot, the look that a leaping doe casts back at the falling ass and the hunters, all possess a vibrancy that comes from being close to the subject rather than from well-used clichés. Other details abound and need to be picked up: the emperor's sword-case carried by an attendant on horseback behind him, suddenly raised in the air as if in reflex action, the little reservoir of water next to the pyramidal structure at the back, the two tiny figures carrying heavy loads and walking swiftly far in the distance.

This folio of the *Baburnama* is mounted, like many others, on a page of the *Farhang-i Jahangiri,* the lexicon compiled for Jahangir in the early 17th century.

This painting has been discussed by Smart (1978:121) who attributes it to the painter Bishan Das. The same author also mentions the corresponding versions in other illustrated *Baburnama*-manuscripts. In composition, the Moscow (Tyulayev, 1960:no.26) and the New Delhi (Randhawa, 1983:no.192) versions are very close to the present painting.

Publ.: Smart, 1978, no.95 in Falk, 1978; S.C. Welch, 1985, no.83.

52 The Emperor Babur storms the fort of Bajaur

Folio (319) from a dispersed *Baburnama*-manuscript
Inscribed with the words: 'Drawing by Basawan, painting by Nand Gwaliori'
24.4 x 14.7 cm; page: 26.7 x 15.2 cm
Akbar period, c. 1590
Private Collection

Referring to his taking of the fort of Bajaur, Babur speaks with tremendous animation and provides graphic detail of the action. The Bajauris being unfamiliar with matchlocks which Babur's army was carrying, the destruction that this dread weapon wrought spread great panic. After its great power had been demonstrated, Babur's forces attacked the fort again at the first dawn of light, swarming up with "mantelets in place", ladders fixed, preparations for mining a part of the fort wall all made. Babur recounts the individual feats of the matchlockmen and his many brave fighters who distinguished themselves and "won the name and fame of heroes." What followed the taking over of the fort is also described in detail: the general massacre, the capturing of wives and children, as many as 3000 men meeting their death, and just a few escaping from "the eastern side of the fort."

This superbly composed page succeeds not only in catching nearly every specific detail of the action, but all its tumult and confusion. While Babur is singled out in the lower left corner of the painting, a space being carved out for him and the royal standard proclaiming his status, an energetic, furious melée is portrayed: the rendering fits well into the general scheme of close engagements in front of forts of this kind, yet it is also possessed of strong specificity of detail. The high fortress with its compacted, telescoped buildings and defenders, the energy of the attacking army, the horses pushing their way into the gate, the guns, the matchlocks, the maces and bows and arrows make for explosive impact; but such details as a part of the garrison escaping at the top right-hand corner bring the narrative uniquely to life. This no longer remains a distant engagement that one reads of in remote books; here it turns into a real event, palpable and only as distant as the cuirass of the next man.

The painting has been identified by Ellen Smart (1978:122). She points out that the famous painter Basawan who is responsible for the composition, had emulated European painting techniques, "making figures appear distant by drawing them smaller than those in the foreground."

Publ.: Smart, 1978, no. 96 in Falk, 1978.

غنیم برویی کرده تیرو کمان ایشان را ذره درنظر نیاورده شکافتن

قلعه و ویران ساختن او مشغول و مشعوف بودند چاشت بود که بج

ماین شتق و مثال راکه مردم دوست پیک میکافند شکافته پیشه

مردم دوست پیک غنیم خودرا کریزانیده بالای برج برامدند

53 Humayun takes the city of Kabul

Folio from a dispersed *Akbarnama*-manuscript
Inscribed with the words: 'Painting by Mahesh, principal faces by Padarath'
33.2 x 21.4 cm; page: 37 x 24.4 cm
Akbar period, c. 1590
Collection of Prince Sadruddin Aga Khan

Easily the single most important source of our information for Akbar's reign, the *Akbarnama* of Abul Fazl, starts not simply with the beginning of the emperor's reign but a reconstructed account of his ancestors and principal events connected with Babur and Humayun, Akbar's grandfather and father. The details of these two earlier reigns are not as dense or by any means as graphic as those of Akbar's own times, but there is no lack of vividness, the historian having taken great pains to acquaint himself both with written accounts of the earlier reigns and with oral information that was constantly being gathered under Akbar's orders. A real sense of Humayun's tribulations, for instance, comes across even though his misfortunes are spoken of discreetly.

This painting relates to the point in the narrative when Humayun's star is in the ascendent again, and he carefully wends his way back to India. But he has to settle many matters even within his own family, including taking back the city of Kabul from his own brother, "that confounded master of hypocrisy", Mirza Kamran. Humayun first tries sending messages of peace and reconciliation but, these being of no avail, he decides to take Kabul.

The action here is not easy to follow, initially at least: a segment of the army seems to be coming out of the walled city of Kabul; this is separated by a rocky mass in the middle of the painting from a spirited area of action; two principal figures on horseback, one in the upper section directly below the camel at the very top and the other in the middle of the painting, carrying a lance in hand, at first look identical, something that led S.C. Welch (1953:138) to see it as a page in which Kamran Mirza is shown "in continuous narration", first leading his troops from the gates of Kabul, and then battling the forces of Humayun, below. In fact, the principal figure on horseback in the upper part is Mirza Kamran, and the one in the middle of the painting is Humayun. The similarity between the two figures is striking, but it is evidently due to their being real brothers. However, the painter takes great care to distinguish them in matters of detail: Humayun's coat of mail is all golden as would be appropriate to an emperor; his helmet has a prominent plume, and his horse is differently and more richly caparisoned than that of Mirza Kamran. For the painter to draw such a distinction was evidently important, for not only is continuous narration exceedingly rare in Mughal painting, here the two persons also need to be carefully distinguished from each other.

The action, as laid out by the painter, consists of Humayun's contingent in the lower half falling upon a section of the Mirza's army and routing it; in the upper part, Mirza Kamran who, as the text says, "took to flight", not being able to maintain his ground against the emperor, is shown quitting Kabul with his followers. There is carnage in the lower half of the painting but only panic and dismay in the upper half, with no actual killing shown. The isolated camel with drums at the very top of the painting needs to be noticed, for though it might simply stand for the drums of war being beaten, it might also make a reference to what follows Humayun's taking of Kabul: his finding two camels on the field of battle, loaded with boxes. When these boxes were opened, the text says, they were found to contain, "by a beautiful coincidence", those treasured, royal books which had been lost in an earlier battle, still in perfect condition. This became an "occasion for a thousand rejoicings."

This folio comes from the famous first illustrated *Akbarnama* of 1595/1600, known as the Victoria and Albert-*Akbarnama,* as S.C. Welch (1959:138) first noticed. Besides the 117 illustrations in the Victoria and Albert Museum, several leaves of this, "the finest of... historical manuscripts" prepared for the Emperor Akbar (A. Welch, 1982:155), exist in various collections. This leaf belongs to chapter 48. The painter Mahesh whose name appears on the margin is mentioned in Abul Fazl's list of outstanding court painters.

Publ.: S.C. Welch, 1959, no. 7; A. Welch, S.C. Welch, 1982, no. 52; Falk, 1985, no. 129.

54 A cavalry engagement

Folio from a dispersed *Akbarnama*-manuscript
24.4 x 12.8 cm; page: 28 x 17.8 cm
Akbar period, 1604/05
Private Collection

The episode is not easy to identify in the absence of any clear support from the text and the difficulty is compounded by the fact that this might well be one half of a double-page illustration. In this part, the principal figure clearly is the man with a long flowing white beard on horseback at the very top of the painting. He carries a double-headed spear in his right hand and issues instructions to a lieutenant as suggested by the extended left hand; his royal status is established by the attendant walking behind the horse and carrying the yak-tail fly-whisk that is ordinarily waved over only a monarch's head. The figure is obviously not Akbar, nor either of his two immediate predecessors, Humayun or Babur; nor is he some general of the emperor conducting a victorious campaign, for the clear indication of royal status would negate that possibility. Under these circumstances, one wonders if it is not an adversary, someone like Ibrahim Lodi whom Babur defeated on the battle-field of Panipat in 1526. From the manner of soldierly dress, it is not possible to tell to what faith the principal figure belongs. If it is indeed a king that one of the Mughals had to combat on the field of battle, the possibility of this leaf being part of a double page becomes all the greater, for the focus would then have been on the Mughal ruler in the other part of the leaf.

As compared with numerous other folios of illustrated Akbar-period manuscripts showing battle scenes, the number of figures here is limited, but the nature of the action is fierce. With swords and spears and bows and arrows, soldiers on horseback direct relentless attacks against foot soldiers on the enemy's side; bodies and heads and severed limbs lie scattered on the ground: much blood obviously has been shed. The only area of relative quiet is at the top part of the painting from where the action is being controlled. Three clear areas are demarcated through the skilfully used device of diagonally-running rocks, the painter's way of suggesting in a limited space the extended nature of the engagement and the expanse of the field of battle. As is to be expected, except for the principal figure, the faces of the soldiers are generalized, but much else is based on direct, sharp observation: the coats of mail and cuirasses, the accoutrement of the horses, the dresses worn by men, the weapons they carry. All this must have been part of the painter's own experience of Mughal India.

This folio, formerly in the Pozzi Collection, belongs to the Chester Beatty *Akbarnama,* the second of the two major *Akbarnama* manuscripts, and generally dated to c.1604. The page is, however, recently mounted (possibly by the dealer Demotte) on a *Farhang-i Jahangiri* page which is later in date and is entirely unconnected with the text from which this illustrated page comes.

Publ.: Falk, 1978, no. 11.

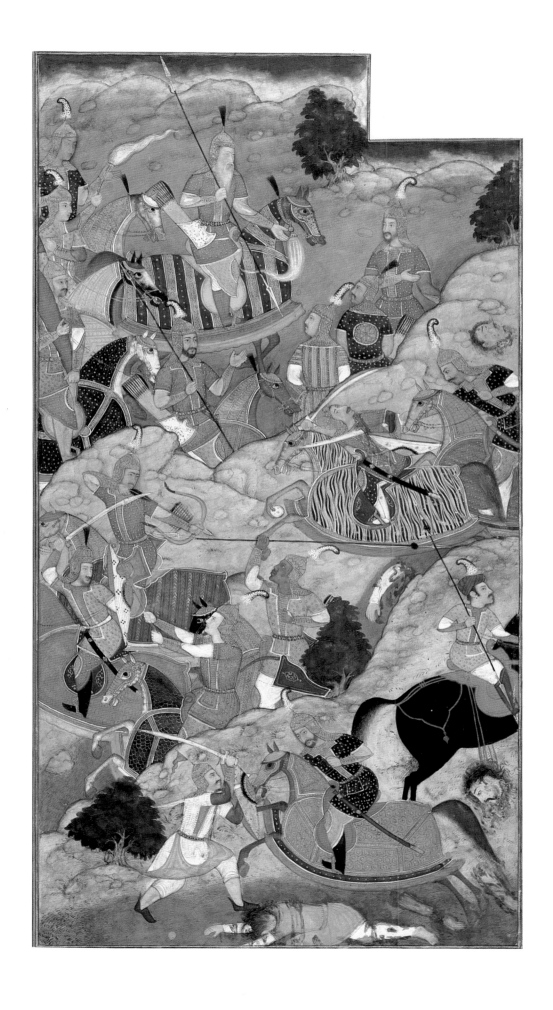

55 Work in an atelier

Folio (196) from the same *Akhlaq-i Nasiri* as no. 11
21 x 10.5 cm; page: 23.3 x 14 cm
Akbar period, 1590/95
Collection of Prince Sadruddin Aga Khan

In the third discourse of his celebrated work on ethics and conduct, the *Akhlaq-i Nasiri,* Nasir-ud Din speaks among other things of 'the basis of the virtuous city' in which many communities become involved, including men of virtue, the perfect philosophers, the masters of tongues, the measurers, the warriors, and the men of substance. This leads him into a discussion of the question of authority which can be of different kinds: derived from an absolute king who holds the authority of wisdom; the authority of tradition; that of the most virtuous ones; or that of the holders of tradition. "As for the other authorities, subject to the Supreme Authority, in all one must have regard to craft and to acts; and the culmination of all heads, in authority, is in the Supreme Head." (Wickens, 1964, p. 217) Among these authorities, interestingly, Nasir-ud Din speaks of the kind in which "one (individual) is capable of imagining the end from within himself, and has the (practical) understanding for the discovery of dimensions; while the other does not have this faculty, but once he has learned the laws of the craft (in question) from the first individual, he becomes able to carry the craft into effect..." This, in his view, makes the first individual clearly superior to the second.

Even in this, there are many degrees, and the two lines of the text that appear on this page refer to the last degree of all, "that of the person totally lacking in the capacity for invention, who preserves the directions of the master craftsman on the matter in hand, carefully follows them out so that the task is completed. Such a person is an absolute servant, having no authority in any respect whatsoever."

The context is long and involved, and one would have wondered how, given the task of illustrating a passage like this, the painter would go about it. Most interestingly, the painter of this page decides to render and interpret the kind of authority he best knew, that of an *ustad* or master in a painting and calligraphy workshop. Even though in the cited part of the text there is clearly no reference to such a workshop, the choice is fortunate, for it allows us an all too rare look at the inside of an atelier. At the highest level within an elaborate architectural complex, in a section of the building, sits an old *ustad* holding his hand in a gesture of offering instruction, while a young man practices writing on a wooden tablet that he rests on his knee in front. At a lower level, directly below this platform, in the middle part of the chamber, sit a calligrapher and a painter, each shown at his task, but at this moment looking at each other as if discussing a point,

while two other persons sit close to them, one of them peering over the shoulder of the painter who has just begun outlining a rocky landscape on the sheet in front of him. At their level, towards the left, somewhat isolated, sits another young man, not in the act of painting a page but of regarding one, a galloping horse drawn on a sheet of paper that he holds. Still further down at the right, in the two areas demarcated by a small channel of running water, a man kneels on the ground, burnishing a sheet of paper on a wooden plank while a young man stands respectfully close to him; towards the left, as if ready to serve from the goblets and carafes placed on a low stool, another attendant stands respectfully, with hands reverently folded in front. A guard leans on a stick at the bottom right hand corner.

Much can be seen in the painting apart from the elaborate architecture that dominates and clearly interests the painter of this page in itself; but much can also be read into it. The atmosphere is one of great industry, of ideas being thought out and discussed and work being carried out at all levels; the instruments of writing or painting that are carefully spread on the carpets close to the painters and calligraphers are, as always, of interest; one gets the feeling that exchanges and discussions are part of the entire process that is shown here. But one also sees a clear hierarchy of levels, precisely the kind of point made in Nasir-ud Din's text. Undoubtedly, the *ustad* is the grave-looking, dignified old man wearing a dark brown *jama* and a green shawl at the top right, for we see him instructing his distinguished pupil while seated on the highest platform; the other painters and calligrapher are at the middle level: while they hold a discussion between themselves, one other person looks up at the *ustad* and a second examines from behind the work being done by the painter; at the lowest level comes the act of preparing paper, the most mechanical of these, with an artisan shown vigorously at his job.

Those who look obviously like 'pupils' are shown of young years. The most interesting and important of these is the princely-looking character seated in close proximity to the *ustad*. He is clearly set apart by his rich, brocaded dress, the *sarpesh*-ornament that he wears in his turban, and an attendant who respectfully waves a cloth fly-whisk over his head; one is tempted to see in him the painter's visualisation of the young Akbar when he used to take lessons of this kind before he became emperor. Even if this is to read too much into the painting, the work remains of quite remarkable interest not

only for what it shows, but also for what it implies: the whole question of the authority of the *ustad,* he who is "capable of imagining the end from within himself", and his pupils, those who, initially at least, are "totally lacking in the capacity for invention", but preserve "the directions of the master craftsman on the matter in hand, carefully follow them out so that the task is completed."

This page has been published at least thrice earlier (A. Welch and S.C. Welch, 1982: 172f; Brand and Lowry, 1985: no. 127; Falk, 1985, no. 127) but identified each time as illustrating the class of the "communication specialists" whose craft comprises "the sciences of scholastics, jurisprudence, elocution, rhetoric, poetry, and calligraphy." The two lines of text on the page, however, suggest a different identification which also lends to the scene a different interest, perhaps even significance, being a statement of a painter's view not only of an atelier but of the nature of authority and the process of learning. The inscription at the bottom of the page has been taken to refer to the painter Sajnu. It is too rubbed for this to be clearly made out, but in its present state, the last part of the word seems to read more like "jiu" than "Sajnu".

Publ.: Sotheby's, November 27, 1974 (Bibliotheca Phillippica), no. 684; A. Welch, S.C. Welch, 1982, no. 58; Brand, Lowry, 1985, no. 19; Falk, 1985, no. 127.

56 Taking care of the needy

Folio (254b) from the same *Akhlaq-i Nasiri* as no. 11
18.3 x 10.4 cm; page: 20.5 x 13.2 cm
Akbar period, 1590/95
Collection of Prince Sadruddin Aga Khan

Much is said about the virtues of magnanimity and philanthropy in books devoted to the conduct of kings. Nasir-ud Din, towards the very end of his work, speaks of the many categories into which a king's subjects fall and recommends how they ought to be treated. Thus, those that are willing to learn should not be kept from learning and those that have depraved natures should be asked to correct their dispositions but at the same time be restrained "from any science that may be a means of their attaining to corrupt purposes." In this very section, mention is made of the need for a careful distinction being drawn "between the needy and the covetous man; the covetous man should be restrained from his desire and not assisted to what he seeks... but the needy should be given gifts and comforted, and aided with the wherewithal of daily life. Indeed, so long as it does not lead to an upset in the affairs of his own soul and of those dependent on him, the needy man should be given preferential treatment."

In his own times, Akbar, who had received much counsel from the wise and referred constantly to books on conduct, certainly attached great importance to alms, according to Abul Fazl. To these *Ain* 17 is devoted: "His Majesty bestows upon the needy money and necessaries, winning the hearts of all in public or private... Presents (were) made daily to beggars... (and) eating houses... were established for the poor. There is a treasurer always waiting at court; and every beggar whom His Majesty sees is sure to find relief."

It is Nasir-ud Din's words and a sight that must be within his own experience that the painter of this page draws upon. Clearly, it is not the Emperor Akbar whom we see here on the balcony of the palace (even though the giving of alms was no uncommon occurrence at the Akbari court): in fact, if one notices it carefully, the prince is dressed in Hindu fashion, with the *jama* tied under the left arm, but no specific individual seems to be hinted at. The painter is intent upon capturing, in the abstract, an image which records the distribution of alms and charity. The landscape in the background, the architecture, the small group with the prince on the balcony, the attendants respectfully standing in the courtyard at the extreme right, only help to establish a setting; for the painter the real interest lies in the two groups of people reaching out to receive what is being handed down. Inside the courtyard, within the sight of the prince whose *dewan* or minister scatters coins, is a superbly grouped assortment of men that greedily reach forward with outstretched arms and

fluttering scarves to catch the coins as they fall; one attendant even tries to drive a person away, possibly the 'covetous' man of Nasir-ud Din's description. Just outside the outer wall of the palace is yet another sensitively drawn group of the truly needy, men and women of different persuasions and complexions, who line up to receive some clothes from a court functionary sitting atop the outer gateway. There is obvious want, even penury, among these people, but also a sense of contentment, perhaps even reconciliation to their state even though they crowd around the royal gate. The scrambling group in the courtyard is a generalised crowd, but the beggars and the needy seem to be sharply observed, as if they were men and women whom the painter in his own life could have reached out to and touched.

Unlike some other pages in this fine manuscript, this one does not bear any signature or attribution.

For other representations of beggars waiting outside the palace walls for alms see Brand, Lowry, 1985: nos. 18 and 32.

Unpublished.

57 "The man who strays from his course"

Folio (181) from the same *Akhlaq-i Nasiri* as no. 11
Inscribed to Bhim Gujarati
20 x 10.9 cm; page: 23.6 x 14 cm
Akbar period, 1590/95
Collection of Prince Sadruddin Aga Khan

In his text, Nasir-ud Din carefully distinguishes between men of different kinds: those that are lovers of God; those that are intelligent or good or virtuous; and those that follow the course of evil, of idleness and sloth. The evil one essentially 'shuns his own soul', and therefore remains continually in quest of something to distract him from concern with himself; thus he becomes "intent on things such as games and the means of accidental pleasures which will put him beside himself." He loves friends who will keep him remote from himself; there are, in his nature, conflicting attractions that lead to "diseases like grief, anger, fear and the rest." Torn within and unable to reconcile opposites in his nature, the evil man, Nasir-ud Din says, mixes and consorts with his own likes, "and by applying and devoting himself to games, his imagination is diverted from sensing that state."

What looks initially to be a scene of a master chiding his pupil for wrong-doing is really the painter's way of rendering the complex state of mind to which Nasir-ud Din's text refers. Here the 'evil man' is the princely figure in the very centre of the painting, surrounded by his friends and companions, 'those that he mixes and consorts with' in order to be able to divert himself from his own vexed state. Some details are clearly picked up from the text: the gameboard lying on the floor of the courtyard; the goblets of wine filled and empty and scattered. Thus are some 'accidental pleasures' clearly set forth. The attitudes and gestures of the central figure's seven companions who sit virtually surrounding him are, however, not as easy to follow. The senior-most man, the one sitting in the loggia at left with a lilac bolster behind him, is perhaps a kind of father-figure who stretches his hands rather helplessly, possibly remonstrating with the young man in the hope of guiding him back to the right course. In the others a mix of emotions is to be observed, false praise at the young man's deeds, encouragement in his ways, surprise at his state of indecision, and the like. Different psychological states are sought to be expressed or established.

The subtlety with which varying characters and attitudes are brought out in this painting is reflected also in its delicacy of colouring. The top-most part with a peacock proudly prancing on roof-tops is like a remote idyll; the architecture is fine and unobtrusive, slender columns tracing a simple but elegant pattern across the page; there is much fine workmanship in the rendering of the carpets with their gold and red edges and blue floral grounds; the figures are quite remarkably drawn, especially those of the young man and the older father-figure at the left. The painter seems entirely in control of the situation, for he is not unfamiliar either with this kind of setting or possibly with the complex mental states that he depicts.

The fact that the principal person is made out to be a princely figure is not without interest. Almost certainly, the painter was aware of a whole tradition of works devoted to instructing young princes on how to find their ways securely in the tortuous paths of life. Many of these texts were of classical Indian origin and had become part of the awareness of countless Indians, for they established codes and values through absorbingly told tales in the *Dasakumaracharita* or the *Hitopadesha.* To this painter, a Hindu from Gujarat, Nasir-ud Din's Persian work was possibly only restating what had been stated before, and its form was in consonance with his times.

The name of Bhim Gujarati, the painter whom an inscription identifies at the bottom of the page, is known from many major Akbar-period manuscripts. Here, in this undertaking, he was working with several other Hindu colleagues, among them Dhanraj, Khem Karan, Nand Gwaliori, Gang Singh, Tulsi the Elder, and possibly Madho.

Unpublished.

58 'The business of life'

Folio (102b) from the same *Akhlaq-i Nasiri* as no. 11
22.3 x 11.5 cm; page: 23.5 x 14 cm
Akbar period, 1590/95
Collection of Prince Sadruddin Aga Khan

There is much wit and great sharpness of observation with which the painter depicts this scene of the ordinary goings-on in a small town. The context in the text is nothing that truly warrants this kind of rendering, for Nasir-ud Din is speaking at this point of the distinction between possessing the faculty of discrimination and lacking it. While, in his words, there is cleverness and ingenuity in what pertains to action when the faculty of discrimination is actively employed, "depravity of this faculty is represented by a yearning for sciences that do not yield certainty or perfection of the soul, as for the science of disputation, and for argument and sophistry in the case of a person employing them in place of the certainties; or as for the science of divination and omen-taking, conjuring and alchemy, in the case of a person who designs thereby to attain to the gratification of these appetites."

The painter decides to divest his rendering of the scene of all suggestions of moral judgment, and simply renders a day in a small town, not by any means ignoring the references to the "science of divination and omen-taking, conjuring and alchemy" that figure in the two floating text panels on this page, but investing a genre scene with feeling and astute observation. The middle part of the painting is taken up by a bearded soothsayer-cum-astrologer who has set up temporary quarters, as it were, on a platform in the main street of the town. He has a whole paraphernalia of impressive looking objects with him: a large tome that he holds in his hand and opens at an appropriate page, a book rest, a prominently displayed astrolabe mounted on a tripod, writing materials, an hour-glass. That he does well from this business is evident, for he seems to travel with attendants, one of whom waves a cloth fly-whisk over him while two others stand in attendance; also indicative of the money he makes while telling fortunes, interpreting omens and casting horoscopes, are the three money bags lying tied up by his seat. His business proceeds briskly, for a sizeable group is beginning to form around him: a middle-aged woman respectfully crouches close to the platform and listens to what the 'learned' man has to tell her, while three women veiled in *burqas* stand awaiting their turn, one of them unable to resist the temptation of listening in on what the other lady is being told, for she prominently leans forward. Waiting in the line, a young lady whiles her time away by looking at herself in a thumb-mirror; a young woman carrying a child is evidently in some state of distress and urgently needs to consult the astrologer and omen-interpreter; other women, young and old, simply patiently stand around.

That the soothsayer excites great curiosity – interestingly, nearly all his clients are women, something that the painter must have very carefully observed – is mirrored in the little vignette of a well-clad young woman, perhaps the maid of a well-to-do household in the door of which she stands, peering at the scene from a distance with irrepressible eagerness. This young lady is evidently unable to free herself from her duties in the household or else, the painter seems to say, she too would be in the line awaiting her turn to consult the soothsayer. A couple seems to be moving into the town at the right of the painting, just outside the wall of the town, perhaps also wending their way to the soothsayer, having heard of his arrival, but they are doing this not without some kind of argument going on between them.

Besides the soothsayer, other people have set up temporary shop in the main street: watermelons are being sold, ground nuts are being weighed to be delivered into the outstretched cloth of a prosperous customer, a small *pan*-shop with heart-shaped *pan*-leaves prominently displayed. A textile-hawker squats on the ground selling white and chequered cloth. This apart, there are permanent shops in the bazaar, and although we cannot see many of them, at the far end, a shop-keeper leaning out of his own shop carries on an active conversation with his neighbour, possibly a gold-smith or jeweler who displays in his little shop some secure-looking boxes and what appear to be daggers, handles of which he might have inlaid with precious stones. In the foreground, in the right corner, a man quenches his thirst with water being poured into his cupped hands by another person who sits keeping watch over large pitchers, a service that he does out of a sense of fellow-feeling and philanthropy; what transpires in another business premise in the foreground is not easy to determine: the man in the middle has an open bag of coins in front of him, another tied-up bag by its side; the man on the left is busily engaged in scraping something off from an object that he has taken out of a scientific-looking contraption, possibly the painter's reference to the mysterious science of alchemy; and a third person at the right looks on and holds a conversation. In the market street are to be seen an old *yogi* with prominent earrings, accompanied by a disciple; two men seem to be trading in cloth of different patterns and weaves; as always, there are also idlers and simple onlookers.

All this detail is of great absorbing interest, for it is not often that one sees so much. There is an air of intimacy and of clear involvement in the scene. Nasir-ud Din's tones of morality and value judgments have been completely dropped, and a living, vibrant segment of life is presented by the painter who brings to his task not only observation and wit, but remarkable painting skills.

It is interesting to see how singularly close some details of this market scene come to the French physician Bernier's description (in 1663) of the astrologers in the bazaars of Delhi who "remain seated in the sun, on a dusty carpet, handling some old mathematical instrument, and having open before them a large book which represent the signs of the zodiac." Bernier goes on: "Silly women, wrapping themselves in a white cloth from head to foot, flock to the astrologers, whisper to them all the transactions of their lives, and disclose every secret with no more reserve than is practised by a scrupulous penitent in the presence of her confessor."

Unpublished.

59 A prince receiving homage

Folio from an unidentified series
30.8 x 20.4 cm
Akbar period, c. 1590
Private Collection

The pages of Mughal chronicles are densely packed with descriptions of so many ceremonials at the court that one event seems to melt into another: the weighing of a ruler or prince against gold and precious objects on a birthday, the reception of embassies from other countries, offerings of lavish gifts by princes and grandees, the holding of elaborate feasts in honour of the divines, and so on. Very precise rules of etiquette and conduct were laid down and observed, and each occasion must have been far more different from another in the eyes of the contemporaries than it seems to be in ours, for much subtle detail evidently escapes us.

The prince seated on the throne in all his regalia in this painting is not easy to identify: it is clearly not Akbar to whose period the painting belongs, nor is it Humayun, his father, or Babur, his grandfather, whose appearance and dress were different, known as they are to us from other works of this period. To identify even the exact nature of the ceremony or the event here is again not easy, for the scene falls somewhat outside the known representation of 'rituals'. While the usual group of grandees and courtiers and attendants stand in the court and arrivals are seen outside the court walls, some benedictions seem to be showered on the prince by people standing around him, possibly flowers from the golden platters held by them. An older man, in a mauve *jama* standing facing the prince and bending humbly, holds in his hands a piece of cloth that is simply laden with flowers that look much like saffron: possibly the suggestion is that he brings these in offering without being able to afford the gold platters the others are carrying. But something in this fine page, some detail that would be essential to identification, clearly eludes us. There can be little doubt, at the same time, that the scene in general reflects a painter's personal awareness of much that happens within the ambiance of a court, large or small, imperial or provincial.

The court that we see here is clearly not Akbari, but Akbari workmanship in colouring and drawing is evident in the work. Of marked interest is not only the grave in the midst of hills in the far distance, something which might have provided a clue to the identification had we known a little more about it, but also the angle at which the whole scene is set. The pillared pavilion is seen frontally but the rest of the courtyard is set at an angle, somewhat diagonally, creating a different kind of space than is generally seen. This gives to the page an air of movement.

Publ.: Palais Galliera, Collection Pozzi, 1970, no. 61.

129

60 The 'unfaithful' wife

Folio from an unidentified manuscript, mounted as an album page
31.5 x 19.5 cm
Akbar period, c.1590
Rietberg Museum, Zurich
(Acquisition funded by Balthasar and Nanni Reinhart)

The few lines of text being now blocked out, it is not easy to identify the context. But it would seem as if the husband who had been away has just arrived at his own home only to find, unexpectedly, a camel stationed outside and a man sneaking out of his wife's chamber. Perhaps he already suspects something and now, his wrath aroused, he cuts down with a stroke of his sword the man whom he suspects to be his wife's lover. Then, before the wife has had time to recover, he rushes in, and while she protests her innocence and falls at his feet, he lunges at her with the same sword and cuts her down too. Perhaps, as he enters, the husband has taken in objects by the side of the faithless bed that bespeak of a night of luxury and merry-making: a wine flask, perfume bottles, and a platter full of *pan*, betel leaves. Now these objects simply stand there, like the inert architecture all around, witnessing this gory deed.

In the absence of any indications from the text, we cannot be quite as certain as the husband of his wife's guilt. Perhaps it is all a grievous misunderstanding: the man leaving the house might be an innocent bearer of some news; the wife's protest might be all too genuine; the objects at the foot of the bed might be indications of the wife's preparations for the happy return of her husband. But whether there is guilt or innocence, blind jealousy or just anger, one will not be able to determine. All that one can take in is the human drama and the remarkable energy with which the painter invests this page. The faces and bodies tell the tale perfectly through the firm set of the jaw and the anger in the eyebrows of the husband, the half-open mouth of the wife as she lets out a piteous cry, the lifeless look on the lover's face as he lies beheaded. The fury of the husband is again expressed through every single detail of the stance of his body as he rushes forward and bends, holding the scabbard of his sword aloft in the left hand and lunging forward at the wife, the pointed ends of his *jama* flying, his shoes being indicative of his having 'just arrived', the ends of the girdle agitated like his own mind.

Quite remarkable is the manner in which the painter treats the figures of the wife and the lover, both sprawled out in identical fashion: but while her body is still possessed of life in its dying moments, the face, hands and feet still capable of motion, the body of the 'lover' is inert, hands more or less like stumps and feet incapable of motion. It is all superbly rendered, the effect of the drama enhanced by the silent but knowing look on the camel's face, and the senselessness of the deed by the inside of the comfortable

61 An altercation in the bazaar

Folio from the same *Kulliyat* of Sadi as no. 12
27.9 x 15 cm; page: 41.7 x 26.4 cm
Akbar-Jahangir period, 1600/05
Collection of Prince Sadruddin Aga Khan

looking, well-appointed house. It is more than likely that some old tale is being told in the text, but the painter invests the scene with a remarkable sense of reality, of immediacy. For him, the context is not the past, a story that belongs to the domain of imagination, but firmly here and now. The event, as he sees it, could have happened in the year, perhaps the day, before he painted this work.

It speaks for the painter's ability to immediately engross the viewer so that one takes in the fine details of the painting only later. But it is worth noticing his skilled handling of space, the combination of massiveness and slender delicacy in the architecture, the exquisite rendering of the trees which have an occasional dash of yellow in a leaf turning colour, the orderly ends of cypresses at the top becoming split, the fineness with which patterns on the tiled floor, the carpet, the split-bamboo screen, the balustrades and the wooden doors are rendered. The awkwardnesses in perspective, like the wall at the right or the ceiling of the bed chamber seem, in the context of the time in which the painter was working, to be hardly relevant.

Crimes of passion are only infrequently depicted in Mughal painting. For another scene of individual violence see no. 83, which may well be from the same manuscript as the present work. For a depiction of a man killing his unfaithful wife, produced 150 years later in Rajasthan, see S.C. Welch (1985: no. 252).

Unpublished.

The text refers to past debts, and the painter of this remarkably sophisticated page dips into his own experience to present a vivid scene of an altercation in a bazaar. An elegantly dressed, seemingly well-to-do man is having an unpleasant exchange with a vendor of fruits and vegetables whom he lays hold of by his collar and pulls towards himself, while the green-grocer gesticulates and responds in anger. This seems to be enough to involve nearly everyone inside, people in the street, across the street, in neighbouring houses, on roof tops, all who do not simply look on idly but become participants by responding to the situation. An older man, a *shaikh* standing under the arch at the left, makes a gesture as if trying to placate the two; a younger person behind the wealthy man, possibly his attendant, tries to support him physically as he is about to fall back; two men behind the green-grocer express surprise and furtively exchange glances; two other persons on roof tops look down intently and one of them extends almost involuntarily an arm towards the disputants; a young boy seems to have picked up something from the ground, possibly a coin, and holds it prominently in his left hand while he gestures with the other; in the middle of the painting a man dressed in a pointed hat extends one end of his cloth waistband as if to garner something in it; in the foreground people across the street look on with a mixture of surprise and distress; an older man comes out of a rich house and stands in the doorway bearing an expression of regret on his wizened face. Perhaps the only person who keeps to himself is the seller of bread which he has displayed on a stepped stand; discreetly he stays out of all this and is content with chasing flies away.

The scene is remarkably well studied, for a feeling of immediacy, of the dispute having just broken out, comes resonantly alive in the work. One becomes so wrapped up in the goings on in the bazaar that only slowly does one see the many subtleties woven in, not only in the colouring and the way in which the figures are drawn and disposed, but in such detail as the painter presenting as wide a variety of people as possible. If one only takes into account the headgear that different men wear, one would notice that no two of them truly match; the colours of the apparel sported by the figures again differ quite remarkably from one another. All this is the painter's way of representing a wide range of people of different classes and extraction. This wide variety is presented with such natural ease that it does not obtrude upon the viewer: it truly seems to belong to the situation. There is much else that is both precise and subtle: the combina-

tions of colour in the dresses, the fine rendering of the arches and the receding space behind them, the gold in the sky, throwing into relief that isolated gabled room on the roof and the tree in the far back.

Unfortunately this painting is not inscribed with a painter's name. In some aspects it recalls the stylistic qualities of the "Visitation" (no. 23), which of course is a European theme.

Unpublished.

بعد ازین قاضیها جهوری آورده ام تا شیخ این بابوی هم هزار درم بوسیده و درم بوسیده خود نخیری قبول می کند زود برخاست

و بیرون رفت و مشهور بپت که ملک عادل مرحوم شمس الدین تازی کوی ارجهر خاطر شیخ خرما و بهای خرما که بقالان جاده بود بفرمود تا تمامی بسخنند

و مبلغ ازیشان باز پرسید و مدد علم بالصواب و الیه المرجع و الماب شد رساله باسپه حکایت باتمام رسید بعون الله و توفیقه و سلم تسلیما

132

Curiosity and Observation

62 A family of *cheetahs*

Single folio on cotton
29.6 x 18.7 cm; page: 40.1 x 27.4 cm
Akbar period, 1575/80
Collection of Prince Sadruddin Aga Khan

"Men through blindness do not observe what is around them..." This simple statement, cited by Akbar's biographer, Abul Fazl, as one of the emperor's sayings, expresses a great deal about his attitude towards life, towards the here and now. There is almost a tone of regret in the way the sentence is phrased, and one can see from the manner in which Akbar himself observed and wanted others like his historians and chroniclers and administrators to observe, that he approved of no part of this 'blindness' that so afflicts men.

It is possible to cite countless examples from contemporary accounts of Akbar's wide-eyed wonder at the world around him, but there is a peculiarly touching one in his own words as cited by Abul Fazl. It relates to the year 1560 when Akbar must have been a young man of only 18 years (*Ain*, vol. III: 446–448). In his words: "In the year that Bayram Khan received permission to depart for Hijaz, a hunting leopard (*cheetah*) killed a doe near Sikandra; a live young one was taken from its stomach. I separated the flesh from the bone myself and gave the leopard its fill. In doing so, something pricked my hand. I thought it was a piece of a bone. When carefully examined, an arrowhead was found in its liver. The doe must have been hit by an arrow when young, but by God's protection it had touched no vital part, and did not hinder the animal from waxing strong and becoming pregnant." A passage like this shows that penetration of observation, that same desire to learn all about the wonders that life holds, which characterises Akbar so succinctly.

Much of the energy of the painters working in the imperial atelier was obviously taken up with producing a large number of illustrated manuscripts, many of them of historical interest; but the world of fauna received its own share of attention when pages of a text like the *Anwar-i Suhayli* were taken up, the painters essaying remarkably sensitive studies of animals as parts of tales. Not many singly-done studies of birds and animals seem to have survived from the Akbar period, and this distinguished work on an altogether unusual subject, a family of *cheetahs,* stands out from this small group. Ordinarily *cheetahs,* referred to as *yuz,* in translation often as "leopards", are heard of in connection with hunting in Mughal India, and one sees them ever so often in scenes showing a forest or a wilderness. That they were prized hunting animals is clear from the long section devoted to them in the *Ain* by Abul Fazl, who speaks not only of the two hundred keepers who keep charge of the royal *cheetahs* and of the system of train-

ing them, but of the allowances of food fixed for them, the wages of their keepers, and the many skills exhibited by them. Interestingly, however, Abul Fazl starts his section on *cheetahs* by speaking of their nature: "Leopards (*cheetahs*), when wild, select three places. In one part of the country they hunt; in another part they rest and sleep; and in a third district they play and amuse themselves. They mostly sleep on the top of a hill. The shade of a tree is sufficient for the *cheetah*. He rubs himself against the trunk. Round about the tree they deposit their excrements, which are called in Hindi '*akhar*'."

The painter of this quite remarkable study of a family of *cheetahs* seems to know all this, and perhaps a little more. The top of the hill, the tree, are accurately brought in to suggest the place where the *cheetahs* rest and "play and amuse themselves." While the male crouches with an amused expression on his face, the female tenderly licks a cub clean and suckles another one, while two others, that make up the litter, frolic around. As a study of animals in their natural setting, as a reading into their nature when left to themselves, this is superb. The impeccable drawing and the singularly subtle colouring seen in the animals are extended to other things around them, especially the remarkable tree, gnarled with age, a little 'burnt' from the inside, that twists and stretches among the rocks, affording the *cheetahs* the shade they need, and a perch for birds and squirrels and monkeys. The stylised rocks, the decorative gold of the sky seem not to affect in the least the feeling of warmth with which the painter invests this entire segment of life.

Mughal paintings on cloth, apart from the great and extensive *Hamzanama,* are rather uncommon. The present painting has been attributed to Basawan (Falk, 1978:13), to whom A. Welch (1982:no.50) refers as "the painter perhaps most responsible for the development of classical Mughal painting." A noteworthy essay on Basawan was published as early as 1934 by W. Staude. Beach (1981:89) remarks that Basawan "was a rationalist, with an interest in physical form and texture and a sympathetic comprehension of human individuality..."

Publ.: Falk, 1978, no. 3; A. Welch, S.C. Welch, 1982, no. 50; Brand, Lowry, 1985, no. 46.

63 A family of elephants

Folio from a *Baburnama*-manuscript, inscribed with the words:
'Drawing by Kanha, painting by Ikhlas'
22.5 x 13.6 cm; page: 34 x 22.5 cm
Akbar period, c.1589
Collection of Prince Sadruddin Aga Khan

With his customary candour, Emperor Babur recorded in his memoirs that he found the towns and countryside of Hindustan "greatly wanting in charm", there being "no walls to the orchards", most places being "on the dead level plain", and woefully little "running water" except for the major rivers. But 'disappointments' of this kind did not keep Babur from entering upon a most remarkable description of the many new things that he found in Hindustan, including its fauna. His first entry under this head, understandably, concerns the elephant, an animal virtually unknown in the Islamic world outside of India as is evident from the uneasy renderings of it in the hands of the Persian painters. Of the elephant, "one of the wild animals peculiar to Hindustan", Babur leaves a detailed account, recording the principal regions in which the elephant is found in his wild state, how elephants are caught, how the state keeps control of elephant catching, and so on. "The elephant is an immense animal and very sagacious. If people speak to it, it understands; if they command anything from it, it does it. Its value is according to its size ..." Then follows a sharp description of its size, how it eats and drinks entirely with its trunk and how, if it loses the trunk, it cannot live; the tusks of the elephant are spoken of, and the fact that it has no hair is recorded. "One elephant eats the corn of two strings of camels."

By the time the great imperial ateliers under Akbar had been formed, the elephant was no stranger to anyone, Mughal or Hindustani, patron or painter. When the first *Baburnama* was taken up for illustration, and it was decided to include renderings of many animals and birds as described by the emperor, curiosity about them had become clearly mingled with warmth and sympathy. The manner in which Kanha and Ikhlas, two of the many gifted artists of the imperial atelier whose work is found in this early *Baburnama* manuscript, render this family of elephants reflects the remarkable feeling that Abul Fazl brings to his description of elephants in the *Ain* (vol.I:123–131). His account of the imperial elephant stables is long and wonderfully detailed, but after establishing that this animal is "in bulk and strength like a mountain; and in courage and ferocity like a lion", and stating that "it adds materially to the pomp of a king", Abul Fazl speaks of the nature of the elephant: "In vehemence on one side and submissiveness to the reins on the other, the elephant is like an Arab (horse), whilst in point of obedience and attentiveness to even the slightest signs, it resembles an intelligent human being ... An elephant never hurts the female, though she be the cause of his captivity; he never

will fight with young elephants, nor does he think it proper to punish them ... Female elephants, when mourning the loss of a young one, will often abstain from food and drink; they sometimes even die from grief."

This is just a brief fragment of Abul Fazl's account that goes on to describe the various kinds of elephants, their habits of breeding, the books that the Hindus have written on them, the areas in which they are found; but he repeatedly returns to the elephants' nature: how they stick together in families, care for their young ones, and so on.

This finely painted page, drawn by Kanha who was to contribute many an animal study to imperial manuscripts and with whom the great Mansur was associated on several works, quite clearly establishes surroundings and locale, as also the appearance of elephants; but more than that, it concentrates on bringing out the nature of these animals, their intelligence and their gentleness of nature. While the female is somewhat in the background, keeping all the same a watchful eye, the tusker lightly nudges with his front left foot, the young one as he moves towards the waterhole, as if instructing him firmly but with innate affection. The precise draftsmanship of the work apart, it lucidly and affectionately captures the feeling of togetherness in a small family of elephants.

This leaf comes from the 'first' *Baburnama* manuscript which was dispersed in 1913, the majority of which is now in the Victoria and Albert Museum, London. The manuscript is generally dated to 1589 (Smart, 1973 in Beach, 1981:75–81).

Publ.: Christie's, April 1, 1982, no. 222.

64   Portrait of a standing noble

Single leaf mounted as an album page; on verso, calligraphy in *nastaliq*,
signed by Muhammad Hussain Kashmiri
16 x 10.1 cm; page: 23.2 x 15.2 cm
Akbar period, c. 1590
Private Collection

The earthiness that belongs to so many Akbar period portraits and is so much in consonance with the character of the times, is evident in this simple but affecting work. The identity of the noble whom we see standing here is uncertain, even though there is a suggestion in the largely illegible inscription on the top border that he is connected with a member of the family of the celebrated Bairam Khan. But whoever the person, there is great dignity in his visage and manner, no grandeur but quiet authority. The body is somewhat heavy and the build broad, but there is lightness in the manner of standing and ease in the way the hands are disposed.

The general look is very Akbari and one prominently notices the relatively small flat turban on the head and the extremely fine cotton *jama,* almost diaphanous, that ends in six sharp points. The *jama,* secured around the waist by a gold and flowered *patka,* is in fact so thin that the outlines of the somewhat heavy hips underneath are clearly visible; only the bright orange of the *pyjama* is somewhat dulled where this film-like garment covers it. Under the armpits, again, dark shadows appear on either side – in fact small strips that were often attached at these points, sometimes with a dotted pattern and musk-scented – and help establish further the fine quality of the fabric worn by the noble who, being a Muslim, ties the *jama* under the right arm.

The figure is placed against a flat jade-green ground that takes it out of any specific space and allows one to concentrate on the form and the character of the noble. The features are remarkably well studied: the broad forehead, the sharp aquiline nose, the relatively heavy neck, the mustache still black but the beard steadily turning grey. All this the painter brings in without getting too close to the noble, almost as if it would be impolite to peer at someone from so close. But this distance also enables the painter to combine convention with observation. The figure conforms to an established pattern on one hand: head seen in profile, the body in three quarters, the feet slightly separated, the hands held in a given position; but it is also a study of a specific individual, a real person. If this were not so, the portrait would hardly have served the kind of purpose that Abul Fazl hints at in his brief account of painting under Akbar when he speaks of those 'immense albums' of portraits that had been formed under the emperor's orders. Quite clearly, these portraits served more than the purpose of conferring 'immortality on those that were alive'; being a remarkable judge of men that he was, the

emperor was, in this form, keeping visual notes for himself on the countless men who served and surrounded him.

The inscription in *shikasta* on the top border seems to contain tantalizing information, but it is not easy to decipher it fully. Bairam Khan seems to be mentioned, who served in Akbar's early years as a tutor and whose son, Abdul Rahim, inherited his grandiose title of *Khankhanan,* 'Khan of Khans'. Unfortunately one cannot read the small squarish seal that appears at the right. The calligraphy in the hand of Muhammad Hussain, on the verso side, consists of four diagonally written lines in *nastaliq:* they contain a *rubai* or quatrain. The date below Muhammad Hussain's signatures is incomplete, part of the leaf having been trimmed.

Unpublished.

65 A Hindu 'shrine of great sanctity'

Single leaf, possibly intended for an album
14 x 7.5 cm
Akbar-Jahangir period, 1600/10
Collection of Prince Sadruddin Aga Khan

The second book of Abul Fazl's *Ain-i Akbari* serves as a gazetteer and administrative manual of Akbar's empire. In it, after a discussion of the various eras obtaining in India and the laying out of the revenue system, the machinery that ran it, the land and its classification, and what was due to the state, follows an account of the twelve *subahs* or provinces of the Mughal empire under Akbar. Detailed statistics are provided, major cities and places of interest are described, a brief history of the previous rulers of those regions are gone into. In the Kabul-*subah,* Abul Fazl mentions prominently the *sarkar* (region) of Kashmir. In the context of this unusual painting, one note is of special interest: "Between Great Tibet and the abovementioned *parganah* (on the eastern boundary of Kashmir) is a cave in which is an image in ice called Amarnath. It is considered a shrine of great sanctity. When the new moon rises from her throne of rays, a bubble as it were of ice is formed in the cave which daily increases little by little for fifteen days until it is somewhat higher than two yards, of the measure of the yard determined by His Majesty; with the waning moon, the image likewise begins to decrease, till no trace of it remains when the moon disappears. They (the Hindus) believe it to be the image of Mahadeva and regard it as a means (through supplication) of the fulfillment of their desire."

Abul Fazl here gets the name of this celebrated centre of Hindu pilgrimage – certainly the most famous in Kashmir – right, if not every detail of it. The 'bubble of ice' that he speaks of is a natural stalactite that forms a phallic-looking column that the devotees regard as one of the miraculous *lingams* of Shiva and to which, at that great altitude, thousands of pilgrims go for paying homage every year. Abul Fazl makes no comment on the phenomenon, with his usual and remarkable lack of prejudice, and only speaks of the place 'as a shrine of great sanctity.' His information was not based on personal observation, but was taken from other sources, written or oral. He did not visit the place himself and, most certainly, the painter of this page had very little idea of what Amarnath looked like. He simply conjures up, from imagination, a place up in the high, snow-clad mountains, where this remarkable image is naturally formed to the great astonishment of those who go up to see it. The astonishment is clearly registered on the faces of the six men who, wearing Akbari dresses for the most part, stand around it; but the *lingam* is shown as if standing on a clear piece of land, not inside a cave as it is in reality. The column here is beginning to melt a little in the heat of the sun which is

prominently shown, this detail obviously brought in to suggest a natural phenomenon that appears and disappears; if this melting had not been shown, the *lingam* as represented here could have easily been mistaken for a solid column of masonry which it was not meant to be.

What is being rendered here is one of the many 'wonders' of India, a visualization rather than a recording. The quality of the painting suggests no connection with the imperial atelier, and it is possible that the work was made for a sub-imperial, perhaps even a Hindu, patron to whose curiosity the painter was trying to respond in his own fashion.

Publ.: Soustiel, 1973, no. 2; Pinder-Wilson, 1976, no. 84.

66 A woman wearing a *Chaghatai*-headdress

Single leaf mounted as an album page
22.7 x 13.2 cm; page: 45.9 x 30 cm
Akbar period, c. 1595
Private Collection

In India, portraiture in the sense of approximation to a true likeness, not a sum of cognizable features, most of them idealised, begins properly only in the Mughal period. It certainly received tremendous fillip under Akbar, as we can judge from Abul Fazl's account: "His Majesty himself sat for his likeness, and also ordered to have the likenesses taken of all the grandees of the realm. An immense album was thus formed: those that have passed away have received a new life, and those who are still alive have immortality promised them."

This oft-cited passage places in perspective the considerable number of Mughal portraits of men of all kinds of rank that have survived from the Akbar period. Portraiture of women, however, evidently still remained a highly restricted activity. Mughal ladies of noble birth stayed mostly behind 'veils of chastity', and entrance to the ladies' apartments was severely restricted, only the most privileged men, apart from the members of the royal family themselves, being allowed access. The number of women whom we see in Akbari paintings is not small, for they figure in palace scenes, especially where celebrations are in progress or the birth of a prince is being recorded, but these depictions of women remain highly generalised rather than specific, unlike in the case of men. In this context, therefore, the portrait of a woman of rank comes as a surprise.

That this is no generalised portrait is evident. The face of the lady, but for its obvious fleshiness, might not look too specific, but the rest of her certainly is. That she is of noble rank and is of Chaghatai or Mughal origin is signified by the tall hat that she wears topped by a plume and a *sarpesh,* as also by the large bolster placed behind her and the jewellery that adorns her figure. She is uncommonly rotund, and the painter emphasizes, without necessarily poking fun at her, her large breasts, her very large belly and full thighs. There is also intricate detail in her dress and her setting, much attention going to the pattern of her brocaded cap, the plume, the little scarf that falls over her chest and covers her neck at the back, the folds of her garment, as also the bolster, the carpet, and the range of flowering plants in the background. All of this makes for a vivid and lively – if slightly startling – painting.

It is not easy to identify the lady, but possibly the painter was aware of those numerous ladies whom Gulbadan Begam in her *Humayun-nama* talks about from her own familiarity with the imperial household. Not without interest is a brief reference to May-wa-jan, daughter of a chamberlain, who was taken by Humayun as one of his minor wives. Gulbadan Begam's account mentions two of these wives of Humayun being in the family way at about the same time, and great anticipation arising about at least one of them bearing a son. While Bega Begum gave birth to a daughter, Maywa-jan, whose claim that she was in the family way had led to much preaparation for celebrations if a son were born, produced nothing. Ten months went by without anything happening, as Gulbadan Begam reports: "The eleventh also passed. Maywa-jan said: 'My maternal aunt was in Mirza Ulugh Beg's harem. She had a son in the twelfth month; perhaps I am like her.' So they sewed tents and filled pillows. But in the end everyone knew she was a fraud."

It is not being suggested that this is a portrait of Maywa-jan during her 'false pregnancy'. But the harem was evidently filled with interesting women, Chaghatai Mughals, Miran Shahis, Qibchaq Mughals, Dughlats and the like; and it is one of them that the painter renders here perhaps.

Publ.: Falk, 1978, no. 8; Falk, 1985, no. 128; Brand, Lowry, 1985, no. 51.

67 Portrait of a Mongol warrior

Single leaf mounted as an album page
16.2 x 10.3 cm
Jahangir period, c. 1620
Private Collection

The name of the great Persian master, Bihzad of Herat, who was active at the end of the 15th century and the beginning of the 16th, has long continued to reverberate throughout the Islamic world; wherever painting was held in any esteem, in fact. Great 'illustrations' apart, Bihzad painted some remarkable portraits, including one of a Mongol warrior taken prisoner, but shown seated like a courtier, his head and arm in a wooden, y-shaped stock; this work, among many others, inspired several later copies and versions in the hands of his pupils and followers and imitators.

This portrait of a Mongol warrior does not show him as a prisoner and it comes a full hundred years later or more after Bihzad, but the Persian master's work stays clearly in the awareness of the Mughal painter who has rendered it. The Mongol features are instantly recognizable, the high cheekbones, the slant of the eyes, even the manner of wearing the beard and the mustache; also recognizable is the domed pointed cap with a plume stuck in it, and the warrior's 'cognizances'. These comprise of many weapons that include a bow resting in a decorated leather case that follows its shape, a quiver filled with arrows marked by black and white feathers at the lower end, a prominent curved sword, a dagger with a jewelled hilt stuck in the waistband and another one in the bow-case and, prominently, a mace that is quite unlike the maces we ordinarily see in Mughal painting, for it has a stiff handle, but its bulbous head is attached to it loosely so that it curves on the carpet next to the warrior. The manner of sitting, once again, is reminiscent of Bihzad's portraits of this description: there is self-assurance in the stance, and the figure exudes a feeling of great, latent energy. This warrior is certainly no prisoner.

Energetic Mongol characters, never very far from the awareness of the Mughals, still excited interest in India, and the Jahangiri painter seems to have decided to bring an early work up to date by imparting to it a clear Mughal air. Whether it is a portrait of a real person or not is difficult to determine, but it looks all too real in the hands of the Mughal artist who provides what could be regarded as more or less contemporary references in the manner in which the warrior is coloured and flanked by two delicately flowering plants on either side. The quality of observation in the face and the stance comes close to the level of the great portraits that came from the court of Jahangir.

The first publication of this painting by Falk (1985: 164) already points to earlier Persian versions. A small matter of detail needs to be mentioned. The warrior is shown wearing his tunic or *jama* tied under the left arm from which streamers or lappets seem to hang down in a decorative fashion along the flank. At the Mughal court, at this point in time, this fashion of wearing the *jama* was confined to the Hindus. It seems to be reasonably certain, therefore, that the painter is taking over this detail from a model that belongs to a date earlier than the Akbar period (in which this distinction between two different modes of wearing the same garment seems to have been clearly established).

Publ.: Falk, 1978, no. 19; Falk, 1985, no. 142.

68 A bird study

Single leaf mounted as an album page
8.9 x 5.7 cm; page: 27.2 x 16.4 cm
Jahangir period, c. 1625
Private Collection

A note of passion enters the words of Jahangir in his memoirs when he describes his interest in painting. One brief oft-cited passage (see Section IV of the Introduction) speaks of his astounding connoisseurship, proudly mentioning his own ability to take in the minutest detail. He speaks of portraits, but much the same feeling and penetration of observation manifest themselves in the emperor's words when he describes wildlife, especially birds. At the end of his account of the eighteenth year of his reign, to give an example, the emperor writes: "At this time one day on the hunting ground, the chief huntsman Imam Wirdi brought before me a partridge that had a spur on one leg and not on the other. As the way to distinguish the female lies in the spur, by way of testing me he asked me if this was a male or a female. I said at once, 'A female'. When they opened it, an egg appeared inside its belly. The people who were in attendance asked with surprise by what sign I had discovered this: I said that the head and beak of the female are shorter than the male's. By investigation and often seeing (the birds), I had acquired this dexterity."

This kind of keenness on the emperor's part was matched by the best of his painters who turned out remarkable studies of birds and animals and flowers at his asking. This superbly drawn and coloured spur fowl has clearly been observed as sharply as the celebrated Jahangiri paintings of the turkey-cock and the peacocks. The two palely coloured flowering plants on either side of it only throw its brilliant feathers and its proud stance into relief, and the bird seems almost to be aware of the great delicacy and variety of its own plumage. The exact name is not known, but different species of spur fowl were constantly being brought to the emperor. On one occasion, in the Panjab, Jahangir received a gift from one of the petty rulers of a state on the foothills, and proceeded to record the matter: "Basoi, the *zamindar* of Talwara, brought me a bird, which the hill people call *jan bahan*. Its tail resembles the tail of the *qirqawul* (pheasant), which is also called the *tazru,* and its colour is exactly like that of the hen-pheasant but it is half as large again. The circle around the eyes of this bird is red, while the orbit of the pheasant is white. The said Basoi stated that this bird lived in the snow mountains and that its food was grass and other stuff. I have kept pheasants and have reared young ones..."

This very small miniature has obviously been 'enlarged' by the addition of floral borders and panels taken from some illuminated manuscript and a wide blue border with birds and animals and trees in gold at a later time. The panels of illumination with Persian writing directly above and below the painting are also unrelated to it.

Unpublished.

69 A leopard stalking a mountain goat

Fragment of a drawing from a painter's sketchbook
4.7 x 10.4 cm
Jahangir period, c. 1625
Rietberg Museum, Zurich
(Alice Boner Bequest)

The Mughal emperors loved leopards, not as animals to hunt, but for training and hunting. In Akbar's time an entire imperial department was devoted to the catching of leopards, their keeping and training. Several methods of capturing leopards are detailed at length, the allowances of food approved of for the leopards and the wages of their keepers are specified; the manner in which these animals are transported to the hunting grounds and how the grandees were appointed to superintend the keepers of each leopard, is all painstakingly recorded. The fondness for leopards is explained not only by the lithe beauty of these great cats, but also by their remarkable hunting skills. Thus Abul Fazl: "Leopards will go against the wind, and thus they get scent of a prey, or come to hear its voice. They then plan an attack ... It is impossible to describe the wonderful feats of this animal; language fails to express his skill and cunning. Thus he will raise up the dust with his forefeet and hindlegs in order to conceal himself; or he will lie down so flat, that you cannot distinguish him from the surface of the ground."

An account of the time of Jahangir records his father's passion for hunting with leopards and says that he had "caught about nine thousand leopards collected during his reign." Like his father, Jahangir also kept leopards and hunted with them. Among the 'curious events' of Jahangir's reign, the author of the *Iqbalnama* mentions that a leopard in captivity covered a female leopard which gave birth to three cubs. This was an extremely rare occurrence, considered worthy of being prominently recorded.

One sees leopards frequently both in Persian and in Mughal painting. In the former, they form part of a wild landscape where they are often seen descending from rocky outcrops in pursuit of a deer or some other animal; in Mughal painting they are rendered alike in their wild state (for a distinguished example see no. 62), or as trained animals being taken out for hunting. This very fascination for the animal is recorded in this fragment of a drawing. From behind the cover of a rock, a leopard advances from the left towards his prey, an ibex. This is obviously no routine drawing, for not only does one see great skill of draftsmanship, one also senses the moment of hushed silence as the great cat advances with amazing grace and soft-footedness, preparing to pounce; at the same time one feels as if the ibex senses danger and nervously stops in his tracks, listening to the approaching sounds. The moment is one of palpable tension.

Mughal drawings of animals are far less common than paintings of them. The present work represents not the recording of a specific moment witnessed by a painter, but a keen reconstruction behind which lie sharp, sustained observation and a clear measure of feeling for the drama that belongs to the field of hunt.

Another drawing from the same sketchbook depicting a hunter is in the Rietberg Museum.

Unpublished.

70 A Safavid portrait

Single leaf mounted as an album page
Inscribed: '*Shabih-i* (portrait of) Isa Khan (?); (the work of) Bishan Das'
15.8 x 8.1 cm; page: 34.1 x 22.4 cm
Jahangir period, c. 1620
Collection of Prince Sadruddin Aga Khan

The Mughal concern for 'likenesses', so evident from the time of Akbar onwards, seemed only to accelerate with time and became permeated with an eager desire to seize the reality behind appearances. At the more obvious level, portraits had always served a need, for they offered a peculiar means of 'revealing' the character of those countless men that flit through the pages of Mughal history; but in the hands of the best of painters they were works that had a life and a power of their own.

Jahangir put likenesses to a variety of uses, including incorporating them into political allegories, apart from valuing them in their own right as works of art. When he sent an embassy under the distinguished Khan Alam to the great court of Shah Abbas of Persia, he made certain that a pictorial record of the visit was brought back. In his own words: "At the time when I sent Khan Alam to Persia, I had sent with him a painter of the name of Bishan Das, who was un-equalled in his age for taking likenesses, to take the portraits of the Shah and the chief men of his state, and bring them. He had drawn the likenesses of most of them, and he especially had taken that of my brother, the Shah, exceedingly well, so that when I showed it to any of his servants, they said it was exceedingly well drawn." The emperor's praise for Bishan Das is only just, for this gifted artist, who was capable of investing his figures with remarkable warmth, created a body of highly refined work. Of the record of his stay in Persia, probably the best known single work is that in the Museum of Fine Arts in Boston which shows Shah Abbas, the Iranian monarch, in select company in a small open-air party where the Indian ambassador and some of the Shah's intimates are seated and some servants stand in attendance.

This remarkable portrait belongs clearly to the group that Bishan Das painted while in Persia or soon after his return to India. It shows a slimly built man dressed in a long, dark purple-blue garment against a plain green ground. The severity of the garment throws the long orange boots into relief, the elaborate Safavid turban with its many folds and a cross-band of striped gold and white cloth, above all the superbly crafted waist-band intricately patterned in gold, blue, yellow, and white: this is somewhat loosely tied around the waist and the dignitary, "cool calculation and determination" reflected in his face, tucks both his hands in it. The face is shown in three quarters; a prominent downward drooping mustache extends very slightly beyond the profile. This very attention to detail is visible in the striped under-shirt, a small part of which is visible under the outer dress close to the neck. In the portrait, as A. Welch observes (1982:203), there is "a deftly balanced combination of the spare and the extravagant, all directed at presenting a penetrating, almost 'psycho-logical', study." The work comes across as a vital and warm characterization, full of life as in many another Bishan Das work.

The brief inscription in Persian close to the bottom of the painting has been read as 'likeness of Ali Khan' (A. Welch, 1982:203) but has been discounted as being a later inscription, "for the person portrayed by Bishan Das is the great Safavid Shah of Iran, Abbas I (r. 1587–1629)." The inscription reads, however, possibly differently, as 'Shabih-i Isa Khan' (the likeness of Isa Khan) and not of Ali Khan. In any case, there is a marked resemblance between the figure here and the noble who sits to Khan Alam's right in the Boston Museum painting *(The Meeting of Shah Abbas and Khan Alam)* whose name is inscribed below it as 'Isa Khan Qurchi Bashi'. The similarities in the form, the face, the dress including the large turban and the decorative waistband are striking. It is to be recalled that Bishan Das was also commissioned to bring back, apart from the portraits of the great Shah, those of "the chief men of his state." As Jahangir says, "he had drawn the likenesses of most of them ..."

Robinson (1972) notes that the Persian painter Riza-i Abbasi painted the meeting of Khan Alam and Shah Abbas at the same time as Bishan Das.

Publ.: A. Welch, S.C. Welch, 1982, no. 67; Falk, 1985, no. 141.

71 Portrait of a standing aristocrat

Single leaf intended for an album
Inscribed: 'Work of the humble Murad (or Murar?)';
at the side: '*Shabih-i* (likeness of) Hakim-al-Mulk'
14.3 x 8 cm; page: 38.2 x 29 cm
Shahjahan period, 1630/40
Private Collection

The study is sensitive, partaking of the quality of many another portrait of the Shahjahan period; attention is immediately drawn to the sharp-featured face and the general gravity of bearing. Against a dark green ground, the figure is flatly, simply placed, so that its colours glow: the yellow of the *jama,* the earthy red of the double-sided shawl, the brilliant gold-patterned mauve of the outer garment, a *qaba,* the striped red and gold of the *pyjamas* and the lapis lazuli blue of the slippers. More details are worked in in the girdle's reddish flowers against gold and in the light stripes of the turban that is secured by a solid cross-band of patterned golden cloth. The workmanship is deft and precise, the painter obviously taking great delight in rendering effects like on the 'bangled' sleeves of the garment through fine shading and the wrinkles on the tight *pyjamas,* only a small part of which is visible. Likewise, the lining of the garments, or the inner side, is shown with meticulous care; also the inside of the sleeve of the *qaba,* its edges in front where it is lightly folded to reveal an orange coloured piping and a green lining, the green reverse of the wrap and the gold edging of the blue slippers. It is not that the noble's features are ignored: there is much fineness of observation and crispness of detail in the rendering of the nose, the eyes, especially the fine hair on the beard; likewise the hands are nimbly depicted. But, with all this, the impression persists that the work has become as much a likeness of the person as of what he wears.

An inscription in Persian, placed vertically on the painting, reads *'Shabih-i Hakim-ul-Mulk'* (the likeness of Hakim-ul-Mulk). Hakim-ul-Mulk is not easy to trace. There is a detailed mention of one famous Hakim-ul-Mulk whose real name was Shamsuddin and who came from Gilan, but he relates to the period of Akbar and appears to have died in about 1580, a date far too early for the present work.

It has been suggested that the inscription might possibly be by Shahjahan (Sotheby's, April 3, 1978), but this is unlikely, for the Emperor Shahjahan's hand shows a consistent and frequent use of *nuqtas* or dots which are completely missing from this inscription. The other inscription, the one which gives the name of the painter, is in much smaller characters and appears on the hem of the yellow *jama* worn by the noble. This mentions that the painting is in the hand of the 'humble Murad', but the word 'Murad' as it is written here looks far more like 'Murar' (Murari), which could be the name of a Hindu painter.

This name, in this very form, occurs also on a *Shahjahan-nama* leaf.

Publ.: Sotheby's, April 3, 1987, no. 87.

72   Portrait of Baqir Khan

Single leaf mounted as an album page
18.2 x 10.9 cm; page: 36.5 x 25 cm
Shahjahan period, c.1635
Private Collection

The grandee portrayed here was a familiar figure, both in the times of Jahangir and Shahjahan. Jahangir speaks on occasion of Baqir Khan in his memoirs, referring to his coming to the court from Multan where he was governor and being honoured by the royal gift of an elephant. He was then raised to the *mansab* of one thousand, interceding on behalf of a deserter, and later appointed to the governorship of the *subah* of Oudh. Baqir Khan continued to serve under Jahangir's successor, Shahjahan, obviously winning distinctions and staying 'on the road to loyalty'.

The painter seems to be aware of all this and renders Baqir Khan in the manner of many contemporary portraits of this period against an uncoloured background that helps to emphasize the noble's figure. There is much that appears sumptuous in Baqir Khan's portrait: the elegant green turban with a plume, possibly a royal gift, stuck in it; a spotless white *jama* which shows to great advantage the colourful red and gold *patka* or waistband, with a dagger tucked into it; the crossband from which is suspended an elaborate black shield, a long sword at left, the *pyjamas* of delicate 'onion-pink' colour and the slippers in red and black. Significant is the manner of standing with hands lightly crossed and held against the waist as if in respectful attendance upon the emperor. The sensitively drawn face confirms the suggestion made by the disposition of the hands. It is as if the painter were keen on showing in Baqir Khan, at least as he is portrayed here, power, but not authority. In his own province, Multan or Oudh, Baqir Khan must indeed have wielded great power, but his authority clearly came from above, and we see him here as if in the presence of that authority.

Other portraits of Baqir Khan have survived, one in the India Office Library and another possible one in the British Museum, and it is of interest to see that each time it is the same air about Baqir Khan that the painter seems to communicate. Baqir Khan knew his place and the painter seems to have known how to show it. It is all discreetly but meaningfully stated, even when the portrait consists of a single leaf, seemingly without a context.

The small inscription at the bottom left identifies the grandee as "Baqir Khan Najm-al Sani." The second part of the name appears to refer to a title or honorific which Baqir Khan carried. We know that he descended from Yar Ahmad of Isfahan (Falk, Archer, 1981:71, no. 67). Steingass' Persian-English Dictionary mentions the fact that Najm-al Sani was a name given to a grandee of the king Ismail Safavi of Persia, and transmitted to his descendants. Possibly, Baqir Khan belonged to this very family that later settled down in India and took up service with the Mughals.

This painting is mounted on a contemporary album page with beautiful floral borders. It is not necessarily based on the more simple version signed by the painter Bulchand (Mulchand or Balchand?) (see Falk, Archer, 1981:71).

Unpublished.

Word and Image

73 "The hunting ground of the heart"

Single leaf mounted as an album page
13.5 x 8.2 cm; page: 36.5 x 24.8 cm
Painting: Jahangir period, c. 1610; borders: Shahjahan period, 1630/40
Private Collection

"Poets strike out a road to the inaccessible realm of thought, and divine grace beams forth in their genius." (Abul Fazl, *Ain-i Akbari,* vol.I:617)

Like most cultivated men of their age, the Mughals were greatly moved by poetry. Some of them composed poems, others calligraphed them, still others recited them. Abul Fazl records Akbar's poor opinion of poets, for many of them bartered away the high value of their talent 'from a wish to possess inferior stores', but of poetry Akbar was evidently fond. There are occasions when he is said to have suddenly quoted a verse from Hafiz entirely appropriate to an occasion, or even offered suggestions to poets to replace one word by another to heighten the poetic meaning of the verse. Clearly, poetry was much in the air and we hear of 'thousands of poets' being continually at court, among them many who had completed a *divan.* Abul Fazl quotes from nearly sixty of them in his works, and Badauni, likewise, leaves a detailed account of the poets active at the Akbari court. Their compositions apart, works of the great poets of the Persian tradition (Firdausi, Jami, Sadi, Rumi, Hafiz, and others) were as intimately known in Mughal India as they were in much of the Islamic world.

The painters in the Mughal ateliers were obviously affected by this situation. They were called upon to provide 'illustrations' to great poetic works in Persian; but this certainly was not their only contact with poetry. Mir Sayyid Ali, the Persian master who came to India with Humayun, was a poet and wrote under the pen-name of Judai; Sharif Khan, Khwaja Abd-al Samad's son, was also a poet himself. In this context, relating words, especially poetic words, to images must have had a special meaning for the more sensitive among Mughal painters.

In this regard, the two traditions to which the Mughal painters were working parallel, the Persian and the Rajput, offer distinguished examples of how word and image could relate to one another. In the Rajput-tradition paintings depict continuous stories 'synchronically' (see p.15), whereas in Persian painting the poetic 'moment' was often crystallized, being shown through elegant single figures placed in idyllic settings, a book or sometimes a goblet of wine by their side. Of that kind of painting we do not find many from Mughal India, but it is likely that behind many a work lies a poetic text (as distinct from a poetic suggestion) or verse now lost to us. The present page, thus, could be seen simply as a painting of a courtier feeding a hawk; on the other hand, it might equally well be a visualisation of some verse which, if known, could enhance its meaning considerably. The hawk, the hunting ground, the feeding of the bird figure all too frequently in poetry that concerns love of the earthly kind on one hand and divine love on the other, as in the Sufi tradition. To take only two examples from the works of Akbar period poets: the poet Faizi, Abul Fazl's distinguished brother, wrote: "If on this hunting ground thou wouldst but unfold the wing of resolution, thou wouldst be able to catch even the phoenix while possessed of the feathers of a sparrow."

A verse of Khwaja Hussain Sanai runs: "I exposed the prey of my heart to death, but the huntsman has given me quarter on account of my leanness and has let me wing away."

One reads, again, of verses with a Sufi ring in which the beloved/devotee rues the fact that he, whom he fell in love with, turned out to be 'a hawk', and much as he fed his own heart to it, it still refused to become his and his alone. Perhaps it is a thought like this that lies behind this quiet, elegant work.

The painting is mounted on an album page of the Shahjahan period which has an outer border of delicate, regular floral patterns that run a circular course in gold and colours.

Unpublished.

74 The slaying of a dragon

Double-sided illustrated folio from the 'Chester Beatty'-*Tutinama*
15.7 x 12 cm; page: 23.9 x 16 cm
Akbar period, 1575/80
Private Collection

It is the fifty-second night and the parrot who has so far succeeded in keeping the lady Khojasta from going out to meet her lover in the absence of her husband, keeps her engaged with yet another tale. The immensely popular Sanskrit classic, the *Shuka Saptashati* ('Seventy Tales of the Parrot') was translated into Persian first in the 13th century, and then again by Nakhshabi in the 14th, under the title *Tutinama*. But the span of the Sanskrit work had been by this time condensed into 52 tales. It is the last of the nights before Khojasta's husband returns, and the parrot whom he had left behind to keep a watch over things in his absence, tells the lady the tale of the pious man's son who was destined to be king, for he had unknowingly eaten the head of the miraculous bird of seven colours that was intended by his mother for her secret lover.

The young man in the tale leaves his country and lives incognito in another land where he falls in love with the king's daughter, but his only hope of marrying her lies in killing a dreaded beast, a dragon that "seizes human beings with its tail and devours them", for such was the promise made by the king to his people. Possessed of uncommon courage, the young man arrives at the spot where the dragon resides: finding him asleep, he renders him senseless with poisoned arrows, and then, coming close, cuts off his head. The contest was wholly unequal and yet, as the text says, "when the hour arrives for annihilating someone and the time for the death of a person approaches, an elephant-like *Namrud* can be destroyed by a gnat..."

"When fate decrees that a certain deed be executed
even the bite of an ant can a snake exterminate."

From this killing much else follows. The young man hides the head of the dragon, then reports his slaying to the king who, full of surprise and admiration, does finally fulfil his promise and takes the young man as his son-in-law. Thus, the prophesy comes true, and the young man succeeds the king on his death. It is as a king then that he returns to his own parents' house where his father, the pious man, had returned but been completely misinformed by his unfaithful wife about all that had happened in his absence: the man was now led to believe that his son, his old nurse and of course the magical bird had all met accidental death. The base act of the pious man's wife is finally exposed by the son's return. The tale ends by the parrot telling Khojasta not to proceed to the rendez-vous, for in her absence her husband may return and "you may be just as embarrassed because of your lover as the wife of the pious man was before her husband."

The story is long and involved, like most stories in the *Tutinama,* but the painter certainly chooses the most dramatic moments from it to illustrate. On the page, the long text leaves for him little space, but the painter uses the narrow strip at left to fill in a detail of the mountainous rocks, the dragon's habitat. The dragon's tail more or less merges with the rocks and as the beast comes down, belching fire and smoke, the young man on horseback gallops forward and smites it with a powerful stroke of his sword. On the verso side of the leaf, the action of the story continues: the king arrives and finds the dragon slain with the young man pointing this out to him. Here, however, we find the head of the dragon missing and the dragon disposed differently. The absent head of the dragon is pointedly mentioned in the tale, for the young man had hidden it lest someone else might find it and claim the deed. The king is duly wonderstruck as are the courtiers.

On this side of the folio, the text having shifted towards the left, the painter shows the rocky feature at the extreme right, using a painterly privilege to shift things about like parts of a theatre set. The painter understands perfectly the needs of the situation, the context of the story and the drama that inheres in this part of it. He uses the brief space available to him, therefore, with economy and intelligence. Since the killing of a sleeping dragon on the recto side would not be adequate in dramatic terms, the dragon is seen as descending from the rocks and full of that dread energy which had stricken terror into the hearts of the populace. One compares this energetic rendering with the other side, where the dragon lies slain and dead, its tail curled up motionlessly, and its limbs inert. The painter clearly bases himself on the text, but is not subservient to it. He knows what the essence of the tale is, but he also knows where to go beyond it pictorially. One also notices that by leaving the background very lightly tinted, unlike in most of the pages of the same *Tutinama* manuscript, he is able to throw into sharper relief the drama of the moment.

This folio relates to the near end of the manuscript, but some others must have followed it for Nakhshabi to round the story off, and to end it by stating that after having heard all that the Tuti had to tell about Khojasta and her faithless intentions in his absence, Maimun set the Tuti free, decapitated Khojasta, shaved his hair, put on woollen clothes and entered a hermitage with the intention of devoting his life to the worship of God. As in the case of the Cleveland *Tutinama,* some leaves of the Chester Beatty *Tutinama* are scattered.

Publ.: Falk, 1978, no. 4.

پنهان کرد و اسپ خود را بهمانجا گذاشت و بر یکی از اسپان پوشا سوار شد و
در شهر آذری چون وقت دفع یکی نزدیک شود و هنگام قلع کسی قریب کرد و
پس یکی چون مرده باشد پیش هلاک شود و آتشی چون فرعون پای به مضحا کرد و لیکن
که آنچنان مار بر ما مور بر باشد که نتوان کشت و آنچنان عفریتی را آید

قطعه

چه نوع هلاک توان کرد را
شبی که ربسته وقت است   وقت او خوش که او بنا باشد شاک
چون بنجوا باد قضا کند کار پی   مار کرد و به دست مور هلاک

روز دیگر کسی پیش پادشاه بر یا پادشاه آنجا گذاشت و رفت و گفت آنچنین خدمتی کرده ام و آنچنان
در دریا کشته ام و از برای یا ز پیاده تا که اسپ خود را بهمانجا گذاشته اسپی دیگر که لای

آورده ام و زیر یم پیش از آن بر پادشاه آمده بود و از رفتن او خبر کرد و
پادشاه و زیر را گفت این بهمان جوان باشد که تو حکایت التمام او میکرد بی
گفت باشد پس پادشاه در آن مغزا رفت از در دریا دید که بیکرا کشته بی سر پادشا
گفت ای جوان سر این اژدها در چه شد گفت این بریده ام و در کوی پنهان کرده
نباید که کسی دیگر ببرد و بر پادشاه آرد پادشاه بر سرهامات او آفرین کرد و
بر حرفت او تحسین نمود و از آنجا بدل فارغ باز کشت بمیر زا دگفت پادشاه

وعده کرده بود و هر که این مزاحمت در از میان ناد و رکند من دختر خود بدو دهم
من خود خدمتی کرده ام پادشاه را لیم وعده خود و فایا یک کرد و قطعه

75 "Like a bird in a cage am I"

Folio from a dispersed manuscript of the *Divan* of Shahi, mounted as an album page
12.9 x 8.7 cm; page: 26.7 x 20.4 cm
Akbar period, c. 1595
Collection of Prince Sadruddin Aga Khan

The words belong to the 15th century Persian poet Amir Shahi of Herat but the treatment is wholly Mughal. Set the task of illustrating the poet's verses, the painter picks and chooses (or is helped to pick and choose), since not every single verse can be visualised. Here, two meaningful couplets are what the painter stops at: "Like a parrot am I, sacred but caged; where is that mirror-like face of yours that, seeing it, I may begin to talk?" The painter sets the scene near a cave in the wilderness which a man of God has made his home. The recluse sits in front of it on a deer-skin, clad in heavy but simple robes, with a book by his side; his earthly belongings seem to consist of a parrot in a cage, and his companion, a dog, sits close to his feet. A prince has come to visit the hermit; far in the distance lies 'his' large city with its palaces and fort-like structures and humble dwellings. He seems to have been accompanied by a small group, as if on a hunting expedition: companions, trusted retainers and huntsmen. A horse from which the prince has just dismounted occupies the bottom right of the painting, and a young boy, a prince, stands close to the ruler, with hands lightly folded in front, listening respectfully. The other retainers are busy, but not necessarily paying attention to what is going on in the middle of the painting, where the ruler, seated on a small carpet, holds a conversation with the holy man. Only an older man, a minister perhaps, listens intently.

As the painter renders the scene, a somewhat mystic turn is given to the words of Shahi. The words "like a caged bird am I" bespeak the king's state of mind who, with all the trappings of power and comfort that are his, longs to soar free and high, at the kind of altitude which only men of God, like the hermit, seem to be able to attain. It is as if, trapped in his present state, the king turns to his preceptor to whom alone he can address words that express the innermost state of his mind. That 'mirror-like face' alone can summon this kind of talk.

The painter, fully aware of the favourite Persian juxtaposition of the Shah and the dervish, the king who has everything and the mendicant who has no material goods, invests Shahi's words with a new poignancy through his interpretation. The verse is no longer about a common lover who is encaged in the passion of his own heart and longs to see the face of the beloved; it is about a man who hankers after what he has not, and struggles to turn his back on all that he has.

Throughout the painting, meaning is endowed upon seemingly commonplace conventions. In the faces hidden in the rocks directly above the head of the hermit, something of a standard device in Persian painting, the painter is not harking back to a tradition; it would seem as if he were giving tongues to the rocks, much as the royal visitor is giving utterance to thoughts that have lain locked up inside of him. There may be meaning also in the intertwining roots of the tree placed directly in the middle of the painting; there is certainly much meaning in the large architectural complex of the city in the distance, for in it the painter is not simply using a cliché borrowed from European sources, but subtly pointing to the world of pomp and circumstance which now tires the prince. If there is refinement and delicacy in the words of Shahi, the painter matches it in his own fashion. The image takes off from the words but, in the final analysis, gives them new wings.

This leaf comes from a dispersed manuscript of the *Divan* of Shahi whose miniatures, as A. Welch (1982:176f) says, show "a grasp of atmosphere and perspective more accomplished than in earlier, larger works done under Mughal patronage." The copy is small in size and must have been meant to be carried around as a sumptuous work, a companion that brought words and pictures together for a discriminating patron. S.C. Welch (1963:223) attributes the present painting to Miskin, and A. Welch (1982:177) believes that the text might have been scripted by Abdul Rahim, *Anbarin qalam*, who was one of the most honoured calligraphers at the Mughal court.

Publ.: S.C. Welch, 1963, no. 5; Falk, 1979, no. 14; A. Welch, S.C. Welch, 1982, no. 59a.

76 "He whom they call mad"

Folio from the same dispersed *Divan* of Shahi as no. 75
12.5 x 8 cm; page: 33.5 x 22 cm
Akbar period, c. 1595
Collection of Prince Sadruddin Aga Khan

Poets in Persian speak with eloquence of madnesses of different kinds: that which comes from inconsolable grief at the loss of a beloved; that which comes from such intensity of feeling that one is no longer fit for civilised company; or that which seizes man when he longingly, achingly looks for that which cannot be found, the peace that comes from the cognition of the ultimate reality. Love both earthly and unearthly can drive men to this state. If Majnun in his distracted state wanders about pining for his beloved, Laila, the boys in the street throw pebbles at him and mock him as if he had lost all reason; but, as the poets say, as easily could Majnun have picked up stones and pelted those that did not know what his love was like. "When love reaches the emporium of madness, it builds in the desert triumphal arches with the shifting sands."

The man whom we see in the very heart of this painting is a love-maddened one. Turban askew, clothes flying open, he hits out with small stones and people flee in fear and amusement from him. He clearly has made a spectacle of himself, for women look at him from their safe perches and exchange comments; those that have not jeered at him and are therefore not targets of his missiles simply stand and wonder. His state has caused enough concern for people to carry complaints to a prince. But the prince, instead of moving into action, stands and wonders himself, much more able perhaps to identify with this man's stricken state of mind than those that bring him these complaints. For if love has its madness, grief has its resonance.

The painting is possessed of remarkable energy and swirling rhythms that are enhanced by the stillness of the structures surrounding the city square in which the action is placed. The painter isolates the 'mad man' with great care so that he can then proceed to explore and render the varying responses to his state. Shahi's words, that speak of madness in the same breath as a certain joyous intoxication, are rendered by the painter as a scene that is seemingly common but touches off uncommon trains of thought. Much is changed and shifted about, the perspective, the scaling, the angles of vision, but everything enhances the intensity of feeling that the verses, the poet and the painter bring to surface.

A. Welch (1982:179) has identified the theme. The calligraphy is ascribed by him to the famous Abd al-Rahim al Haravi, called 'Anbarin Qalam'.

Publ.: A. Welch, S.C. Welch, 1982, no. 59b.

77   A sinner's passionate plea to God

Folio from the same *Kulliyat* of Sadi as no.12
27.6 x 15.3 cm; page: 41.7 x 26.4 cm
Akbar-Jahangir period, 1600/05
Collection of Prince Sadruddin Aga Khan

The Persian poet Sadi tells in his *Bustan* the tale of a drunkard, "heated with liquor", who ran into the sanctuary of a mosque and cried out aloud: "Lord! Take me to the highest paradise!" At the point of being unceremoniously thrown out by the *mulla* as being unworthy of even entering the house of God, the old drunkard tearfully sent up a moving, passionately eloquent plea to God reminding Him of His own words that "repentence's door is open, and the Truth holds out a hand." Ignoring the *mulla*, the sinner called upon God again and again: "But if you cast me down, then none will take me up; / Who will do me violence if you give support? / Who will take me captive if you give release?" Citing Joseph, who saw so much affliction in his life and yet forgave all those who had done this to him, the drunk sinner pressed on with the words that appear above this illustration:

"Oh Mighty! Forgive this wareless one;
None's to be seen with a record blacker than mine,
For I have no acceptable deeds to offer –
Merely my trust in your support,
My hope in your forgiveness:
No wares I have brought but hope:
Oh God! Let me not cease to hope for pardon!"

The writing is too minute, but quite possibly it is the very last verse from this tale of the *Bustan* that is inscribed on the book lying open close to the 'sinner' who kneels on a parapet and holds his hands, palms joined, in prayer, his head tilted upwards and his eyes lightly closed.

The painter of this brilliantly coloured page takes liberty with the text and changes the setting completely. There is no mosque here to serve as a setting, no angry *mulla* who throws the drunkard out. The only architecture we see is in the distance: a walled city and a garden (clearly not a mosque) in a marble enclosure at a slight distance from it. The scene has shifted, far from habitation, to a quiet corner at the edge of a stream where two learned men of God engage in a conversation over a point in a book that lies open between them, and another devotee, also with a book by his side, kneels at the edge of a stream, performing ablutions apparently in preparation for his *nimaz*-prayer. Here also, higher than the three other persons in the foreground, the 'sinner' sits devoutly on a rocky parapet, his knees tucked under him. A small grove of trees and stylised bare rocks of many a hue set this segment of the painting apart from the far distance with its architecture and a vista with herdsmen watching their cattle grazing. The entire scene has become so 'generalised' that had it not been for the verses inscribed above, it would be impossible to link it with an episode from Sadi's *Bustan*. To be sure, there is a wine flask set close to the 'sinner' where he kneels, apparently an indication of his weakness for drink, but this is hardly sufficient to establish the nature of the man, for in all other respects he appears devout and, at this moment at least, deeply inwardly turned.

As in so many other works of this period, the drawing is highly refined, and the colours glow with a saturated richness, jewel-like in brilliance against an artfully introduced dark background. Everything is viewed with great clarity, and while a European-inspired view of a city in the distance figures here too, it is articulated with great attention to specific detail and is not on the point of disappearing in the haze of aerial perspective. In terms of the relationship of text to image, the painter views it all with marked freedom, using the words only as the barest cue to set up a scene, and not letting it dictate every detail in the picture.

Unpublished.

بصاعات مرجا نشان ین کرد	بکردار بدسان مقید نکرد	که مغنی بود بصورت خوب را	نه عفو کرد آل یعقوب را
که میم فعالی پسندیده نیست	کپس از من پسنه نامه ترد نیست	برین بی بضاعت ینخش اغنیم نیز	رلطفت میم چشم داریم نیز
خدایا زعفوم مکن با امید	بضاعت نیاور دم الامید	امید م برآمزر کاری نیست	بخیا بس کاعتقاد م بیاری نیست

159

78 Written by a 'Golden Pen'

Calligraphy in *nastaliq* by Muhammad Hussain (Kashmiri), called *Zarrin Qalam*,
('Golden Pen'); on verso, a scene of a literary gathering
31.8 x 22.4 cm
Calligraphy: Akbar period, c. 1580; painting: Jahangir period, c. 1610
Private Collection

Abul Fazl's passion for the arts of writing is quite remarkable. His account of the written letter, though long, is never without interest: "The written letter looks black, notwithstanding the thousand rays within it; or it is a light with a mole on it that wards off the evil eye. A letter is the portrait painter of wisdom; a rough sketch from the realm of ideas; a dark night ushering in day; a black cloud pregnant with knowledge; the wand for the treasures of insight; speaking, though dumb, stationary, and yet travelling, stretched on the sheet, and yet soaring upwards."

He goes on about the written word in this strain at considerable length, speaking of it as a heavenly traveller, which in the realm of thought is communicated through words, occasionally giving its "course a different direction by means of man's fingers, and having passed along the continent of the pen and crossed the ocean of the ink, a light on the pleasant expanse of the page, returns through the eye of the reader to its wanted inhabitation." Like many others in the Islamic world, Abul Fazl regarded calligraphy as the more important of the two arts of writing and painting, and he gives a detailed account of the many styles of writing and the most distinguished practitioners of them: "His Majesty shows much regard to the art, and takes a great interest in the different systems of writing; hence the large number of skilfull calligraphers. *Nastaliq* has especially received a new impetus. The artist who, in the shadow of the throne of His Majesty, has become a master of calligraphy, is Muhammad Hussain of Kashmir. He has been honoured with the title of 'Zarrin Qalam', the golden pen. He surpassed his master Maulana Abdul Aziz; his *maddat* and *dawair* show everywhere a proper proportion to each other, and art critics consider him equal to Mulla Mir Ali."

The high praise accorded to Muhammad Hussain here is reflected in the manner in which specimens of his writing were preserved and mounted in Mughal albums along with those of the reputed masters of Iran. The common practice was to have, on the two different sides of an album leaf, a panel of calligraphy and a painting. This is so here, too. The four lines in elegant, exquisitely crafted *nastaliq* by Muhammad Hussain appear diagonally across the page; the triangular spaces left at the top right and bottom left are separated, but treated in an equally decorative fashion, the top right having an elegant arabesque design and the bottom left the signatures of the calligrapher against a floral ground. This, in itself, does not complete the page, for around it is another floral border which is surrounded by yet another, in which little fragments of illumination separate narrow panels of calligraphy, very likely from the work of the great poet Jami. On the other side appears a painting, but it is also enclosed by similar small panels that run along its sides, calligraphy mixed with illumination. The painting shows a prince seated in the company of some literary men, listening to poetry and music while the group entertains itself with drinks. Clearly, the painting is accomplished, but as it stands now, sharing the same album leaf as Muhammad Hussain's fine *nastaliq,* it seems to serve more as a foil to the words than to offer it serious competition.

Calligraphy unpublished; painting published in Croisier, 1984, no. 82.

79 An unseemly quarrel

Folio from a dispersed manuscript of the *Gulistan* of Sadi
9 x 13.3 cm; page: 36 x 28.5 cm
Jahangir period, 1610/15
Private Collection

The moral tone of Sadi's celebrated works is mixed with flashes of great wit, sometimes even relish, and in it there are passages that were too frank for some translators of his to render. Some early editions even omit certain parts of his work in translation, or turn to the Victorian convenience of rendering them in Latin. One such tale is told in Book VI of the *Gulistan* that centres on feebleness and old age. The story here is of an old man who, when asked why he would not take a wife, said he knew better than doing that, for he had himself heard of a very old man who had married "a lovely young virgin, Gauhar ('pearl') by name", whom "like a casket of pearls, he hid from other men's eyes." But because of his advanced years, much as he desired her, their marriage could not be consummated. Natural discord arose between husband and wife, and the husband started complaining to his friends, accusing her of "making a clean sweep of all her property", not admitting to his own inadequacy. Marital strife came finally to such a point that the case went first to the head of the police, and then to the Qazi. The tale ends in Sadi's words who says: "After reproving and abusing (the husband), the (Qazi's) verdict was 'What is the girl's fault? Thou, whose hand trembles, what shouldst thou know about piercing a pearl?'"

Much of this is said in delightful verse, but as the painter of this page renders it, it becomes a straightforward case of marital discord being judged by learned men of law. We recognise the characters immediately: the infirm old husband and his very young-looking wife seated, looking eagerly at the Qazi and his companions who expound the law; the police chief who stands behind the couple, with a rod in his hand and a sword at his side; and other functionaries or neighbours of the couple. The scene is well laid out, and there is much fineness of workmanship in the page. However, the poetic dimension of the tale is not explored; nothing here truly enhances the delight that Sadi's words yield. Not only is the pun on the word pearl (Gauhar), the young wife's name, missed; nothing truly hints at other, poetic possibilities. The painting looks far too sober for a visual interpretation of what, in words, is witty and poetic.

This leaf comes from a dispersed manuscript of the *Gulistan* of Sadi which, Falk (1985:no.138) believes, "was probably intended as a companion volume to the 1605–06 *Bustan*" that belonged to Jahangir.

Publ.: Falk, 1985, no. 138.

80 A folio from the *Divan* of Hafiz

From the 'Bute Hafiz' manuscript
24.3 x 17 cm
Calligraphy: Iran, c.1500; border decorations: Jahangir period, c.1605
Rietberg Museum, Zurich

The pride, apart from the delight, that the Mughals took in owning sumptuously produced volumes is reflected repeatedly in the kind of entries that the emperors made in their own hands on the fly-leaves of some of the most precious books that they owned. They certainly commissioned great works themselves, but they also collected works that had history behind them, were reminders in a way of their heritage. There seems to have been a constant flow of books into India from the lands west and northwest of it: books were purchased, received as gifts, brought as humble offerings by men in search of employment or patronage at the Mughal court. One knows of many works predating their times and others that are contemporary but not of Mughal or Indian origin, that entered the libraries of Akbar, Jahangir and Shahjahan. When one sees fly-leaves on which more than one emperor has entered in his own hand the fact that this volume came into his possession "with the grace of God" on his accession to the throne, and when one sees the seals of virtually all the great Mughals from Babur to Aurangzeb on the same leaf, together with seals of minor functionaries like librarians and store keepers, the great sense of value that was attached to these volumes comes vibrantly across.

This folio comes from a manuscript of the *Divan* of the great Persian poet Hafiz of Shiraz. The manuscript to which it belongs is now in the British Library and goes under the name of the 'Bute Hafiz', having been once in the family of the Marquis of Bute. The fly-leaf has autographed entries by Jahangir and Shahjahan, the latter mentioning, among other details that he records, that the hand in which this manuscript is written is that of Sultan Ali of Meshed, evidently the master calligrapher whose writing was "among other writings as the sun upon the other planets." Not many examples of the work of Sultan Ali of Meshed are known from Mughal India, and this *Divan* must have been highly valued when it entered the Mughal library.

At what point this happened is not certain, but of interest is the fact that, having come from outside of India, the *Divan* was taken up for 'refurbishing' or decorating under Jahangir, close to a hundred years after it was penned. As Losty (1985) notes, border decorations, known to start hesitantly in the last years of Akbar's reign, were taken up with a new enthusiasm in the studio of Jahangir when he was still a prince, and then received a further fillip when he ascended the throne of India. Jahangir did clearly possess this manuscript at the time of his accession, for

a note in his hand appears also on the fly-leaf, but it would seem as if the border decorations were undertaken in that very year, A.D. 1605. Losty states that: "The Bute Hafiz must have been one of the first manuscripts to have been refurbished when Jahangir finally gained possession of the throne and the vast imperial studio and library in 1605."

As a matter of rule, every single folio was provided with new decorative borders except for the opening pair of pages which has a more ambitious scheme of decoration. The normal pages have five gold cartouches disposed around the text panels with half-cartouches at the inner end where this would go into the binding. The cartouches, as on this folio, are differently shaped, and in the volume they range from round to oval, to pear-shaped, to stellar and triangular shapes, each with a serrated or flame-like edge. Within the cartouches diverse subjects are introduced, mostly men, animals, birds perching or in flight, with an occasional woman or winged *peri*. A remarkable diversity is seen, from young men poetically or artistically disposed to workmen shown working with their tools; furthermore, also artists and scribes, astrologers and devotees are represented. The birds and animals are ordinarily in gold outline and only rarely in full colour; the human figures, on the other hand, have fully coloured heads with clothes in various tones of gold. Very little colour seems to have been used in general, as if not to take away from the severe nobility of the calligraphy.

On this page, one sees birds in flight, a deer, young men seated in a landscape as if reciting or drinking; a standing man, possibly admiring the beauties of nature, a pair of birds, a musician playing on a *shehnai*, a clarinet-like instrument. What exact connection, if any, subsists between the verses on each page and the figures in the cartouches around them is not easy to establish. It is possible that the painters took their cues from one or the other of the couplets on each page. What is remarkable, however, is this painstaking effort to add images to words close to a century after the words had actually been scripted. A new emphasis, a renewed appreciation, is brought to the volume through this act.

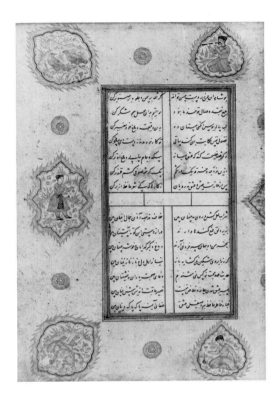

Losty (1983:13f) found the date of production on folio 58r and has later (1985) attributed some of the best vignettes in the 'Bute Hafiz' to the brush of Daulat, a possible portrait of whose is among the artists shown in the cartouches on two pages. He remarks: "His work here is a trial run as it were for the spectacular pages he contributed to the (Berlin) album, where for the first time full colour is used for all the marginal portraits. Other artists did not favour this technique for marginalia, and in this respect Daulat's work is ahead of its time, for it became a usual practice in the albums put together in the reign of Shahjahan (1627–1658)". Other leaves are in the Keir Collection, published by Skelton (1976:251); in the Ehrenfeld Collection (Ehnbom, 1985:54); and a further leaf has been published by Brand and Lowry (1985:no.11).

Unpublished.

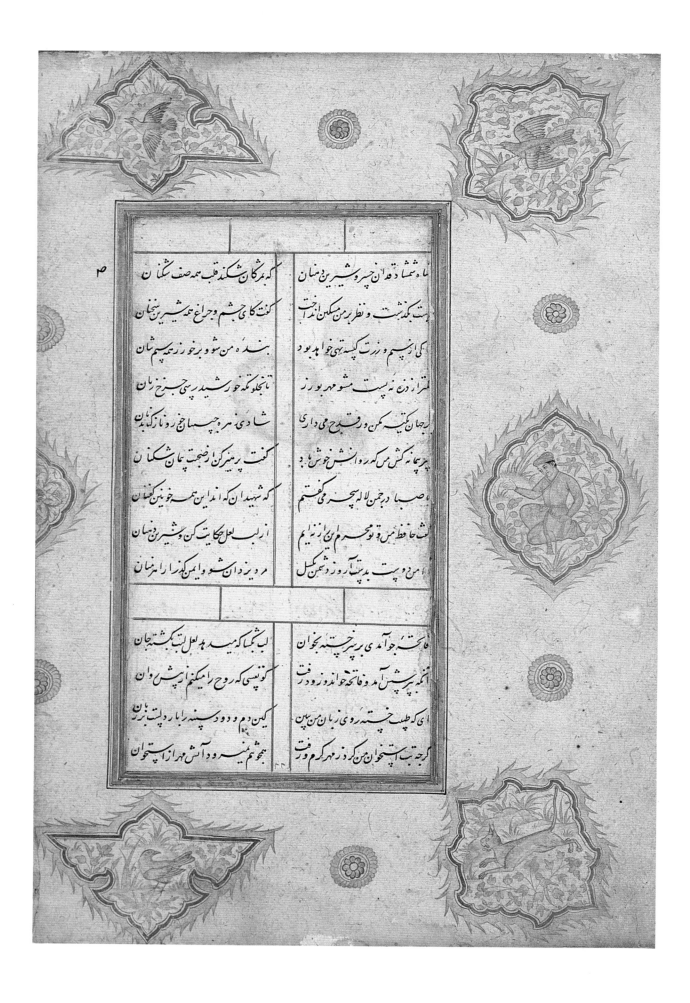

Inward Turning

81 "Difficult is the path we tread"

Lightly tinted drawing, mounted as an album page; on verso, four lines of calligraphy in *nastaliq*, signed by Jugal Kishor
12.9 x 9.2 cm
Drawing: Akbar period, 1580/85; calligraphy: 1620 or later
Collection of Prince Sadruddin Aga Khan

The work has much delicacy, not only of form, but of feeling. A Hindu ascetic stands at the foot of a stony hill, his head turned towards it, and a long staff that he carries pressed firmly against a small boulder. His hair is long and brown and matted; the only garment worn by the holy man is a coarse cloak draped around the body, leaving the knees and the legs bare; a short garland of dried flowers and leaves is loosely draped around the shoulders. Behind the *sadhu*, but very close to him, stands a younger person, also one 'who is tieless', evidently a disciple. His hair is matted and forms a kind of circle around his head. He wears the same coarse cloak-like wrap; in his right hand he holds up a small begging bowl; with the left hand he holds a simple, rustic fan woven from rush leaves, but looking much like a large halberd; very close to the handle of the fan is the top end of an object which has a long staff attached to it, and evidently tucked at the back. Both men are bare-footed and between their legs appears a recluse's constant companion, a small dog.

There is an emphatic feeling of bareness in this sensitive little drawing. Behind the two principal figures a large area is left 'uncovered': a rock stretches out from the right towards the left, and behind that, far in the distance, is visible a clump of trees in front of a segment of a town with prominent buildings. The bare rocks in front, towards the right of the drawing, are interspersed with little, dried-up shoots, like plants that have never seen any greenery. There is remarkable delicacy of modeling, and the painter shows great skill in the manner in which he handles the faces of the two men and renders their garments. But what is specially affecting is not the technique or the sheer draftsmanship: it is the feeling that permeates the work. The holy man, one senses, is clearly in search of that path which many before him have trodden. It is as if he has seen a light from a distance, but does not quite know how to reach it yet. He has turned his back on the world and there is no return to it; but what road he has to wend his way on is not yet clear. There is no unease in his situation, only uncertainty, the uncertainty that comes from personal inadequacy.

The painter distinguishes the states of mind of the holy man and his younger disciple with wonderful sensitivity. The disciple, as he looks out of the painting and at the world outside of himself, is still 'attached': his concerns are not exactly the same at this stage of his life, as those of his *guru*. But he goes where the *guru* goes, not yet touched by that ray of light but hopeful of it.

The two men are not common mendicants but men of God, and these the painter of Mughal India must have known well. Several painters rendered, each in his own fashion, divines and holy men, and one can imagine their turning to these subjects with quiet enthusiasm, for this would take them away from illustrating histories and chronicles and recording the externals of the world, towards richer themes of inner life. We have to recall the fact that there was much philosophical and devotional thought in the air in Mughal India even as the clang of the battlefield was constantly heard. The great Muslim saints that the greatest of the kings turned to, the *sufis* who were bridging the gap between Muslims and Hindus, remarkable men and women of God like Surdas, Tulsi, and Mirabai, were giving utterance to deep, moving thoughts. If then *dervishes* and *mullas, sannyasis* and *yogis,* are rendered, they only reflect an interest in a segment of life that the more inwardly-turned painters might have been drawn to.

The four lines of fine calligraphy in *nastaliq* on the verso of this album page follow a pattern seen commonly enough in Mughal albums, but there seems to be a connection between what those verses contain and the drawing of the two *sadhus*. The verses are addressed to oneself, as it were, for they say to the heart that 'you have no friend, and no place to turn to except the dust of (His) door; the portico of your eyes, and the dwelling of your heart possess no trace of a ray of their own but for (His) light'.

The calligraphy is of more than usual interest, for even though it starts in praise of God in the approved Islamic fashion, and the verses are in Persian, it is signed by Jugal Kishor, clearly a Hindu. One is initially startled to see a Hindu name appended to lines in a script and a language that one does not easily associate with Hindus in Mughal India, but there is little doubt that much had been mastered by them. Like the Hindu painters working in collaboration with, or under the tutelage of, Muslim masters, Hindu calligraphers must also have bent themselves to the task of acquiring these skills.

Unpublished.

82 A lonely vigil

Leaf from an unidentified series, mounted as an album page
15 x 10 cm; page: 30 x 21.3 cm
Akbar period, c. 1600
Collection of Prince Sadruddin Aga Khan

The setting is strange and unusual. On an isolated tower that rests on a hexagonal platform placed in the midst of wilderness, close to the top, sits a young maiden dressed in a *choli*-blouse and a *sari,* all by herself. The pillar, reminiscent of the monumental 'milestones' that were placed along major roads in Akbar's India, is not part of any architectural complex: it stands by itself, far away from habitation, the nearest sign of human activity being a modest little shrine in the middle distance directly behind a clump of trees. Farther off, tiny little figures of hunters or men wending their way home are to be seen, but there is seemingly no possibility of contact between them and the lady who sits there surrounded by her own isolation. A stylised mushrooming rock, tall and bare, rises to the left; in the far distance and to the right are little hills with signs of trees on them; a shallow mountainous river runs its zig-zag course through them. But close to where the tower is, there is only the skeleton of a tree, denuded of leaves and burnt out; an expanse of wilderness – perhaps soon to be penetrated by a hunter – is hinted at by an antelope with two of its mates running swift-footed towards the right.

Unfortunately it is not possible to identify the subject or the context of this work, but it must come from some tale now lost to us. The high finish of the work, the remarkable painterly qualities in it, are fair indications that the series from which it comes must have involved painters of a very high order. Here the painter turns whatever episode it is into an image of growing, overpowering loneliness. It is not mere physical isolation, a distancing, that is sought to be represented, but a true, inner loneliness. There is despair and hopelessness in the stance of the young maiden as she bends forward and looks down from her uneasy height at some sign of hope, some indication of 'coming'. The hopelessness of her situation is hinted at by the meaningfully placed shrivelled tree at the bottom left, a feature one does not see all that often in Mughal painting; this is emphasized further by the absence of any means by which access can be had to her perch: there is no door, no visible steps that could possibly lead to where she is.

One is aware, through the range of paintings in the Rajput tradition, of states of mind like this being explored and established: of heroines pining for absent lovers, of *raginis,* personifications of musical modes, wandering about desolately in forests and on mountain tops; but in Mughal painting, especially of this period, it is not easy to think of many works that take isolation and loneliness, the pain of separation, as their theme and invest

the entire atmosphere with a feeling of insistent, spiralling silence as here. Perhaps it is a corner of his own mind into which the painter here decides to cast a dim light and peer.

On the top border an inscription identifies the lady as "the daughter of Rai Pithaura", a Rajput ruler of the 11th century, but we do not know of this ruler having imprisoned his daughter in a tower. This theme, however, is reminiscent of European legends (Saint Barbara) and of some oriental tales (Princess Rudaba). The illustration of Rudaba who hauls her lover up a rock (Das, 1982: no. 4) also comes to mind.

On verso there is a painting of yellow flowers with birds and butterflies and animals dispersed over the page. This work appears to be much later in date, possibly the 18th century. An inscription identifies the tree as being of 'yellow chameli', a kind of jasmine.

Unpublished.

83 When the lamp of life is extinguished

Folio from an unidentified manuscript (possibly the same as no. 60)
29 x 20.5 cm
Akbar period, 1585/90
Bernisches Historisches Museum

Inside a chamber set in the midst of a court-yard of a house, a man has hanged himself with a rope from the ceiling. There is hushed silence in the scene: no one else is inside, no sign of human life survives. There is only the body of the man which dangles from the rope, his hair dishevelled, the turban loos-ened and slipping from his head, his *jama* flung open revealing the *pyjamas* under-neath and the bare flesh of the upper part of the body. The head hangs to the side, the mouth slightly open. A small wooden stool lies on the floor of the chamber, close to the dangling, lifeless feet: it is seen upside down and at a very slight remove from the body, to suggest that the man used it to climb up and raise himself and then, at the last moment, pushed it to the side with his feet for the rope to bear the weight of his body. Elaborate, thoughtful preparation for the act is thus established. But we have no clue to the circumstances leading to this gruesome act that has 'extinguished the lamp of life' of this man. A clue would cer-tainly have been provided in the two lines of text that appear at the bottom of the page, but these unfortunately have been covered with pigment so as to make the words com-pletely inaccessible. All we are left with is the image of the hanging man. It is possible that poverty of circumstance led him to this fell decision. There is some suggestion of this in the fact that the house is singularly bare, devoid of all appointments. There is no indication of any affluence on the man's person, no ornaments, no jewellery; the clothes that he wears are barely adequate. It is as if, from a once comfortable state, he has come to straitened circumstances. But this can only remain a guess.

The scene is superbly conceived and exe-cuted with great, painstaking attention to detail. The manner in which the head is treated, for instance, or the falling turban is rendered, speak of a masterly hand at work. One also notices from the disposition of the limbs that the suicide is recent, as if the body were still possessed of some warmth. The introduction of the finely detailed trees behind the back wall of the house, the flow-ering plants in front and the presence of the peacock on the roof of the chamber, seem to be more than mere decorative additions: through them, the painter seems to suggest that while this man's life has come to an end, the world around goes on as usual and continues to be filled with beauty. The col-ouring of the work is exceedingly delicate, with a marked preference for lilacs and mauves, apart from the brown and red sand-stone of the walls and the fine, tiled pattern in jade- green on the floor. The painter has had obvious and usual problems with per-spective but nothing stands out as truly awkward. Nothing, in any case, interferes with the powerful feeling in the painting. The manner in which an atmosphere of utter si-lence is meticulously built up, the fine detail of the water pitcher in the courtyard on a wooden stand turned upside down to sug-gest that all its contents are now emptied out, speak for the intense manner in which the painter seems to have entered the spirit of the situation. The import of a moment of agonizing but irreversible decision seems all to be here.

Tales of suicides are not uncommon either in Persian or in Indian literature. One even hears, in an early Jataka story from Buddhist India, of a painter playing a trick on a col-league by painting himself as having com-mitted suicide so 'realistically' that his col-league who, as he enters hurriedly from the outer door, is completely shattered at finding his friend dead. But what we see here is no 'trick of the eye', no matter of a light-hearted exchange. This suicide is all too real. An event that the painter knew from his own ex-perience could have made a deep, lasting impression on his mind for it to come out in this way. It is useful to remind ourselves of the fact that the brilliant Daswant, among the most gifted painters in the Mughal atel-ier, took his own life. As Abul Fazl tells us: "Daswant. He is the son of a palkeebearer. He devoted his whole life to the art, and used, from love of his profession, to draw and paint figures even on walls. One day, the eye of His Majesty fell on him; his talent was discovered, and he himself handed over to the *Khwaja* (Abd-al Samad). In a short time he surpassed all painters and became the first master of the age. Unfortunately the light of his talents was dimmed by the shadow of madness; he committed suicide."

This work comes from the Tillot Collection, ex Comte de Gobineau.

Unpublished.

84 Mercury in Gemini

Folio from a manuscript of the *Kitab-i-Saat* ("Book of Sidereal Hours"),
copied for Mirza Aziz Koka at Hajipur
20 x 11.7 cm; page: 28 x 20.7 cm
Akbar period, dated *21 shawwal 991* / November 7, 1583
Private Collection

The wide-spread faith in omens and fore-casts, astrology and horoscopes, was shared in Mughal India equally by commoners and rulers and nobility. Even that noted rationalist Babur, when he was to engage Shaibak Khan in one of his many battles, wrote how he hurried on with a fight on a particular day: "The reason why I was so eager to engage was that on the day of battle, the eight stars were between the two armies; they would have been in the enemy's rear for thirteen or fourteen days if the fight had been deferred." In the leaves of the illustrated *Akbarnama* there is strong evidence from the Akbar period of belief in horoscopes and forecasts: the scene of a prince's birth is almost invariably accompanied by a vignette outside the ladies' chambers where Muslim learneds and Hindu *pandits* sit recording the hour of the birth and foretelling the events in the life of the newly born. Again, when Jahangir was in Kashmir, we read that he entered Srinagar on a particular day because "the hour for entry had been fixed for Monday, when two watches of the day had passed."

The work to which the present leaf belongs, the *Kitab-i-Saat,* was not commissioned by the emperor himself, but by a favoured grandee of his, Mirza Aziz Koka, who lived at Hajipur in the east for a length of time. The work has twelve miniatures and four zodiac diagrams and is among the extremely few dated sub-imperial manuscripts.

The text that accompanies the illustrations is detailed and goes into much length about what to anticipate in the life, for instance, of one born under a specific sign of the zodiac. The nature of the person, the likely difficulties that he would run into in the course of his life, the special talents and weaknesses that he would possess, details about marriages, possibilities of travel, dealings with friends and enemies and the like, all figure in the Book of Hours.

This folio refers to "Mercury in Gemini". What gives it special flavour is the fact that while the zodiacal sign, the Gemini, is relatively summarily treated, attention focuses on the figure of the seated man, Mercury, pen in hand, instruments of writing close to him on the carpet, a small scroll of paper, a pen box, a pair of scissors, a brass pot, and two little shallow receptacles. The figure is quite remarkable: it is not only the pensive, thoughtful facial expression that the painter focuses on; he provides other indications of deep involvement in the moment in the slightly forward bent stance, and especially in the manner in which the left hand is held as if a process of cogitation were in progress. The

man is shown prominently carrying a necklace of beads stuck into the waistband; the manner of tying the *jama* under the right arm indicates, as does the rest of his appearance, that the figure is that of a Muslim. The setting is conventional with rocks and a tree and flowering plants and pairs of birds. But it is generalised, not demanding any attention to itself, leaving the viewer to focus on the figures, especially of the man immersed in thought.

To compare this figure and its introspective feeling with others in the same manuscript which are much more outwardly turned, like that of the young lady who encounters Taurus in a landscape, or a man (Mars) who carries a severed head in juxtaposition with a ram, is quite revealing, for the feeling in these paintings varies quite remarkably.

The importance of this manuscript for the chronology of illustrated books of the Akbar period was first pointed out by Falk (1978:19) who read the colophon and identified the scribe as Muhammad Yusuf. Unfortunately the individual paintings are not signed.

Further leaves of the *Kitab-i-Saat* manuscript are reproduced in Falk, 1978, no.5, and Falk, 1985, no.123.

Publ.: Falk, 1978, no.5; Brand, Lowry, 1985, no.56.

بادی مغربی بر طبع خون و بطبع شیرین طفلی بهاری ... قائم بالا درست اعضاکش وه ابر و شبهم جزم

باریک کردن ... نزلات و نفر پس از کلف ... ملوک و اهل دیوان و محاسبان و معلمان

وصیادان و نقاشان و خیاطان و ارباب ملاهی و آلاتی که بدین طایفه منسوب بود و مرغان های صیدی

و درختان میوه دار و بلند و میوه های مغز دار و عطر ها و دارو ها ... دوشها و بارو ها ... سبک و

روحانی مزاج خوش بوی و کرم اخلاق ساکن طبع زیرک لهو و لعب دوست میانه عفت ... زردی که

بسر سینخ زند ... طرابلس و رقه و حمص و مصر و ارمیه و تکریت و کیلان و دیم و طبرستان

و مرو رود و موقان و اصفهان و مازندران و کرمان و قزوین ... صورت برج جوزا و عطارد که صاحب اوست

هر که به طالع برج زاید مردمی باشد و نیکو روی و بدخوی و از مردم نوع بهرمان با بهره باشد اگر برج مشتری

متولد شده باشد سفید پوست و با طراوت بود و فراخ روزی و نفع و به هر کس رسد و لیکن در کار خود کامل

باشد و او را بر پشت یا سینه خالی یا نشانی باشد و بر روی او نیز دلیل کند که علامتی باشد و هر و پشتش جراحتی رسد

و در بازار کار ملی کند و از سفر و تجارت او را بهره باشد و پیشها آنچه بخشش و کار با نیک و کار آتشی و با نیکی بود

85 Words that move

Folio from a dispersed manuscript of the *Gulistan* of Sadi; above,
three lines of text in *nastaliq*
21.5 x 11.3 cm; page: 25.5 x 12.8 cm
Akbar period, c. 1600
Private Collection

The tale that the painter picks up for visual rendering – illustration is hardly the appropriate word –, is from Shaikh Sadi's celebrated Persian classic, *Gulistan*. The choice is somewhat surprising for there is not the usual narrative interest in the tale that would provide the painter much opportunity. In the text, Sadi speaks of how, while preaching in the metropolitan mosque at Baalbek, he noticed that his words had little meaning for his audience until in the context of a verse from the *Quran,* Sura Qaf, in which God speaks of being 'closer to man than the vein on his neck', he explicated: "We know what dark whispers come to him from his soul." Hearing this utterance, the tale goes on to say, a casual passer-by felt suddenly deeply moved and cried out aloud, as if in recognition of some message that had lain dormant inside him. This man's ecstatic response then suddenly started a chain reaction, and the entire congregation became agitated, seemingly turned inward. An ordinary moment had turned into a moment of magic.

Even though the preaching *shaikh* is introduced here standing, almost levitating, on a pulpit in an open pavilion, and the mosque of the text has been transformed into a lush garden with wonderful foliage and blossoming flowers (possibly a pun upon the word *Gulistan,* literally a garden of flowers), it is not a tale that the painter keeps in sharp focus, but an experience. The whirling dervish-like figure, who looks curiously like the other self of Sadi himself, is evidently in some kind of trance. But equally sustained is the artist's exploration of the other members of this diverse congregation, remarkably varied-looking and dressed pointedly differently. Among these men, scarcely anyone is looking at Sadi anymore; everyone seems to search somewhere within himself: there are those that raise their hands in amazement, others that bend their heads gently as if gazing at unseen mirrors within themselves; still others cover their eyes as if unable to contain emotion. Every person is shown as touched, each in his own manner, to the depth of his being. All of this makes the painting into much more than the fine study of different characters that it is: it becomes a record of that elusive moment that comes to everyone, if all too rarely, in which one confronts an inner self.

This miniature, which has been attributed to the painter Miskin by Falk (1978:25), belongs to a now widely dispersed group, and seems to have once belonged to a manuscript copied in Bukhara in 1567, mixed with works by Bukhara artists. The work is clearly, however, of Mughal origin, having been done close to 1600. The paintings seem to have been dispersed fairly early; the present folio bears a note mentioning its being viewed by King George V and Queen Mary whose signatures appear on it, possibly on the occasion of the Darbar in Delhi in 1911.

Publ.: Falk, 1978, no. 9; Das, 1982, no. 4; Falk, 1985, no. 33.

در ینع امدم تربیت پینوران و اینه داری در محله کوران ولیکن در معنی باز بود

و پله سخن دراز در معنی این آیت   و نحن اقرب الیه من حبل الورید

پسانیده بودم

سخن مله جاا

قطعه

86 "Giving from toil's own hand"

Folio from the same *Kulliyat* of Sadi as no. 12
27.6 x 15.3 cm; page: 41.7 x 26.4 cm
Akbar-Jahangir period, 1600/05
Collection of Prince Sadruddin Aga Khan

The words are the Persian poet Sadi's from his celebrated *Bustan;* the context, that of kindness; the setting a wilderness, far from any habitation. In this wilderness Sadi speaks of a man who found a thirsty dog:

"With nought of his life but the last gasp left;
That man of seemly ritual made his hat a bucket,
Binding his turban thereto as a rope;
His loins he girt in service and opened up his arms
And gave the helpless dog a draught of water."

This simple act of kindness, the poet says, made "that man's condition worthy of being pardoned by the arbiter of sins." The moral is then stated further in the words:

"Be as generous as within you lies:
The world Lord never shut on anyone the door of benefit;
Though in the wilderness you own no well,
Yet set up a lamp in a place of visitation!
Giving gold from your treasury by the quintal
Is not like one carat's worth from toil's own hand..."

For the painter who set himself the task of illustrating this tale from the *Bustan*, the setting presented no problem whatsoever, for 'a wilderness' had, in the tradition in which he was working, an established iconography of its own: distance from the city, a group of bare, denuded rocks, isolated trees sprouting at short distances from each other, wild animals like lions and deer and foxes moving about freely, a generally sparse look. But, beyond this, the painter goes on to flesh the picture out, giving it a sense of warmth. The necessary elements of the tale have to be brought in: an emaciated dog, a man, a well, the means by which the man draws water from the well, namely a turban and a skull-cap. But what he makes of these elements and how he goes about turning this into a truly moving work is of deep interest. Sadi's text makes no mention of the age or the station of the man who performed this kindly deed: it is the painter who visualises him as a man with no belongings of his own, bearing the weight of age, bent and indigent, a *dervish* in fact. He does this evidently because, through this, he is able to establish a special bond between man and animal, between two beings that have a certain poverty in common. The patched cloak that the man has taken off and kept at the edge of the well in order to exert himself to draw water, is the very badge of mendicancy; and his age draws compulsive attention to his own relative helplessness. At the same time, the manner in which the painter treats the well says something about the entire situation: like the *dervish,* it looks dilapidated from the outside, broken and is in a state of disrepair; but it provides a generous, kindly heart, a reservoir of life-giving water.

The *dervish* and the dog are placed in the very heart of the painting, and the manner in which – solicitously, tenderly, the *dervish* bends over and holds the skull-cap filled with water down for the dog to lap up water from is curiously moving. Further poignancy is added to the scene if one recalls to one's mind the fact that in India, even today, a dog that wanders about is frequently referred to as 'a *dervish*', one who moves about from door to door in search of the barest means of sustenance. Almost certainly, this kind of painting would linger long in the mind of the discerning viewer not only because of its subtle composition or its fine colouring but because of the feeling with which it is permeated.

Unpublished.

87 Intimations of mortality

Single leaf mounted as an album page; inscribed with the words: '*amal-i Nadir al-Zaman*'
(painted by *Nadir al-Zaman*, 'Wonder of the Age', i.e. Abul Hasan)
11.6 x 6.5 cm; page: 36.6 x 24.6 cm
Jahangir period, 1618/20
Collection of Prince Sadruddin Aga Khan

It is with deep feeling that poets, alike in India and Persia, speak of old age, of the coming of that time when "the lamps of the eyes will begin to grow dim, and the lotuses of the hands start to wilt." "Years will roll over Thee", as Sadi says, along the path "thou will take to the grave of thy father." But it is not merely of the wrinkles on the face, the infirmity in the knees, that the poets speak of; it is of a time of life when, finally, the meaning will dimly begin to unfold itself, or when the hollowness of it all will make itself manifest. For the man of God, however, the poets say, this is the time to sit out and wait with patience and dignity, with submission and resignation rather than regret or defiance, for one knew it all along that this edifice of life is built on walls that are but sand and rests on pillars fickle as the wind.

The painter Abul Hasan, to whom the inscription in a minute hand on the right shoulder of this bent old man ascribes this painting, is known for far more spectacular work: ambitious groups of people, allegorical portraits, virtuoso copies of European etchings, and the like. But here, in a quiet, hushed tone, he renders an old, bare-footed man who leans on his staff and slowly makes his way forward. The body bears the marks of the ravages of time: the bent back, the stooped shoulders, the snow-white beard, the lean desiccated frame. But the mind, like the eyes, is still keen and the thoughts are pious, as is indicated by the rosary of beads that this pilgrim-like figure carries prominently in the right hand. All the signs point also to a state of indigence, for the body is bare in the lower part, the feet are unshod, and the apparel consists mostly of a coarse cloak roughly wrapped around, a folded shawl-like sheet on the left shoulder, a bag and, of course, a white turban.

The painting is technically brilliant with superb attention to detail – consider, for instance, the roughness of the skin at the knees, the slenderness of the fingers of the hands, the rendering of the beads in the rosary, each shrivelled and varying in size, above all, the virtuoso treatment of the face with its noble lines of age and experience. But the painting goes far beyond brilliance of technique and finish. Abul Hasan seems here to impart to this isolated figure of an unknown old man a universality of feeling, turning the seeing of it into an experience even for the most casual viewer. It is nearly perfectly thought out and meanings are hinted at, allusions created. That vast uncharted area of darkness behind is not without significance, nor is the delicately rendered flowering plant in the foreground a mere decorative detail. It is of age that Abul Hasan speaks here, but also of renewal.

Abul Hasan's powers of observation and interest in a face like this holy man's puts one in mind of his patron, the Emperor Jahangir, who speaks in his memoirs of one of his intimate attendants, Inayat Khan, whose portrait as a dying man is one of the finest Mughal works to have survived. In this very context, he refers to painters "striving much in drawing an emaciated face." When he saw Inayat Khan, who was addicted to opium and had become exceedingly low and weak, he writes: "...yet I have never seen anything like this, nor even approaching to it. Good God, can a son of man come to such a shape and fashion? These two couplets of the *ustad* occurred as appropriate:

"If my shadow do not hold my leg
I shall not be able to stand till the Resurrection
Nor, from weakness, does my soul see a refuge
Where it may for a while rest on my lips.

"As it was a very extraordinary case I directed painters to take his portrait... Next day he travelled the road of non-existence."

Publ.: Brown, 1924, no. 17; Goetz, 1958, no. 4; Robinson, 1976, no. 93; A. Welch, S.C. Welch, 1982, no. 68; Falk, 1985, no. 140.

88   Sadi in conversation with Hindu priests

Folio (78b) from the same *Kulliyat* of Sadi as no.12
Inscribed to Dharamdas
24 x 13.2 cm; page: 41.7 x 26.4 cm
Akbar-Jahangir period, 1600/05
Collection of Prince Sadruddin Aga Khan

The Persian poet's visit to the famed temple of Somnath in Western India is associated with a contest between him and the Hindu priests of that temple. In this, the Muslim *shaikh* has the better of the exchange, being able to expose the clever mechanical device by which the priests surreptitiously moved the idol in the temple to the astonishment of the devotees.

Dharamdas, the painter of this fine leaf, however, sharply alters the focus of the episode. His interest is to show the kind of earnest, spiritual argument that was so much in evidence in Mughal India, especially in the 16th century. It was not only at the highest level, in Emperor Akbar's presence, that keen philosophical debates were held between protagonists of different faiths. The times seem to have been astir with a spirit of enquiry in which everyone participated: Hindus and Muslims, Jainas and Zoroastrians, Christians and Buddhists. The point of Sadi's tale, as interpreted by the painter, is somewhat blunted, for no superiority of any kind is established. Here the atmosphere is one of equal but deeply involved exchange: the *shaikh* gesticulates with his right hand while he holds a text in his left; the Hindu priest facing him refers to the scripture in front of him. They both seem to hold their own, utterly self-possessed, for each thinks he is the one that knows. Of equal interest to the painter are the other characters in the scene: the devout disciple with the *chauri*-fly-whisk; the acolytes carrying peacock tail fans; the priest's assistant looking like his double-image; the young female devotee; the sage-like, bearded old man who seems to know it all but does not participate in the debate. Attention is paid to the finely etched, dark-skinned wandering ascetic who arrives at the door of the shrine and to the attendants who move up and down. The whole setting has little to do with the Somnath temple and architecturally a major liberty has been taken by the painter: the outer wall is more reminiscent of a *dargah* or Muslim shrine rather than a Hindu temple. But all this is not of much consequence from the painter's point of view. He establishes the essentials of a sacred Hindu atmosphere, domed temple with its fluttering pennants and a stately *banyan*-tree. But then he moves on to his dominant concern: the animation of argument, that collision of two minds which one sees in the figures of the *shaikh* and the priest.

Dharamdas, the painter whose name is inscribed at the bottom of the page, was only one of the many painters involved in the production of this fine manuscript. Interestingly, a drawing, like a first sketch, of this very scene has also survived (Sotheby's, July 9, 1979, no.75). Only minor changes have been introduced in the finished painting, such as the female devotee and the young mendicant now looking towards the viewer (curiously reminiscent of the way in which self-portraits in European painting are introduced).

Publ.: A. Welch, S.C. Welch, 1982, no. 64; Falk, 1985, no. 134.

89 "In the desolate land of love"

Tinted drawing mounted as an album page
21.3 x 12.7 cm; page: 40.5 x 30.5 cm
Shahjahan period, c. 1630
Rietberg Museum, Zurich
(Alice Boner Bequest)

From among the many episodes of the tragic romance of Laila, 'beautiful as the dark night', and Majnun, that quintessential tale of tragic love in Persian literature, the painters often rendered Majnun in the company of wild animals, a scene meant to interpret the hapless lover's desolate state. Betrayed by fate, mocked by all and sundry, crazed by the loss of his love, Majnun renouces the world and takes to the wilderness. Emaciated and unkempt, there he lives all by himself, all hope 'extinguished like a flame'. With his mind in this state, he neither fears nor expects anything. In this heartless setting, wild animals gather around him, for no human company seems to be fit anymore for 'the mad one'.

The way the Mughal painter laid out this scene – and he did this quite often –, he bent to his own use the considerable repertoire of animal drawings and paintings that he had acquired by this time. Lions and leopards, rhinoceros and buffaloes, horses and wild asses, antelopes and mountain goats and deer and ducks, were all inhabitants of a world that he knew all too well. These denizens of the forest he could draw upon in a variety of situations, in hunting scenes, in depictions of Noah's ark, or of the court of Solomon, for instance. There is also little doubt that tracings or pounces with single figures of animals or pairs were freely in use. But what he made of these depended evidently on his understanding of a context, or his involvement in a theme.

Here, after rendering the bony, tragedy-wracked figure of Majnun in the very heart of the work, he sets about establishing a setting through his depiction of rocky formations, a few trees, some running water, a vignette of a distant town in the top right hand corner. But then he manipulates this conventional format and uses its various elements to underscore the mood of the work. The mountain goats that gaze at each other across ledges on the rocks, the marked expanse of bareness in the greater part of the painting, the isolation of the tree, all serve the theme of the drawing well. But what greatly enhances the mood is the manner in which the painter renders the various animals, emaciated as Majnun himself. One sees this markedly on the bodies of the rhinoceroses, whose thick hide hangs loosely on their frames, of the horses that are reminiscent of those shrunken creatures that one finds in some sensitive Mughal drawings, in the hungry-looking lioness who crouches despondently, its rib-cage prominently shown. Even the leopard and the tiger who nestle close to Majnun are not fleshed out as they ordinarily are in many another

painting. Unlike in other versions of this theme, not every animal sits looking at the skeleton-like figure of Majnun, for some of them wade towards water and others lie panting; but those that do, wear expressions that show a mixture of puzzlement and sympathy. Because for them, as for the viewer, Majnun is a bare breath away from his end, his devastated face and body a study in pain and despair.

A large number of Mughal paintings representing 'Majnun in the wilderness' have survived, one rather similar one in the National Museum, New Delhi, dated 1614 (Goswamy, 1986, no. 100).

Unpublished.

90 Two saintly men in a landscape

Tinted drawing mounted as an album page
Inscribed with a painter's name, possibly Anup Chattar
7.1 x 8.1 cm; page: 34.3 x 22.4 cm
Shahjahan period, c. 1640
Private Collection

The life of the mind is the subject of this small but intense work. The two holy men seated here face to face, both of them Hindus, are seen by the painter as being two entirely different characters. The older of the two, the *sadhu* with long matted hair and a full beard, seated wrapped up in a coarse sheet with his knees hunched up, one hand holding a rosary resting lightly against them, has on his face a certain peace, the air of one who has been able to resolve the conflicts within himself. A marked feeling of relaxation belongs to him as he lightly leans back against the trunk of a tree; one can visualise a visitor, a devotee, drawing solace from the very fact of being near him. The younger *sadhu,* on the other hand, his head and beard shaved clean, and a plain sheet wrapped lightly around his body, sits more alertly, his legs crossed, the back straight, gaze fixed directly in front, hands open but held as if involuntarily pressed against the body. The air about this figure is far from relaxed: the keenness of look in the eye suggests involvement, passion, almost an eagerness to pronounce judgments and take sides. One can see him as being possessed of a quick temper, the kind of irascible *sannyasi* that stories are current about. He, like the other *sadhu,* has also clearly left the world behind, but this is viewed by him as an achievement, something that brings a glint of hauteur to his eyes.

The relationship between him and the older *sadhu* is not easy to perceive: it is unlikely that they are *guru* and disciple, or holy men of different orders who come together to discuss issues of philosophy; at the same time theirs seems to be more than simply a chance encounter in the wilderness.

There is much refinement in the manner in which the painter approaches the subject. The display of sheer technical skill is remarkable, and details are deftly handled. The quality of line is seen at its best in the treatment of the faces and hands and in the fineness with which hair is rendered. Apart from this, textures and shapes are sensitively realised, as seen in the coarse wrap of the older *sadhu,* the fan of peacock feathers that lies by his side, and the stick meant to be placed under the armpit that belongs to the younger one. But of an altogether superior order is the painter's decision to place the characters in the open against a vista that stretches far into the distance, and to leave colour mostly out of the work. It is as if, through these decisions, he hints at a different kind of space that the two figures inhabit and makes at the same time a reference to these men having bleached all colour of attachment from their own lives. The work, for all its smallness of size, perhaps because of it, is curiously moving.

The elaborate panels of illumination that have been used to 'enlarge' the small work do it little justice. They are obviously unrelated (originally meant for a vertical painting) and have been used here to turn the tiny study into a regular album page.

The minute writing on the drawing is not easy to read, but it possibly contains the name of the Shahjahan period painter, Anup Chattar.

Unpublished.

91 Two Rajputs visiting a recluse

Single leaf mounted as an album page
21.1 x 14.1 cm; page: 36.4 x 24.1 cm
Aurangzeb period, c. 1660
Rietberg Museum, Zurich
(Acquisition funded by Barbara and Eberhard Fischer)

The need to get away from it all – the glitter and the gore, the noise and the tumult that made up life in Mughal India – must have overtaken many who were in the heart of the action themselves. When Akbar walks bare-foot to the shrine of Khwaja Salim Chishti, or Jahangir seeks out the Hindu *sannyasi,* Jadrup, and spends time in his company; or, when Dara Shukoh engages in philosophical discussions with holy men of various descriptions, including Baba Lal, one senses this rising need within men to whose hems the dust of the world clung all too persistently. Paying homage to holy men must at least in part have been an act of politics, but it could not have been that alone. One perceives this quite clearly in paintings that leave out all pomp and show the quiet, eager coming together of men who are in search of an inner peace and those who seem to have found it.

The setting here is exceedingly simple: a small hut with a thatched roof and a unostentatious terrace on the bank of a river, far from the other side where life lives out its normal course. Here lives a recluse, surprisingly young of years, with a female companion, also a recluse, both of them wearing ochre-coloured simple clothes and necklaces of small *tulsi*-beads that characterise Hindu ascetics of the Vaishnava order. The man smokes a simple hookah-waterpipe and by his side on the floor lie small objects: a water ewer, a pair of tongs for coal embers, two bowls, a fan of peacock feathers. Belonging to him or to his companion is an arm-rest, and yet another water vessel. A quiet conversation seems to be in progress with two men dressed as Rajput princes who have come to visit; the younger of whom, more richly dressed than the other, holds his left hand gently forward to betoken his being engaged in talking. The other man, older and more soldier-like, sits up alertly, his large shield resting in his lap, and his eyes fixed on the holy man.

The youthful look of the recluse and the fact that in his clothing is still visible a trace of his connection with the world – a little glint of jewellery, an upper garment cut like a *jama* – raise the suggestion that the recluse might have once been a prince who decided to turn his back upon the world. The men visiting him might well come from the same family or at least from the same background. But this can only remain a speculation. Whatever be the subject of the conversation here between the two visitors and the recluse and his companion, there is an extraordinary sense of peace in the painting. One especially notices this on the faces of the recluses which are touched by remark-able softness. The face of the woman-ascetic is particularly subtly treated, for it shows not wisdom but an inner contentment, a refusal to be drawn into the matters of the world even as her companion fixes the visitors with a gentle gaze and listens with quiet intentness. The painting is possessed of marked delicacy, alike in its soft finish and in the mood that it captures: a juxtaposition of those that are caught up in the snares of the world and those who seem to have broken free of them.

An inscription in Urdu on the reverse identifies the scene as *"Raja Chhattar Singh visiting Guru Nanak,* and goes into some detail of identification, stating that the persons dressed in ochre robes are Guru Nanak and his sister Nanaki, and that Guru Nanak is a Khattri Bedi by caste. This however has to be disregarded, for Guru Nanak would not be shown smoking a hookah, and there is little else to connect this painting with him. The inscription is evidently of the 19th century. Another brief note on the back mentions the names of Sayyid Muhammad Kazim Hussain *urf* ('also known as') Nawab Bahadur, and Sayyid Kasim Abbasi. It seems as if the painting exchanged hands in February 1913, the date mentioned in a pencilled note. The painting was acquired in Paris in 1986.

Unpublished.

Single leaf mounted as an album page
29 x 19.1 cm
Aurangzeb period, c.1660
Private Collection

With that blend of candour and bitterness that is so characteristic of him, Badauni, the author of the *Muntakhab-ul Tawarikh,* opens the third part of his work by stating that he has no interest in an account of the "nobles of the realm" of his own times. Therefore he says: "I will refrain from polluting the nib of my pen with a description of such worthless wretches, and will commence with the enumeration of some of the holy men of the age, for an account of noble men who have chosen the way of God is in every way to be preferred to an account of scoundrels and debauchees."

Badauni goes on in this strain, speaking of some remarkable men whom he knew or knew about, all belonging to the period of Akbar. But, as he says, now, "for the most part, they have withdrawn, as the *anqqa* retires to the mountains of Qaf, to the neighbourhood of the great God. It is as though they had all conspired together to roll up and remove the baggage from this dwelling of care and deceit and to take up their reward in the home of joy and bliss." But his memories of these holy men seem to be remarkably sharp: he speaks in some detail of their withdrawal from the world, of finding pleasure only in the company of others equally devoted to God, or in giving instruction to those who showed any promise of recognizing the true path and setting out on it. These include accounts of exceedingly weak and feeble men who would lie all day long not able to move, and yet rise up without anybody's assistance, put on their shoes, perform ceremonial ablutions and stand, the moment a call for prayer was heard; men for whom the sound of a holy song felt as if "a violent wind had risen, and was blowing through a fiery tempest"; whose utterances "would turn flint into wax". He also speaks of many a *shaikh* admitting with the greatest reluctance someone to the ranks of their disciples: then, once granted the privilege of admission, the newcomer had to commit texts to memory, would receive "the cap and the tree", the latter meaning a genealogical tree going back to the time of Muhammad that was formally drawn up each time, and remained with the disciple who thus became a *murid.*

The painter of this quiet, somewhat withdrawn work, catches some of the spirit of spiritual animation that belonged to gatherings of the kind that Badauni speaks of with such vividness. The setting is somewhere 'far away', on the bank of a river, in a simple unostentatious structure; the time is night; the company consists of two white-bearded old men, both *shaikhs,* and between them a young man dressed so as to suggest that

93 *Sufis* and *Mullas* in conversation

Single leaf mounted as an album page
26 x 15.5 cm; page: 43.6 x 34.3 cm
Aurangzeb period, c. 1670
Collection of Prince Sadruddin Aga Khan

he still has ties with the outside world. While these three share a simple carpet, two other men, one on either side, look intently upon the three-some. The remarkably well-drawn bare-headed old man in red holds a book from which he recites something that the young disciple is about to write down on a rolled up sheet: he is already dipping his pen into an ink pot and the instruments of writing are by his side. The other *shaikh,* in a large turban, grey-bearded and wearing a striped yellow and black gown, sits watching, a small fly-whisk lightly held in his left hand. The two other persons looking on seem to occupy a lesser rank, and perhaps are visitors drawn to the expounding learned man. The person at the right, with a musical instrument prominently placed next to him, is dressed in a worldly fashion and is a Muslim; the person at the left, in robes that are suggestive of ochre, is possibly a Hindu: by his side lies an armrest on the floor and a bunch of peacock feathers. Prominently placed in the middle are two trays full of fruit, obviously offerings brought to the holy man whose simple abode this is.

Some late additions to the painting, like the boat on the river, the elaborate clouds in the sky and the slightly awkward wall at the left, distract somewhat, but not enough to take away from the intense atmosphere of concern with inner meaning that the painting suggests. There is delicacy in detail and the colouring is precise: the pink and black stripes of the underrug, the texture of the peacock feathers, the seemingly careless curl of the rosary, the 'night effect' with an occasional cast shadow from the candle are not to be missed. But the focus rightly remains not on these but on what is going on in this gathering.

An inscription in a minute hand at the very bottom of the painting states this to be the work of "the humblest, Abd-al Samad". If it is Khwaja Abd-al Samad of Shiraz, the famous Akbari master who is meant by this, the inscription has to be completely discounted, for the painting is much later in date. The likelihood of there being another painter by the same name as the Shiraz master cannot, however, be ruled out.

Unpublished.

Eight learned men, each of them seen clearly as an individual and not belonging to a type, sit on a marbled terrace on which is spread a coarse but beautifully patterned mat. Two of them hold books; others fold their hands in their laps; still others make gentle gestures as if emphasizing a point. A discussion is in progress: ideas, philosophical or mystical, are being exchanged; some finer points possibly need to be looked up in books. No one is specifically seeking instruction or enlightenment from another; it is as if they are all collectively engaged in a search, each bringing his own experience and perceptions to this gathering. These saintly Muslim characters are seen by the painter as differing quite sharply from each other: some of them deeply introspective like the bare-headed man in a coarse shawl at the bottom left; others eager to participate in a discussion, like the man holding the book at the edge of the group at the right. The principal exchange seems to be going on between the *mulla* who has his arms covered by the long *dervish*-like sleeves of his garment, and the slightly older man who sits with his knees hunched up and his hands lightly crossed against them.

As if to emphasize the fact that they have removed themselves from the world, from the company of ordinary men at least, the painter provides an idyllic setting in the background, a stylised, sharply rising hill from which a waterfall cascades down into a lake. Perhaps the idea is to suggest some place in Kashmir which certainly was highly favoured among men of God who wanted to be by themselves or in communion with God through the beauties of His nature. In the foreground, at the very bottom of the page, a beautifully painted panel of lotuses further emphasizes the Kashmir setting. The stylisation of the grassy hill with its body of water in the background is in marked contrast to the sharp observation with which the holy men are rendered.

A little like those groups of royal and princely personages belonging to different generations who were brought into the same painting, the painters frequently showed holy men of different persuasions and times, sometimes within the same frame. These served as visual reminders of the learning that once existed or as auspicious 'presences' that a viewer liked to surround himself with. Also characteristic of some Mughal paintings of holy men in conversation, is that some figures, although seemingly very sharply observed, were taken out of one setting and incorporated into another so convincingly that they seemed to have always belonged to that group. The figures

we see here, however, are not identified through any inscriptions, and it is not easy to make out if, despite their strong differentiation, they too come from a finely established repertoire of saintly figures developed by the painter.

This painting is strikingly close to another of a group of six holy men in conversation, now in the Berlin Museum. The figures in the Berlin painting are different, even though they are all men belonging to one or the other of the holy orders; but the setting is nearly identical: the water reservoir, the waterfall, the rocks in the background, the identically patterned mat, the narrow panel with blooming lotuses in the foreground. The treatment of the hills and the waterfall is slightly different, but there can be little doubt that there is a connection between the two works. Linda Leach (1986:128) has recently suggested that the present work was possibly done in Kashmir in c. 1650 where Zafar Khan, "an intimate companion of *sufis* and poets", maintained an atelier and offered serious patronage to painters, poets, and calligraphers.

Publ.: Leach, 1986, no. 6.

Chronological Framework

94 Rustam and the "Seven Champions" hunting

Folio (135v) of Shah Tahmasp's *Shahnama*, mounted as an album page
Ascribed to Mir Sayyid Ali of Tabriz
47 x 31.8 cm
Iran, c. 1530
Private Collection

The inexpressibly refined Persian work which this folio represents stands at one end of the chronological framework within which Mughal painting can be viewed. The leaf has been attributed by Dickson and Welch (1981:no.96) to Mir Sayyid Ali of Tabriz, one of the master painters who had joined Humayun's service before his return to India from Persia and Kabul in 1555. One knows about the Mir, who was also a distinguished poet, having been placed as a master in charge of the newly forming Mughal workshops of painting, but there is no clearly 'Indian' work in his hand that seems to have survived. One can only sense the hand of this master, upon whom in the words of Abul Fazl 'the ray of royal favour had shone', behind many a painting enterprise in India, including the great *Hamzanama*.

In this very Persian page, a certain boldness, a wish to innovate, is clearly visible. There is that exquisite delicacy that one associates with fine Persian work in the lower half of the painting, where Rustam himself slays a lion and his companions cut down boars with their swords and arrows. But, a little above, the manner in which the rocks are treated with an altogether different kind of amplitude, the foreshortening in the treatment of the horse in the middle of the painting, and the rhythmic movement in the figure of the leopard as it descends from the rocks to move towards the galloping horseman, contain a somewhat different flavour. It is as if between the 'Chinese' clouds at the top and the delicate Persian floral landscape at the bottom, new possibilities were being explored by the artist. There is, of course, precision and naturalism of detail, but there seems to be an urge also to 'open' the leaf out, to let the people in it breathe a somewhat different air.

Publ.: Dickson, Welch, 1981, no. 96; Falk, 1985, no. 50.

95 Amir Hamza escapes from prison

Folio on cotton from a dispersed *Hamzanama*-manuscript
64.5 x 46 cm; page: 72 x 57 cm
Akbar period, 1562/77
Private Collection

The turmoil and energy that seem to run through this and so many other *Hamzanama* folios, must have reflected on the one hand the prodigious military effort through which the Mughal empire was being consolidated by the Emperor Akbar and his generals and, on the other, the excitement of activity in the painting workshops where great new enterprises were set in motion. Little dated material from the first twenty years of the Akbar period is available but, the Cleveland *Tutinama* apart, the *Hamzanama* was easily the most ambitious of imperial painting projects. In the face of slightly conflicting evidence, it is not easy to determine exactly how many years this project took, but if, as is widely believed, it was between 1562 and 1577 that this extraordinary work was executed, the decidedly 'early' look of the folios of the *Hamzanama* becomes easy to understand.

The fusion of diverse stylistic elements in these large folios remains quite constant, even if the quality of the work seems to vary a great deal. There is a certain ease with which Persian plants and rocks and an occasional 'Chinese' cloud commingle with full-bosomed Hindu women, and aerially viewed water channels in these pages. Apart from the winged fairies and delightfully variegated demons who belong to the world of imagination, the painters seem to bring in a great deal of what they must have observed around them, like the small encampment that is being destroyed by rocks and boulders showered on it from the air by angry beings. There is shrewd, sharp observation in several details: one does not miss the long, tangled strip of cotton that must have been made into an Akbari-style turban and now lies close to the fallen warrior in the bottom left corner; the cloth curtain walls being rolled up; or the decorative curving dragonheads with attached yak-tails that form a part of the structure, one of them in the process of falling to the ground, hit by a rock.

But, even as regards factual information, there are surprises in this folio. On either vertical edge, a little removed from the painted surface, are inscriptions in a rough and somewhat incorrect *devanagari* script. These are not easy to read, but their presence reinforces the Hindu contribution to the work. At the same time, one should notice the flowing garments of the two winged fairies leading the group at the top to see how much of a 'European' element they represent at this early date, for in weight and texture the treatment of these garments is quite different from that ordinarily seen in the Persian or the Rajput tradition.

Publ.: Falk, 1979, no. 11; Falk, 1985, no. 119.

Double-sided illustrated folio from the Chester Beatty-*Tutinama*
96   17.1 x 12.5 cm; page: 25.5 x 16.5 cm
97   19.1 x 14.1 cm; page: 25.5 x 16.5 cm
Akbar period, c. 1580
Rietberg Museum, Zurich

In the well-established format of the *Tuti-nama,* that classic of its kind in the category of boxed stories, the Tuti or the parrot tells the lady over whom he is keeping an artful watch yet another story on the fiftieth night. A king marries the daughter of a distant emperor, but she, out of fear, had not told him of her having had a son by an earlier marriage. Longing to see her son, she persuades the king to send for a gifted slave of her father's for he is a great knower of precious stones. The 'young slave' is none other than her son, and when he arrives, in the privacy of her own chamber, she embraces and kisses him, an act that is reported to the king who becomes suspicious and jealous and orders this 'slave' to be put to death. But a kind guard does not carry out the royal orders. Both husband and wife are now greatly troubled, the wife in the belief that her son has actually been killed, and the husband by his lingering doubts about the justness of his orders and the chastity of his wife. Advised by a clever woman of the royal household, the wife adopts a ruse and feigns to sleep while the king, under the same old lady's advice, places a magic talisman on her chest which will make her utter her thoughts candidly in her sleep. The wife is in fact awake, and she makes a statement which clarifies all the facts of the case. The king is deeply distressed, but the situation is saved by the guard who discloses that the son is not really killed. The son is finally brought; mother and son are united, and the king's conscience is cleared of nagging guilt.

The elements of the story are carefully sifted and presented with the usual directness by the painter in this fine, double-sided folio. The wife pretends to be asleep and the king stealthily places the talisman on her chest. Again the drama of the reunion and the feeling of great relief on the king's part are communicated with quiet ease. At the same time, it is of interest to see how the painter establishes two different settings and episodes of the same story: the bed-chamber of the queen is provided with elaborate, billowing curtains tied to the pillars, while the modest court of the king has a far more open and public look; both the queen and the king are dressed slightly differently from one scene to the other: she wears a *choli* and a *sari* while at rest, but a formal court dress in public; and he, dressed in a yellow *jama* in the privacy of his bed chamber is devoid of that *sarpesh* in the turban that he prominently wears in court. To the king's dress the painter also adds the richness of the red of his *jama*, and a dagger is prominently tucked into his waistband, as would befit a ruler. Clearly, these details are metic-

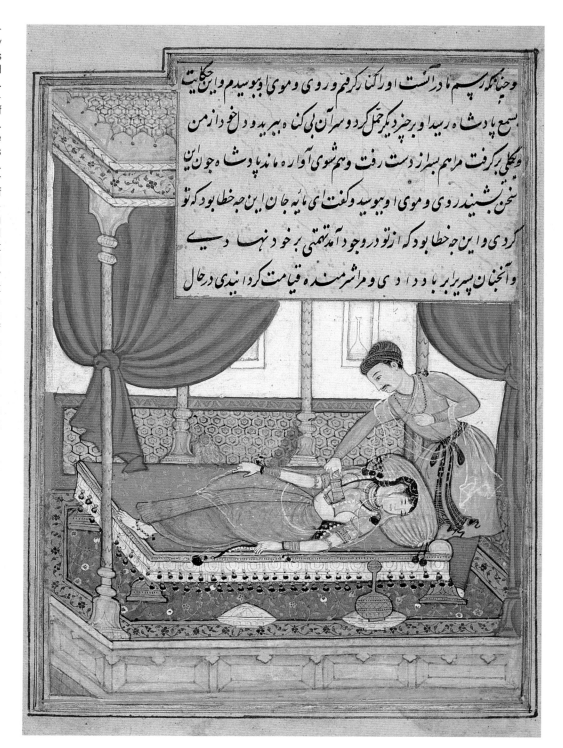

ulously thought out and brought in, in the interest of clarity.

Stylistic elements that help to identify the work as essentially 'Akbari' can be identified: the treatment of architecture with prominent use of hexagonal tiles and crenellation on the roof and the same kind of tiles in different colours on the back wall; the slender pillars, the brick wall, the dominant pink sandstone colouring in the architecture; the characteristic stances of the figures and their distribution over the space; in terms of appearances and dresses, the two-third profiles, the brief Akbari turbans, the relatively full-bosomed form of the queen, the long, slightly wavy ends of the waistband hanging in front, the transparent white scarves. And connecting this manuscript to so many others of this period, is the overall rich, warm colour scheme that is skilfully used to manipulate and establish space.

Publ.: McInerney, 1982, no. 3a, b.

98 The battle of Bilah

Folio from a *Baburnama*-manuscript
24.5 x 13.5 cm; page: 26.5 x 15.7 cm
Akbar period, c.1589
Collection of Prince Sadruddin Aga Khan

The action is bloody and tumultuous: the Emperor Babur arrives with his contingent at a small township in the Panjab, Bilah on the Sind. The 'villagers' take to their heels, cross the water in boats, some of them flinging themselves into the river, with Babur's men, "man and horse in mail", plunging in and crossing to the island to which the villagers escape. Some people are carried by the current; clothes and baggage are lost; one of Babur's men, Qul-i-Bayazid, "the taster", shows remarkable courage, for he single-handedly chases away a segment of the enemy's group, swimming "alone, bare on a bare-backed horse, no one behind him."

As we see it on this spirited page, only a part of the action is laid out, for this is apparently the right half of a double-page illustration of the episode. Things are not seen with excessive clarity, but this is of the essence of pitched engagements: there is courage and chivalry and bloodshed, but also an enormous amount of panic and confusion. What the designer and the painter of this page do is first to establish the setting clearly: a walled city in the background, a large, torrential river, an island-like stretch of land, boats that 'the villagers' use for escape. But all this simply sets the stage for the enormous energy that is seen in the action with which the page pulsates. As cannon fire from the city walls and arrows whistle about in the air, men and horses advance, the boats turn and capsize, people are flung into the river or jump out of fear. The bodies are disposed in an incredible variety of positions and angles, gestures and stances communicating determination, doubt, or sheer mounting panic.

As in so many paintings showing battles of this nature – not necessarily grand actions, but small engagements that are all too tense and real – the viewer is drawn into the very vortex of this tumult. This is true not only of this *Baburnama,* most of which is in the Victoria and Albert Museum in London, or the other *Baburnama*-manuscripts which follow a fairly well-established illustrative programme, but of so many of the Akbar period manuscripts dealing with history and chronicle. In paintings from later reigns, frenzied action is also repeatedly seen – sometimes it is on a grand scale – but the view tends to be taken from a slight distance, or large battle-fields with countless little figures of men and horses and elephants are rendered in the far distance while generals are painted prominently in the foreground. But the feeling that belongs to these pages in the Akbar period is never really captured again, for here the viewer seems to be grabbed and pushed into the heart of the mêlée himself.

Ellen Smart has recently pointed out that the left half of this double-page illustration is now in a private collection in Philadelphia (see Kramrisch, 1986, no. 11, footnote p. 156).

Publ.: Sotheby's, July 13, 1971, no. 132.

99 Moses learns a sad lesson

Folio from the same *Kulliyat* of Sadi as no. 12
28.2 x 15.6 cm; page: 41.7 x 26.4 cm
Akbar-Jahangir period, 1600/05
Collection of Prince Sadruddin Aga Khan

When Sadi expands upon the virtues of contentment in the third chapter of his *Gulistan,* he approaches the subject from varying angles, weaving tales and anecdotes that show the pattern of his thought clearly. The text of this page begins with a continuation of tale 14 in which Hatim, whose generosity is a legend in the Islamic world, admires the self-discipline and contentment of a simple wood-cutter who declines to attend his feast. This is followed by the next story in which the prophet Moses figures. Here Sadi speaks of an indigent, derelict man who, too poor to cover his own nakedness, had half-buried himself in the sand. Seeing Moses pass by, he begged him to pray for him so that he comes into some means of subsistence. Moses offers such a prayer on the poor man's behalf, and walks off. But sometime later he chances upon the same man, this time being led, hands tied, by a guard. On enquiring he learns that this man had come into wealth; however he misconducted himself, became drunk and killed a man and was now under orders of being beheaded. The brief tale ends with Moses seeking the forgiveness of God for having rashly prayed for the conferment of bounties upon that man, for he was obviously unworthy, and Moses had not served him well by wishing riches upon him. The man's nature was such that he could not have contained himself. A verse follows:

"The base man, when rank, and silver, and gold come to him, his head really needs a buffet.
Hast Thou not heard what a wise man said? 'An ant is always best when it has no wings.'"

It is only when one knows the context that the situation in the painting comes within reach: then one sees the wretched man, clad in fine muslin but his hands tied, being led away by a firm-footed guard; one also notices the detail of the king's functionary following close behind, carrying a hatchet, obviously meant for beheading. The prophet, looking much like a contemporary *shaikh,* but nimbate, is followed by a younger person, reminiscent of the manner in which young Joseph is often rendered. The hand of Moses is raised in a gesture of conversation, but possibly also of making the point that the undeserving man should be left to his own fate, as the tale says.

The page, like the others in this manuscript, bears marks of great refinement. The details are precise: the tiny dark strip at the bottom, with some scattered rocks; the very delicately coloured ground in pink and mauve with little tufts of grass; the fine tree with prominent birds; the range of bare 'Persian' rocks, and the telescoped view of a walled, architectural complex surrounded by a moat across which a secure bridge is built. Here the painter does not follow the cliché of showing the faint outline of a Flemish-looking city in the distance, but paints a massive, solid-looking structure touched by gold on its gateway, its crenellations and domes. This area is viewed from above eye level so as to reveal much of its interior. But untypically, there is no living creature present, neither in that 'city', nor anywhere in the background, neither man nor animal except a pair of magpies. This detail is clearly deliberate although its meaning eludes us, unless it be that the city hints at the desolate state of mind of the wretch who is being taken to be beheaded.

Unpublished.

پشته فراهم آورده کنم مهمانی حاتم چراپژوی کف خلقتی بر بساط او کرده آمده اند کفت مردم نان زعل خویش خورد

منت حاتم طایی برد حاتم انصاف داد که من اورا همت وجوانمردی از خود بتر دیدم حکایت موسی علیه السلام

درویشی را دید از برهنگی در ریک پنهان شده کفت یا موسی عاکن یا خدای تعالی مرگ خفتنی میبید موسی مرا بید موسی بخدای تعالی او را نعمتی بداد پس تا خشدوز

100 A presentation scene

Tinted brush drawing mounted as an album page
15.2 x 10.8 cm
Jahangir period, c. 1620
Private Collection

With conscious effort and taking this as some kind of challenge, a European scene is placed in an Indian setting in this sensitive drawing. The subject is not easily identifiable, but all four women are clearly meant to be seen as Europeans, not only by the ample robes that swirl and billow around them and the kind of round-necked, tight-fitting jackets that they wear, but also by their features, especially their long, flowing locks. A few objects prominently seen in the drawing are also European: the curious fluted throne-like seat on which the principal personage lightly perches, the little footstool on which the woman holding an open book in her hands rests her left foot, the ink-pot and the quill. These details are exotic and alien. The chamber visible behind the women, however, has a more Indian look even if the shading, the depth, the clearly defined angle of vision, the curtain gathered at the side, also show European influence. But then, far at the back, the group of trees is completely Mughal, both in the tree types and the treatment the painter accords them. Likewise the objects placed in the foreground – the fruit in a tray, a water-ewer with a human face, a deep metallic bowl – come from nearer home. A keen-looking dog with a furry tail, and a cat that looks like a miniature tiger licking its paw, seem to be at home here even though they are taken from a distant source.

The artist here is clearly preoccupied with details which permit him to show off his skill. The most obvious thing for him to do is to capture the weight and the texture of the garments, through their many folds and curves and repetitive shaded areas that give them a life of their own. But he goes considerably beyond this, even in the figures of the 'European' ladies. Their fingers are elegantly held and sensitively drawn. Their feet with the curvature of the toes, and especially the slight turn of the big toe away from the others, reveal the painter's painstaking commitment to detail. Again the meticulous care with which the painter shows us both hands of the child carried by the woman on the left, and the manner in which its left leg comes out of the crook of her arm and dangles against her side, speaks for the kind of concerns that the painter gave thought to. He seems to be so completely wrapped up in all this, that he makes virtually no attempt at communicating any specific feeling: the work is grave and highly finished, but lacking in warmth, except for the feel of the texture of life in the two animals.

Interest in European themes at the Mughal court starts with a genuine, deep curiosity not only for exotic subjects but for other ways of seeing and making things; this seems to give way slowly to European-inspired works or copies, turning into a vogue in the early 17th century, for they were signs of an eclectic taste, demonstrable proof of expanded awareness and challenge to a painter's skill. But as the 17th century advances, the wave begins to ebb. It does not die and some of what it had brought with it stays, but interest decidedly shifts away from it.

S.C. Welch has attributed this drawing to Manohar, Basawan's son. He also suggests that like another drawing in the Gulistan Library in Teheran, this one derives from engravings "of the circle of Marcantonio Raimondi." As it is now, the drawing has been mounted as an album page, with floral gold and blue borders into which are integrated unrelated little panels of calligraphy.

Publ.: S.C. Welch, 1963, no. 11.

101 Grandees at the court of Shahjahan

Fragment of an illustrated folio from the *Padshahnama* (*Shahjahan-nama*)
24.7 x 17.5 cm
Shahjahan period, c. 1640
Rietberg Museum, Zurich
(Acquisition funded by the Volkart-Foundation, Winterthur)

The imperial copy of the *Padshahnama,* also referred to sometimes as the *Shahjahan-nama,* is generally considered the last of the great Mughal manuscripts. Most of the work, with forty-four surviving paintings still forming part of it, is in the Royal Library at Windsor Castle, but a number of its leaves were separated from it at an early point in time and are dispersed. The present painting seems to be part of a large, double-page composition of the kind that one comes upon so often in the *Padshahnama.* One can visualise this being a continuation of a royal *darbar* or levee, in which the emperor himself must have been painted on the right side, and this group of grandees, respectfully standing at a distance, facing in his direction. A lavishly caparisoned elephant with a younger one appear at the left, the *mahout* of the larger elephant bending his head and raising his hand in obeisance. Like the elephants, horses have been led into the courtyard of the palace. One of them is held by its reins by a groom who, like everyone else, looks towards the right where the emperor in the complete painting would be, seated in all his majesty.

Large groups like these figure frequently in Shahjahan-period works: the levee might have gathered for a specific grand occasion, but even if this were not so, the intention behind paintings on such a scale is to show the sheer grandeur of the court. In a similar, more complete painting, the groups can be easily identified as representing the various sections and levels of those whose attendance upon the emperor was *de rigueur:* princes, grandees, ambassadors, governors from the provinces, lesser functionaries, musicians, singers and dancers, *mahouts* and grooms and the like. One has only to read a contemporary or near-contemporary account like that of Bernier to gain some idea of how grand and lavish these *darbars* were.

An obvious concern of the painter here is to render, in the group of grandees, as large a variety as possible of *types* of men: their appearances, the manner in which they wear their turbans, beards and mustaches and their dresses. Even if these notables are unidentified by inscriptions – unlike many in Jahangir-period paintings – there is little doubt that the painter captures here likenesses of people whose origins can be traced to Iran and Khurasan, to central Asia, or to different parts of India, including the Deccan and the many Rajput courts of Rajasthan.

The emphasis of most paintings in the *Padshahnama* being on grandeur – *darbars,*

battles, processions and state occasions – there is relatively little warmth in the portraits. There is also not enough spontaneity, for groups seem to be predetermined and arranged so as to make a collective impact. But the technique and the ease with which different figures are handled, are singularly impressive. As Losty (1982:100) says: "These pages in the *Padshahnama* along with some of the pages of Shahjahan albums are technically the most brilliant of all Mughal paintings, building directly on the advancement in technique made possible by Jahangir. No longer is there even the slightest clash between the disparate European and Indian elements which can create such unintended tension to a European viewer..."

The identification of some dispersed paintings from the *Padshahnama* in the Windsor Castle Library presents several problems. Begley (1986) draws attention to some of these prickly, unresolved issues.

Publ.: Brinker, Fischer, 1980, no. 16.

102 Portrait of a standing prince

Single leaf on uncoloured ground, mounted as an album page
17.5 x 9.4 cm; page: 36.3 x 24.8 cm
Aurangzeb period, c.1675
Private Collection

The dress is relatively simple but elegant, much like the painting itself. The prince stands wearing a white *jama* over gold-flowered tight-fitting *pyjamas;* but most of the colour in the painting comes from the maroon and gold turban, the finely detailed *patka*-waistband with a dainty, brocaded floral pattern, and the green coloured shoes, as well as from the occasional detail of jewellery, an aigrette stuck in the turban, and a dagger in the sash. The prince's hands rest lightly on the hilt of a straight, uncommonly long sword.

There is much in this precisely rendered, elegant looking figure that brings it close to those technically brilliant studies of princes and grandees from the Shahjahan period. The control over the medium was so firm, and such the mastery of style attained by the Mughal painters by this time, that, for all their fine preciseness, portraits seem to have been turned out in large numbers with relative ease. In them, there is a certain loss of feeling and warmth compared to the earlier periods, but the achievement is still impressive and the paintings fit perfectly into the spirit of the age.

The present study comes very likely from the Aurangzeb period, for the shading, especially in the treatment of the dress, has that slight hardness which enters work done in this period. The turban which the prince wears here is still Shahjahani, not of the typical Aurangzeb type, as is the *patka;* but these things did survive from one reign at least into the early years of the next one. A brief inscription in Persian at the top identifies the figure as 'Muizuddin'. This was the name of the future Jahandar Shah, Aurangzeb's grandson, who sat on the throne for but a very brief period. But it is unlikely that the portrait is quite as late as Muizuddin's period. Clearly, under Aurangzeb, who is known to have been no great enthusiast for painting, competent work continued to be done, but quality was steadily declining, and the imperial atelier slowly dispersed only to be reassembled when there was a renewed spark under Muhammad Shah (ruled 1729–1748) in the 18th century.

The portrait is mounted on an album page of the kind that we associate with the Shahjahan period. There is an inner, gold-decorated border and a broad outer margin of finely executed flowering plants in colours and gold.

Copies of Mughal portraits, especially those of rulers and princes, were produced as a matter of routine at some Rajasthani courts, like Kishangarh and Bikaner. Work of the kind that this portrait represents appears to have been carried to Rajput centres where local painters produced whole sets of versions of these Mughal paintings.

Unpublished.

103 A royal elopement

Single leaf mounted as an album page
39 x 27 cm; page: 55 x 38.5 cm
Late Mughal, 1755/60
Rietberg Museum, Zurich

The scene is set at night, with the full moon seen prominently in the dark sky, and a dense sprinkling of stars. A ruler, no longer young in years, heavy in weight and nimbate, arrives on the back of an elephant in a garden next to a palace wall from where a princess, also seen nimbate, seems to be about to climb down as her companion holds her from behind to keep her steady; an old duenna helpfully balances a shallow tray with a light in it; from behind a door in the women's apartments, a lady peers out cautiously. Outside, the king is attended upon by women, one of whom holds a circular royal standard and two others keep guard, leaning on their long staffs. Seated on the elephant in front of the ruler and carrying a goad in his hand, is a young prince.

Persian inscriptions in a minute hand identify the three principal figures in the painting: the princess about to scale the balustrade and escape is identified as *'Nawab Zeenat Mahal'*; the ruler himself as *'Aziz-ud Din Padshah Alamgir Sani'* (Aziz-ud Din, the king, the second Alamgir), and the prince as *'Shah Alam'*, seen here at a young age. The episode is not easy to identify, but the king and the young prince are known figures, and it is not unlikely that the painting recalls an actual incident. Considering the power wielded by Mughal monarchs, it is hard to visualise a situation in which a royal elopement would be necessary – for the will of the rulers was virtually law in these matters – but there might well have been a real-life romantic episode to which the painting refers.

In the 18th century, painters at the Mughal court moved away from the concerns that the painters of the 16th and 17th centuries had had: royal splendour was still a favourite subject, as were hunting scenes and *darbars;* but what emerged as a clear favourite was the theme of love in romantic settings, often involving the representation of the ruler or clearly identifiable princes. Themes of this kind had always been part of Rajput work, but they were relatively new introductions at the Mughal court. This leaf is treated with a measure of competence, but does not possess the poetic quality that a Rajput painter working in his own setting might have brought to the subject. It also has passages that are slightly awkward and stiff, like the figure of the lady about to be lifted across and the rendering of the elephant. But it is clear that the painter is harking back to work that had elegant figures, spacious compositions and brilliantly contrived night effects.

The Mughal atelier in Delhi had, by this time, been reduced to a shadow of itself, and painters had obviously moved away, drawn by prospects of patronage elsewhere at centres like Oudh, Farrukhabad and Murshidabad, where work in the late Mughal style continued to be produced into the 19th century.

Publ.: Cran, 1980, no. 11.

104   Celebrations at the wedding of Dara Shukoh

Single leaf mounted as an album page
40 x 28 cm; page: 42.5 x 30.7 cm
Late Mughal work at Oudh, c.1760
Private Collection

The hero of this painting, the cynosure of all eyes, is Dara Shukoh, Shahjahan's eldest son and his great favourite. He arrives here as a bridegroom, riding a charger. The Emperor himself can be identified through the nimbus around his head but, following convention, even he rides slightly behind the bridegroom. Behind him, on horse-back, on foot or riding on elephants, is the throng of men and women who constitute the marriage party as it majestically moves towards the right where it is met by the bride's people. According to custom, not only men from the bride's party but also women come out of the house and stand in welcome, each of them eager to catch a glimpse of the handsome prince as his horse comes to a stop. The occasion is aglitter with a display of splendour and wealth on the bridegroom's side, the emperor and the prince himself the very picture of sumptuous elegance; the whole scene is lit up with lights that are scattered over the entire ground, torches and candles in golden stands and burning in large domed glass shades, of course, the spectacular display of fireworks in the distance. The party arrives with an enormous contingent of music-makers: large drums being played from the backs of elephants, and troops of women singers, all on elephant-back, seen at the very top. On the bride's side, there is a clear attempt to match the splendour of the royal party, even though the differences are immediately visible. But there is marked elegance in clothes and stances, and a troupe of performers including musicians and a boy-dancer strike the right notes of merriment. There is fine observation on the painter's part, for so much that belongs to an occasion like this is accurately caught: the entire formation of the marriage party with the bridegroom in front and his 'best man', also a prince, walking by his side; the prince's face behind a veil of strands of pearls, and even his horse decorated in a similar fashion; on the bride's side, the principal figure, the old man in a yellow floral *jama,* holding up his hand in surprise and admiration of the handsomeness of the prince; the group of women gazing at the prince and singing songs full of welcome and mild banter. This entire scene, in which 'night has been turned into day', is set off by the superb rendering of fireworks, inventive and brilliant in colour against a massive cloud of darkness in which golden blazes seem to be coming out of spirals of smoke that look like massive elephants seen frontally, as if in imitation of the real elephants close-by.

The event that the painting celebrates relates to the second quarter of the 17th century. But the painting was made more than

105 Bahadur Shah II, the last Mughal Emperor

Single leaf mounted as an album page
36.2 x 42.2 cm
Late Mughal, dated *Rabi al awwal, A.H. 1254* / 1838 A.D.
Private Collection

a century later, and was possibly produced not at the Mughal court in Delhi but at the provincial court of Oudh, where a major centre of local power had been established. Here, despite far slenderer resources, the *nawabs* not only endeavoured to rise up to the level of the great Mughals in splendour and luxury: their painters also harked back ever so often to Mughal models. Mughal works were copied regularly, and the Mughal manner of seeing and recording was sought to be preserved. It has been suggested that this scene is possibly a copy of an original in the *Padshahnama (Shahjahan-nama),* now lost. The original would certainly have figured prominently in the work, being a record of a royal event of the times of Shahjahan.

The imperial manuscript of the *Padshahnama* now in the Windsor Castle Library was, for some time, in Oudh: it bears the seals of Asafjah, *nawab* of Oudh. A nearly identical version of this painting, copied in Oudh as well, and now in the National Museum in New Delhi, was published by Carroll (1972:80).

Publ.: Falk, 1978, no. 36; Falk, 1985, no. 156.

The empire founded by Babur in 1526 had weakened appreciably in the early years of the 18th century, but a century later it was decidedly tottering and had all but disintegrated. Of Shah Alam II who ruled from 1759–1806, a rule nearly as long as that of Akbar or Aurangzeb, it was often jocularly stated in a doggerel, that the extent of the dominion of Shah Alam ('Lord of the world') was from Delhi to Palam – a distance of less than 20 kilometres! Not only had the provinces grown strong and virtually broken away; the ravages of resolute groups like the Marathas and the Rohillas had also eaten into the very vitals of the empire. The British had all but taken over. The formal extinction of the empire came with Bahadur Shah II who was found by the British to be involved in the most serious uprising against them, 'the Mutiny of 1857'. The monarch was consequently dethroned and sent off in exile to Rangoon where he died soon afterwards. The Mughal empire was no more, and India was declared part of the British Empire.

Bahadur Shah sat on the throne of Delhi for twenty years, but he emerges as a somewhat tragic figure. A poet of some distinction himself, and patron of the most gifted Urdu poets of his day like Ghalib and Zauq, in a different age he might have fared better. But from the very beginning, his was a husk of a kingdom with all the trappings of an empire but none of its power or influence. One sees him portrayed here, seated on a throne, holding the end of a remarkably long and elegant stem of a hookah-waterpipe, attended upon by Nawab Mughal Beg Khan, and with his two sons, Mirza Fakhr ud-Din and the very young Mirza Farkhanda. The painting is densely inscribed, each figure being clearly identified with a long string of titles, the longest of them naturally being that of the emperor himself. But the titles, high-sounding, grandiose, shot with hyperbole, sound as if they were substitutes for real power. Behind the emperor's throne on the wall is other information, for the inscription there states that the work was painted in the month *Rabi al-Awwal* of the year 1254 A.H. (corresponding to the first year of the emperor's reign, i.e. 1837–1838). Everything is made to appear exceedingly rich: the dresses, the crowns, the jewellery, the carpet, the decoration on the wall, but the effect is more ornate than elegant. Much more is said by the visage of the emperor who looks remarkably shrunken, like a flickering flame, than by all the glitter that surrounds him.

More than one painting of the Emperor Bahadur Shah II on his throne in this, or a very similar, setting was made. An almost identical version of this painting, distinguished from the present work only by the fact that Bahadur Shah is seen here with a black beard and in the other with a grey beard (although dated in the same year), is now in the Knellington Collection. There is yet another slightly extended version with more princes and courtiers and a European who commanded part of the garrison; that is inscribed with "the year 2" of the reign, which would make it a year later than the present work.

Publ.: Christie's, June 11, 1986, no. 161.

Changing Times, New Patrons

106 An Entertainment for Colonel Polier

Single leaf mounted as an album page
Inscribed with the words: 'The work of Mihr Chand, son of Ganga Ram'
19 x 28 cm; page: 28.5 x 39.5 cm
Late Mughal work at Oudh, c. 1780
Collection of Prince Sadruddin Aga Khan

The prince-like figure seen seated here, watching a dance performance to the accompaniment of music, while smoking a hookah-waterpipe and attended upon by two servants, is no Indian *nawab* but a European engineer, the Swiss Colonel Antoine Louis Henri Polier. He had left home when only sixteen years of age, and gone to India to serve as an army engineer. From service in the British East India Company he had moved on to that of the *nawab* of Oudh, Shuja-ud Daulah, whose dominion was once part of the Mughal empire but now a state in its own right, with only nominal allegiance to the Mughals. Here, at Oudh, where the paraphernalia of a kingdom was in evidence and the arts were seriously being patronised, Polier 'went native' and, while rendering professional services to the *nawab,* lived and conducted himself like a minor Indian potentate.

Polier took interest not only in the casually itinerant European painter who came through Oudh: local artists including Mihr Chand, the painter of this work, one of the most gifted men active at that time in the area, also interested him. Polier's involvement in art clearly went beyond having himself portrayed savouring a moment of leisure: he was seemingly a serious collector. At least one large album compiled by him has survived, as have some single paintings and calligraphies. Polier returned to Europe and died in Avignon at the hands of robbers in 1795.

In this attractive work by Mihr Chand, everything else appears very Indian except for some furniture and appointments: the bright yellow, brocaded sofa on which Polier sits, the tripod table at the far end with a bottle and caskets, and the glass shades for candles that look different from the usual Indian objects of this kind. The colonel is dressed like an Oudh figure, down to the detail of his *goshpech*-style turban with a brocaded band going around it. One notices that he is rendered appreciably fairer of skin than everyone else in the painting except for the principal dancer, who slowly advances towards him with measured, tinkling steps.

Mihr Chand, who signs his name in a minuscule hand below the sofa, employs here several painterly devices that he had picked up from the European painters who worked in Oudh from time to time, people like Tilly Kettle and Johann Zoffany. He thus shows a concern for cast shadows without drawing too much attention to them. But one notices them all over: at the feet of the dancers and the performers, close to the poles and the legs of the sofa, and the like. He brings in

delicate effects in the back wall where the left half is much greyer than the right and in the lit up area directly above the head of the shorter of the two servants standing behind Colonel Polier. From this scene in the foreground, without making any transitions, Mihr Chand shifts to the distance, where in a fine, minute hand he shows a host of workmen engaged in setting up a whole network of lights, and further beyond them, a virtual forest of fireworks that explodes in the sky. It is as if the *Diwali*-night were being celebrated.

Mughal work of the first half of the 18th century stays somewhere in the background of a painting like this. But, like it, the work has slowly but surely moved away from its 17th century moorings. A new wind was blowing in Oudh and other centres.

On verso of this leaf is an illuminated *shamsa* ('sunburst') of the kind that one finds at the beginning of fine albums. The heart of the *shamsa,* however, where it would ordinarily have contained the patron's name, and possibly a date, is bare. A. Welch (1979:196) has published a calligraphy dated 1781 from the Polier-album.

Publ.: Sotheby's, November 27, 1974, no. 723; S.C. Welch, 1978, no. 34; A. Welch, S.C. Welch, 1982, no. 79.

107 Chess game in the *zenana*

Single leaf, presumably after a European oil painting
61 x 81 cm
Late Mughal work at Oudh, c.1780
Private Collection

This painting deviates so far from the mainstream of Mughal work that it is all but impossible to understand it except in reference to some European original in oil of which this is almost certainly a copy by an Indian painter working in Oudh. The scene is set not in the formal, etiquette-controlled atmosphere of a court, but in the *zenana,* where two princesses sit concentrating on a game of chess, their contest of wits witnessed by an entire household of women and girls, young and old, while some eunuchs dressed as men keep strict vigil. Close to the slightly raised carpeted area, the atmosphere is one of even greater intimacy: children play about under the eyes of nurses; one of them suckles at the breast of a plump woman; a young girl looking like a love-sick person clings to a pillar; a maid, her clothes fluttering in the breeze, is bringing in a hookah-waterpipe with a long stem. The atmosphere is relaxed; there is no lack of decorum, only a sense of general ease. The scene is placed in a chamber with arched openings onto a garden, visible through the fine mesh of the split bamboo screens.

One sees this as an Indian painting primarily because of the atmosphere and because the characters – women, girls, and children – are dressed as the *begums* of Oudh and their intimates were known to have dressed. Also the architecture, the appointments, the carpet, are recognisably Indian. But quite clearly the recording eye is European, judging from the manner in which the painting is composed and the figures rendered bending, turning, in profile, two-thirds, three-quarters, and from the back. Everything is viewed from a fixed point – notice the three arches in the background, the middle one seen frontally and the ones at the right and the left shown 'curving' in opposite directions. The heavy use of shading, the interest in the weight and texture of dresses, the whole understanding and rendering of light, are also dramatically different from the way an Indian painter, viewing the same scene, would have conceived it. But here the Indian painter is painting after a European original, not producing an original work. Even then, the skills he brings to his work are impressive, for he copied the effects of a European oil in a different technique and on a different scale.

It has been suggested that the work is in the hand of Nevasi Lal who is known to have been one of the prominent artists working at the Oudh court. The original that the painter seems to have based his painting on was possibly by the travelling British artist Tilly Kettle, who was active in the Oudh area in 1772–1773. Another painting of the same group of game-players, also an Indian 'copy', is known (see Sotheby's, July 5, 1982, no. 18).

Publ.: Sotheby's, April 16, 1984, no. 21.

108 A group of entertainers

A leaf from the 'Fraser album'
Inscribed on the fly-leaf with the names of the musicians and dancers: 'Saira (or Saiza)
Naqqal, inhabitant of Shahjahanabad, Piru Naqqal, Inayatullah, father of Saira' and others
30.8 x 41.7 cm
Delhi, 1810/20
Collection of Prince Sadruddin Aga Khan

The setting has changed completely. One is no longer in a court or inside a palace: this group of men, so spiritedly rendered, is performing under a small *shamiana* or awning set up in the courtyard of the *haveli* or residence of a minor prince, identified in the fly-leaf inscription simply as 'Mirza Mughal'. That this is no grand mansion one senses from the wall in the background with an empty niche and, beyond that, the brick wall of another house. The ground is covered by a light pink and blue striped carpet. It appears as if some occasion is being celebrated in the household: one can visualize the man of the house sitting on his verandah surrounded by family members and friends at one end of the courtyard and watching this group perform from a slight distance. In this setting, the principal performer, the male dancer who throws up his right hand into the air while holding his left one coyly at the waist, in imitation of a woman dancer, would be looking his patron directly in the eye. A marriage in the family, the birth of a son or some such event could be the occasion for calling in the entertainers, who must be bound to the family by old ties. While they perform, two *chobdars* (ushers) leaning on long staffs flank them under the awning.

The intention behind this painting, and a large number of others in its group, is not to focus on the patron or the event, but on relatively ordinary people. One knows this from albums that were made for discerning British patrons like Colonel James Skinner and William Fraser. The people represented in these fine groups of paintings are not members of a faceless tribe as in the usual 'Company' paintings done in India for the British in the 18th and 19th centuries. The intention here is not to compile a cold record of trades and professions of people in a strange land: the men and women in these paintings are real people, each an individual, each identified through an inscription that gives his name, his profession, even the village or town that he comes from.

One sees that individuals have been closely observed here. The old man who plays lightly on the stringed instrument, perhaps the *pater familias* of this group, seems to have seen it all in his day; the principal performer looks straight ahead as he goes through motions of dance; the young boy, an understudy, also does the same but carries less conviction in his gestures; a dark-skinned old man at the very back, beating time by clapping his hands, is temporarily distracted and looks away to the right; the musicians are keen and alert except for the drummer who looks sideways at a dark, lightly bearded man. Clearly, elements are borrowed from European work – the frontality, the interest in shadows, the shading in the faces and dresses, the variety and ease of attitudes and the like – but the eye and the hand that register the scene are very Indian.

Not many of the paintings in the distinguished Fraser and Skinner albums carry the names of painters; but one painter, Ghulam Ali Khan, is known to have worked for these sensitive British patrons and also, for a while, at the Mughal court in Delhi in the early 19th century.

Publ.: A. Welch, S.C. Welch, 1982, no. 80.

109 A sulphur-crested cockatoo (Cacatua galerita)

A leaf from the 'Impey album'
Inscribed to Shaikh Zain-al Din
71.2 x 57.7 cm; page: 88.7 x 74.5 cm
Calcutta, 1775/80
Private Collection

That 'passionate delineation' which marked the best of the natural history paintings in the high period of Mughal art seems to have lain dormant for close to one hundred and fifty years before it surfaced again in the end of the 18th century: this time, however, not under the patronage of a Mughal ruler or a provincial *nawab,* but of the British. Suddenly, at this time, remarkable interest was taken by some British civil servants in documenting what was around them in India in the form of flora and fauna. The interest stemmed from curiosity and the desire to prepare a scientific record in which botanists and zoologists and others became involved. Gradually, however, the new natural history drawings and paintings came to acquire a life of their own. Private collectors also emerged, among them the senior-most of British officers, the Marquis Wellesley, governor general of India from 1798 to 1805; the chief justice, Sir Elijah Impey and his wife Lady Impey; and Lord Clive. The albums prepared for these collectors were sometimes enormous, the Wellesley album alone consisting of 2'660 folios of natural history paintings showing plants, birds, mammals, insects, and fish.

The painters involved in this extensive enterprise were, with minor exceptions, all Indians, trained originally in the Mughal manner. As M. Archer remarks, the making of these paintings did not suit British natural history painters, for they considered this work "too elaborate, decorative and expensive." The choice of the scientists and collectors then fell upon a group of Indians many of whom came from Patna, which had developed into a centre of 'painting for the British'. The Indian artists bent their great powers of observation and skill in drawing to the new task with remarkable energy and understanding. They had new materials to work on, English paper provided by their employers; they used European watercolours, mixing them with the white that they were used to; they informed themselves of what was required of them by carefully examining models which came from English illustrated books of natural history. It was with a new understanding that they set their hands to this work that was also, in their tradition, old.

The quality of what the Indian painters turned out quite naturally varied, but at its best this work is not only accurate but sensitive and moving. The painters of the 17th century had developed that fine technique of applying layers of pigment and burnishing the pages after the application of each flat layer of colour so that a firm, enamel-like surface was built up on which work was done with extremely fine brushes. The artists succeeded through this technique in reproducing "the lustre of a feather, the roughness of an animal's coat, the velvet texture of a petal, or the tough and leathery surface of a leaf with ... delicacy and precision." No Jahangir was now commissioning these late survivors of the Mughal tradition. Also the scale of these works was enormous. And yet the Indian painters brought to it, for all its seeming scientific sterility, a new passion, as one sees from this superb rendering of a cockatoo perching on the branch of an Asoka tree. The cockatoo is not a native of India, coming as it does from Australia and New Guinea, but it had certainly made its appearance in the country. It is here rendered not only with veracity but feeling, specific detail perhaps only subserving a higher end: that of reflecting the dazzling range of nature's creation.

This leaf comes from an album associated with Lady Impey who had employed both Hindu and Muslim artists. Many of the leaves from these natural history albums carry detailed documentation, giving not only the name of bird or animal or plant but also that of the painter. This cockatoo, according to the brief Persian inscription at the bottom left, was painted by Shaikh Zayn al-Din who, in another painting from the same album, is recorded as being a "native of Patna".

Publ.: Falk, 1984 (cover).

Bibliography

ABUL FAZL ALLAMI: *Akbarnama,* 3 vols., tr. by H. Beveridge, 1902 / reprint 1985 (see also Beveridge).

ABUL FAZL ALLAMI: *The Ain-i Akbari,* vol. I: tr. by H. Blochmann, 1873; vols. II and III: tr. by H.S. Jarrett, rev. by J. Sarkar, 1891 / reprint 1949 (see also Blochmann and Jarrett).

ARBERRY, A., 1967: *The Koran Illuminated,* Dublin.

BABUR: Zahir ud-Din Muhammad, *Baburnama,* 2 vols., tr. by A. Beveridge, 1922 / reprint 1979 (see also Beveridge).

BEACH, M.C., 1978: *The Grand Mogul – Imperial Painting in India,* Williamstown.

BEACH, M.C., 1981: *The Imperial Image – Paintings for the Mughal Court,* Washington, D.C.

BEACH, M.C., 1985: *The Art of India and Pakistan,* Durham.

BEGLEY, W., 1982: "Illustrated histories of Shah Jahan: new identification of some dispersed paintings and the problem of the Windsor Castle *Padshahnama*", in Skelton, 1986, London.

BERNIER, F.: *Travels in the Mughal Empire (1656–1668),* A. Constable (ed. 1891), London.

BEVERIDGE, A. (tr.), 1902: *The History of Humayun (Humayun-nama),* by Gul-Badan Begam, London.

BEVERIDGE, A. (tr.), 1922: *The Baburnama (Memoirs of Babur),* by Zahirud-din Padshah Ghazi, London.

BEVERIDGE, H. (tr.), 1902: *The Akbarnama,* by Abul Fazl, New Delhi.

BINNEY, E., 1973: *Indian Miniature Painting – The Mughal and Deccani Schools,* Portland.

BINYON, L., and ARNOLD, T.W., 1921: *Court Painters of the Grand Mughals,* Oxford.

BINYON, L., 1965: *The Spirit of Man in Asian Art,* New York.

BLOCHET, E., 1929: *Collection de Jean Pozzi – Miniatures Persanes et Indo-Persanes,* Paris.

BLOCHET, E.: *Musulman Painting, 12th to 17th century,* New York, reprint 1975.

BLOCHMANN, H. (tr.), 1873: *The Ain-i Akbari,* vol. I, by Abul Fazl Allami, Calcutta.

BRAND, M. and LOWRY, G., 1985: *Akbar's India: Art from the Mughal City of Victory,* New York.

BRINKER, H. and FISCHER, E., 1980: *Treasures from the Rietberg Museum,* New York.

BROWN, P., 1924: *Indian Painting under the Mughals,* New York, reprint 1975.

CARROLL, D., 1972: *The Taj Mahal – India under the Moguls,* New York.

CHANDRA, M., and SHAH, U.P., 1974: *New Documents of Jaina Painting,* Bombay.

CHANDRA P., 1976: *The Tutinama of the Cleveland Museum of Art* (facsimile), Graz, Austria.

COLAS, R., 1984: "Le Fonds Polier à la Bibliothèque Nationale", *Bulletin de l'Ecole Française d'Extrême-Orient,* vol. 73, Paris.

COOMARASWAMY, A.K., 1924: *Catalogue of the Indian Collections in the Museum of Fine Arts Boston,* vol. VI, Boston.

CORREIA-AFONSO, J., 1980: *Letters from the Mughal Court: The First Jesuit Mission to Akbar (1580–1583),* Bombay.

CRAN, R., 1980: *Miniatures Indiennes,* Neuchâtel.

CROISIER, J.P., 1984: "Islam et Art Figuratif", Musée d'Art et d'Histoire, Geneva.

CZUMA, S., 1975: *Indian Art from the George P. Bickford Collection,* Cleveland.

DAS, A., 1978: *Mughal Painting during Jahangir's Time,* Calcutta.

DAS, A., 1982: *Dawn of Mughal Painting,* Bombay.

DICKSON, M. and WELCH, S.C., 1981: *The Houghton Shahnameh,* 2 vols., Cambridge, Mass.

EGGER, G., 1969: *Der Hamza Roman,* Vienna.

EHNBOM, D., 1985: *Indian Miniatures – The Ehrenfeld Collection,* New York.

EHNBOM (manuscript): *An Analysis and Reconstruction of the Dispersed Bhagavata Purana from the Caurapancasika Group,* in press.

ETTINGHAUSEN, R., 1961: *Paintings of the Sultans and Emperors of India,* New Delhi.

FALK, T. and ARCHER, M., 1981: *Indian Miniatures of the India Office Library,* London.

FALK, T., 1978: *Indian Painting – Mughal and Rajput, and a Sultanate manuscript,* London.

FALK, T. and DIGBY, S., 1979: *Paintings from Mughal India,* London.

FALK, T., 1984: *Birds in an Indian Garden,* London.

FALK, T. (ed.), 1985: *Treasures of Islam,* London.

GAHLIN, S. and VAN BERGE-GERBAUD, M., 1986: *L'Inde des Légendes et des Réalités (Fondation Custodia),* Paris.

GASCOIGNE, B., 1973: *Die Grossmoguln,* Munich.

GLUECK, H., 1925: *Die indischen Miniaturen des Haemzae-Romanes im Österreichischen Museum für Kunst und Industrie in Wien und in anderen Sammlungen,* Zurich.

GOETZ, H., 1930: *Bilderatlas zur Kulturgeschichte Indiens in der Grossmoghul-Zeit,* Berlin.

GOETZ, H., 1934: *Geschichte der indischen Miniaturmalerei,* Berlin.

GOETZ, H., 1958: *The Early Muraqqa's of the Mughal Emperor Jehangir,* Marg XI, pp. 33–41, Bombay.

GOSWAMY, B.N., 1986: *Essence of Indian Art,* San Francisco.

GOSWAMY, B.N., GREWAL, J.S., 1967: *The Mughals and the Jogis of Jakhbar,* Simla.

GRADMANN, E., 1953: *Indische Miniaturen,* Berne.

GRAY, B., 1979: *The Arts of the Book in Central Asia, 14th to 16th century,* Boulder.

GRAY, B. (ed.), 1981: *The Arts of India,* Oxford.

GROUSSET, R., 1930: *Les Civilisations de l'Orient – l'Inde,* vol. II, Paris.

GUL-BADAN BEGAM: *Humayun-nama,* tr. by A. Beveridge, 1902 / reprint 1983 (see also Beveridge).

HAQ, M.M., 1931: "The Khan Khanan and his Painters, Illuminators and Calligraphists", *Islamic Culture,* vol. V, pp. 621–631.

JAHANGIR: Nur ud-Din Muhammad, *Tuzuk-i Jahangiri,* 2 vols., tr. by A. Rogers, ed. H. Beveridge 1909 / reprint 1978 (see also Rogers and Beveridge).

JARRETT, H.S. (tr. and ed.), 1978 : *The Ain-i Akbari,* vols. II and III, by Abul Fazl Allami, New Delhi.

JAUHAR, AFTABCHI: *Tazkirat al-Vaqiat,* tr. by Ch. Stewart, Delhi, 1972.

KAHLENBERG, M.H., 1972: "A Study of the Development and Use of the Mughal *Patka* (Sash)", in Pal, 1972, pp. 153–146, Leiden.

KHANDALAVALA, K.J. and CHANDRA, M., 1969: *New Documents of Indian Painting: A Reappraisal,* Bombay.

KRAMRISCH, S., 1986: *Painted Delight,* Philadelphia.

KRISHNA, A., 1958: "Some Pre-Akbari Examples of Rajasthani Painting", *Marg,* XI, no. 3:18–20.

KRISHNA, A., 1971: "A Study of the Akbari Artist: Farrukh Chela", *Chhavi: Golden Jubilee Volume,* pp. 353–373, Banares.

KRISHNADAS, R., 1955: *Mughal Miniatures,* New Delhi.

KUEHNEL, E. and GOETZ, H., 1924: *Indische Buchmalereien aus dem Jahangir-Album der Staatsbibliothek zu Berlin,* Berlin.

LEACH, L., 1986: *Indian Miniature Paintings and Drawings,* Cleveland.

LEACH, L., 1986: "Painting in Kashmir from 1600–1650", in Skelton, 1986, London.

LOSTY, J., 1982: *The Art of the Book in India,* London.

LOSTY, J., 1986: *Indian Book Painting,* London.

MARTIN, F.R., 1912: *The Miniature Paintings and Painters of Persia, India and Turkey from the 8th to the 18th Century,* 2 vols., London.

MC INERNEY, T., 1982: *Indian Painting – 1525–1825,* London.

PAL, P. (ed.), 1972: *Aspects of Indian Art,* Leiden.

PINDER-WILSON, R. (ed.), 1976: *Painting from the Muslim Courts of India,* London.

RAEUBER, A., 1979: *Islamische Schönschrift,* Zurich.

RANDHAWA, M.S., 1983: *Paintings of the Baburnama,* New Delhi.

ROBINSON, B.W., 1972: "Shah Abbas and the Mughal Ambassador Khan Alam: The Pictorial Record", *Burlington Magazine,* London.

ROBINSON, B.W., 1976: *Persian and Mughal Art,* London.

ROE, T.: *The Embassy of Sir Thomas Roe to India 1615–1619,* W. Foster (ed. 1899), London.

ROGERS, A., and BEVERIDGE, H. (tr. and ed.): *The Tuzuk-i-Jahangiri (Memoirs of Jahangir),* (Third edition 1978), New Delhi.

SEN, G., 1984: *Paintings from the Akbar Nama,* Varanasi / Calcutta.

SIMSAR, M. (tr.), 1978: *Tales of a Parrot,* by Ziya ud-Din Nakhshabi, Graz.

SINGH, CH., 1971: "European Themes in Mughal Miniatures", *Chhavi I,* pp. 401–410, Varanasi.

SKELTON, R., 1957: "The Mughal Artist Farrokh Beg", *Ars Orientalis,* vol. II, pp. 393–411.

SKELTON, R., 1961: *Indian Miniatures from the XVth to XIXth Centuries,* Venice.

SKELTON, R., 1969: "Two Mughal Lion Hunts", *The Victoria and Albert Museum Yearbook,* vol. I, pp. 33–48, London.

SKELTON, R., 1972: "A Decorative Motif in Mughal Art", in Pal, 1972, pp. 147–152, Leiden.

SKELTON, R., 1976: "Indian Painting of the Mughal Period", *Islamic Painting and the Arts of the Book: The Keir Collection,* pp. 233–74, London.

SKELTON, R., 1982: *The Indian Heritage – Court life and Arts under Mughal Rule,* London.

SKELTON et al. (eds.), 1986: *Facets of Indian Art,* London.

SMART, E., 1973: "Four Illustrated Mughal Babur-nama Manuscripts", *Art and Archeology Research Papers,* vol. III, pp. 54–58, London.

SMART, E., 1978: "Six Folios from a Dispersed Manuscript of the Babarnama", *Indian Painting,* Falk, 1978, pp. 111–132, London.

SOUSTIEL, J., 1973: *Miniatures Orientales de l'Inde: les Ecoles et leurs Styles,* Paris.

SOUSTIEL, J., 1974: *Miniatures Orientales de l'Inde,* Paris.

STAUDE, W., 1928: "Le paysage dans l'Akbar-Namah", *Revue des Arts Asiatiques,* Paris.

STAUDE, W., 1928: "Muskine", *Revue des Arts Asiatiques,* vol. V, no. III, pp. 169–182, Paris.

STAUDE, W., 1931: *Abd-us Samad, der Akbar-Maler und das Millionenzimmer in Schönbrunn,* Vienna.

STAUDE, W., 1934: "Contribution à l'étude de Basawan", *Revue des Arts Asiatiques,* Paris.

STAUDE, W., 1955: "Les artistes de la cour d'Akbar et les illustrations du Dastan-i Amar Hamza", *Arts Asiatiques,* vol. II, pp. 47–65 and 83–111, Paris.

STAUDE, W., 1961: "Basawan", *Enciclopedia Universale,* vol. II, columns 469–471, Rome.

STCHOUKINE, I., 1929: *La Peinture indienne à l'époque des grands Moghols,* Paris.

STCHOUKINE, I., 1929: *Les miniatures indiennes de l'époque des grands Moghols au Musée du Louvre,* Paris.

STCHOUKINE, I., 1935: "Portraits moghols, IV: La Collection du Baron Maurice de Rothschild", *Revue des Arts Asiatiques,* no. 9, pp. 190–208, Paris.

STRZYGOWSKI, J. et al., 1933: *Asiatische Miniaturmalerei im Anschluss an Wesen und Werden der Mogulmalerei,* Klagenfurt.

TAVERNIER, J.B.: *Travels in India* (1676), tr. by V. Ball, 1889, 2 vols., London.

TOPSFIELD, A., 1984: *Indian Court Painting,* London.

TYULAYEV, S., 1960: *Miniatures of Babur Namah,* Moscow.

WEBER, R., 1982: *Porträts und historische Darstellungen in der Miniaturensammlung des Museums für indische Kunst Berlin,* Berlin.

WELCH, A., 1979: *Calligraphy in the Arts of the Muslim World,* New York.

WELCH, A. and WELCH, S.C., 1982: *Arts of the Islamic Book – The Collection of Prince Sadruddin Aga Khan,* London.

WELCH, S.C. and BEACH, M., 1965: Gods, Thrones, and Peacocks, New York.

WELCH, S.C., 1963: *The Art of Mughal India – Painting and Precious Objects,* New York.

WELCH, S.C., 1976: *Indian Drawings and Painted Sketches,* New York.

WELCH, S.C., 1978: *Imperial Mughal Painting,* New York.

WELCH, S.C., 1978: *Room for Wonder,* New York.

WELCH, S.C., 1979: *Wonders of the Age,* Cambridge, Mass.

WELCH, S.C., 1985: *India – Art and Culture 1300–1900,* New York.

WICKENS, G.M. (tr.), 1964: *Nasirean Ethics,* by Nasir-ud Din Tusi, London.

WILKINSON, J.V.S. and BINYON, L., 1931: *The Shah-namah of Firdausi,* London.

ZEBROWSKI, M., 1983: *Deccani Painting,* London.

Appendix

It seems useful to reproduce Abul Fazl's most informative chapter on the art of painting in the *Ain-i Akbari* in H. Blochmann's translation in its entirety. Important passages also appear in the catalogue in various places. Spellings and diacritical marks correspond to the original translation.

H. Blochmann, *The Ain-i Akbari by Abul Fazl Allami* (Calcutta, 1927; third reprint of 1977 by Oriental Books Reprint Corporation, New Delhi)

The Art of Painting
(*Ain-i Akbari,* vol. I:113–115)

Drawing the likeness of anything is called *taswîr.* His Majesty, from his earliest youth, has shown a great predilection for this art, and gives it every encouragement, as he looks upon it as a means, both of study and amusement. Hence the art flourishes, and many painters have obtained great reputation. The works of all painters are weekly laid before His Majesty by the Dârôghas and the clerks; he then confers rewards according to excellence of workmanship, or increases the monthly salaries. Much progress was made in the commodities required by painters, and the correct prices of such articles were carefully ascertained. The mixture of colours has especially been improved. The pictures thus received a hitherto unknown finish. Most excellent painters are now to be found, and masterpieces, worthy of a *Bihzâd,* may be placed at the side of the wonderful works of the European painters who have attained world-wide fame. The minuteness in detail, the general finish, the boldness of execution, etc., now observed in pictures, are incomparable; even inanimate objects look as if they had life. More than a hundred painters have become famous masters of the art, whilst the number of those who approach perfection, or of those who are middling, is very large. This is especially true of the Hindus; their pictures surpass our conception of things. Few, indeed, in the whole world are found equal to them.

Among the forerunners on the high road of art I may mention:

1. Mîr Sayyid 'Alî of Tabrîz. He learned the art from his father. From the time of his introduction at Court, the ray of royal favour has shone upon him. He has made himself famous in his art, and has met with much success.
2. Khwâja 'Abdu 's-Samad, styled *Shîrînqalam,* or 'sweet pen'. He comes from Shîrâz. Though he had learnt the art before he was made a grandee of the Court, his perfection was mainly due to the wonderful effect of a look of His Majesty, which caused him to turn from that which is form to that which is spirit. From the instruction they received, the Khwâja's pupils became masters.
3. Daswanth. He is the son of a palkee-bearer. He devoted his whole life to the art, and used, from love of his profession, to draw and paint figures even on walls. One day the eye of His Majesty fell on him; his talent was discovered, and he himself handed over to the Khwâja. In a short time he surpassed all painters, and became the first master of the age. Unfortunately the light of his talents was dimmed by the shadow of madness; he committed suicide. He has left many masterpieces.
4. Basâwan. In back grounding, drawing of features, distribution of colours, portrait painting, and several other branches, he is most excellent, so much so that many critics prefer him to Daswanth.

The following painters have likewise attained fame: Kesû, Lâl, Mukund, Mushkîn, Farrukh the Qalmâq (Calmuck), Mâdhû, Jagan, Mohesh, Khemkaran, Târâ, Sâwlâ, Haribâs, Râm. It would take me too long to describe the excellencies of each. My intention is "to pluck a flower from every meadow, an ear from every sheaf."

I have to notice that the observing of the figures of objects and the making of likenesses of them, which are often looked upon as an idle occupation, are, for a well regulated mind, a source of wisdom, and an antidote against the poison of ignorance. Bigoted followers of the letter of the law are hostile to the art of painting; but their eyes now see the truth. One day at a private party of friends, His Majesty, who had conferred on several the pleasure of drawing near him, remarked: "There are many that hate painting; but such men I dislike. It appears to me as if a painter had quite peculiar means of recognizing God; for a painter in sketching anything that has life, and in devising its limbs, one after the other, must come to feel that he cannot bestow individuality upon his work, and is thus forced to think of God, the giver of life, and will thus increase in knowledge."

The number of masterpieces of painting increased with the encouragement given to the art. Persian books, both prose and poetry, were ornamented with picutres, and a very large number of paintings was thus collected. The Story of Hamzah was represented in twelve volumes, and clever painters made the most astonishing illustrations for no less than one thousand and four hundred passages of the story. The Chingiznâma, the Zafarnâma, this book, the Razmnâma, the Ramâyan, the Nal Daman, the Kalîlah Damnah, the 'Ayâr Dânish, etc., were all illustrated. His Majesty himself sat for his likeness, and also ordered to have the likenesses taken of all the grandees of the realm. An immense album was thus formed: those that have passed away have received a new life, and those who are still alive have immortality promised them.

In the same manner, as painters are encouraged, employment is held out to ornamental artists, gilders, line-drawers, and pagers.

Many *Mansabdârs, Ahadîs,* and other soldiers, hold appointments in this department. The pay of foot soldiers varies from 1,200 to 600 dâms.

Addenda